Communications
in Computer and Information Science 1373

Qun Chen · Jianxin Li (Eds.)

Web and Big Data

APWeb-WAIM 2020 International Workshops

KGMA 2020, SemiBDMA 2020, DeepLUDA 2020
Tianjin, China, September 18–20, 2020
Revised Selected Papers

Springer

Editors
Qun Chen ⓘD
Northwestern Polytechnical University
Xi'an, China

Jianxin Li ⓘD
Deakin University
Geelong, VIC, Australia

ISSN 1865-0929   ISSN 1865-0937 (electronic)
Communications in Computer and Information Science
ISBN 978-981-16-0478-2   ISBN 978-981-16-0479-9 (eBook)
https://doi.org/10.1007/978-981-16-0479-9

This Springer imprint is published by the registered company Springer Nature Singapore Pte Ltd.
The registered company address is: 152 Beach Road, #21-01/04 Gateway East, Singapore 189721, Singapore

Preface

The Asia Pacific Web (APWeb) and Web-Age Information Management (WAIM) Joint International Conference on Web and Big Data (APWeb-WAIM) is a leading international conference for researchers, practitioners, developers, and users to share and exchange their cutting-edge ideas, results, experiences, techniques, and tools in connection with all aspects of web and big data management. The conference invites original research papers on the theory, design, and implementation of data management systems. As the 4th event in the increasingly popular series, APWeb-WAIM 2020 was held as a virtual conference in Tianjin, China, during 18–20 September, 2020, and it attracted more than 600 participants from all over the world.

Along with the main conference, the APWeb-WAIM workshops intend to provide an international forum for researchers to discuss and share research results. This APWeb-WAIM 2020 workshop volume contains two tutorial summaries and the papers accepted for the following three workshops that were held in conjunction with APWeb-WAIM 2020. These three workshops were selected after a public call-for-proposal process; each of them focused on a specific area that contributed to the main themes of the APWeb-WAIM conference. The three workshops were as follows:

- The Third International Workshop on Knowledge Graph Management and Applications (KGMA 2020)
- The Second International Workshop on Semi-structured Big Data Management and Applications (SemiBDMA 2020)
- The First International Workshop on Deep Learning in Large-scale Unstructured Data Analytics (DeepLUDA 2020)

All the organizers of the previous APWeb-WAIM conferences and workshops have made APWeb-WAIM a valuable trademark, and we are proud to continue their work. We would like to express our thanks to all the workshop organizers and Program Committee members for their great efforts in making the APWeb-WAIM 2020 workshops a success. In particular, we are grateful to the main conference organizers for their generous support and help.

December 2020   Qun Chen
                                                                                                          Jianxin Li

Organization

APWeb-WAIM 2020 Workshop Co-chairs

Qun Chen   Northwestern Polytechnical University, China
Jianxin Li   Deakin University, Australia

KGMA 2020

Workshop Program Co-chairs

Zhuoming Xu   Hohai University, China
Saiful Islam   Griffith University, Australia
Xin Wang   Tianjin University, China

Program Committee Members

Gao Cong   Nanyang Technological University, Singapore
Huajun Chen   Zhejiang University, China
Jun Gao   Peking University, China
Armin Haller   Australian National University, Australia
Wei Hu   Nanjing University, China
Martin Kollingbaum   University of Aberdeen, UK
Jiaheng Lu   University of Helsinki, Finland
Jianxin Li   Deakin University, Australia
Ronghua Li   Beijing Institute of Technology, China
Jeff Z. Pan   University of Aberdeen, UK
Guilin Qi   Southeast University, China
Jian Qiu   Alibaba Cloud Computing Co. Ltd., China
Jijun Tang   University of South Carolina, USA
Haofen Wang   Shanghai Leyan Technologies Co. Ltd., China
Hongzhi Wang   Harbin Institute of Technology, China
Junhu Wang   Griffith University, Australia
Xiaoling Wang   East China Normal University, China
Yongli Wang   Nanjing University of Science and Technology, China
Guohui Xiao   Free University of Bozen-Bolzano, Italy
Qingpeng Zhang   City University of Hong Kong, China
Wei Zhang   Alibaba, China
W. Jim Zheng   The University of Texas Health Science Center
                               at Houston, USA
Xiaowang Zhang   Tianjin University, China
Yuqing Zhai   Southeast University, China

SemiBDMA 2020

Workshop Program Co-chairs

Baoyan Song	Liaoning University, China
Xiaoguang Li	Liaoning University, China
Linlin Ding	Liaoning University, China
Ge Yu	Northeastern University, China

Program Committee Members

Ye Yuan	Beijing Institute of Technology, China
Yongxin Tong	Beihang University, China
Bo Ning	Dalian Maritime University, China
Yongjiao Sun	Northeastern University, China
Yulei Fan	Zhejiang University of Technology, China
Guohui Ding	Shenyang Aerospace University, China
Bo Lu	Dalian Minzu University, China
Xiaohuan Shan	Liaoning University, China
Yuefeng Du	Liaoning University, China

DeepLUDA 2020

Organizers

Tae-Sun Chung	Ajou University, Korea
Rize Jin	Tiangong University, China

Workshop Program Chair

Joon-Young Paik	Tiangong University, China

Program Committee Members

Shaoqian Yu	Hunan University of Commerce, China
Seungmin Oh	Kongju National University, Korea
Liangfu Lu	Tianjin University, China
Seungjae Shin	Electronics and Telecommunications Research Institute (ETRI), Korea
Xun Luo	Tianjin University of Technology, China
Yunbo Rao	University of Electronic Science and Technology of China, China
Yenewondim Biadgie	Ajou University, Korea
Ziyang Liu	Kyonggi University, Korea
Muhammad Attique	Sejong University, Korea
Caie Xu	University of Yamanashi, Japan
Huayan Zhang	Tiangong University, China
Gaoyang Shan	Ajou University, Korea

Contents

The First International Workshop on Deep Learning in Largescale Unstructured Data Analytics

Tutorials

Neighborhood Query Processing and Surrounding Objects Retrieval in Spatial Databases: Applications and Algorithms

Md. Saiful Islam(✉) (iD)

School of Information and Communication Technology,
Griffith University, Gold Coast, Australia
saiful.islam@griffith.edu.au

Abstract. A nearest neighbourhood query (NHQ) retrieves the closest group of collocated objects from a spatial database for a given query location. On the other hand, a reverse nearest neighborhood query (RNHQ) returns all groups of collocated objects that find the given query nearer than any other competitors. Both NHQ and RNHQ queries might have many practical applications on mobile social networks, demand facility placement and smart urban planning. This paper also introduces another query, called direction-based spatial skyline query (DSQ), for retrieving surrounding objects from a spatial database for a given user location. The retrieved objects are not dominated by other data objects in the same direction w.r.t. the query. Like NHQ and RNHQ queries, retrieval of surrounding objects also has many applications such as nearby point-of-interests retrieval surrounding a user and digital gaming. This paper presents the challenges, algorithms, data indexing and data pruning techniques for processing NHQ, RNHQ and DSQ queries in spatial databases. Finally, encouraging experimental results and future research directions in NHQ, RNHQ, DSQ queries and their variants are discussed.

Keywords: Neighborhood query processing · Direction-based spatial skyline · Surrounding objects retrieval · Spatial databases

1 Introduction

The location information of many spatial objects including locations of mobile users and point-of-interests (PoIs) are readily available due to the immense popularity of location-based information services, e.g., availability of check-in information of users in social media and location information of restaurants, parks and service centers in Google map. There are many spatial queries proposed in the literature in last decades, e.g., shortest path search, nearest neighbor (NN), reverse nearest neighbor (RNN), keyword matching queries and their variants for spatial databases. These queries are found to be useful for the development of many meaningful applications. Many of these queries optimize their result based on individual objects, e.g., an NN query returns the database object that is closest to the given query location. On the other hand, an RNN query returns the

Q. Chen and J. Li (Eds.): APWeb-WAIM 2020 Workshops, CCIS 1373, pp. 3–13, 2021.
https://doi.org/10.1007/978-981-16-0479-9_1

database objects that find the query location closer than any of its competitors. However, there are many cases where a user wants the system to return a group of objects. The objects in the group need to be close to each other location-wise. In some cases, users also want the system to retrieve objects surrounding a given query location. The existing spatial queries are unable to address the above requirements in spatial databases.

In this paper, we provide an overview of neighborhood queries as well as queries that can help users to retrieve surrounding objects from spatial databases. A nearest neighborhood query (NHQ) returns a group of collocated objects, called neighborhood, that is closer to the query location than any other groups. The objects in the group are bounded by a radius constraint and the group must contain at least a user specified number of objects. An NHQ query is a group version of NN queries. On the other hand, a reverse nearest neighborhood query (RNHQ) returns all groups (neighborhoods) that find a query location closer than any other competitors. An RNHQ query is a group version of RNN queries. Both NHQ and RNHQ might have practical applications in many areas including spatial data mining, clustered kNN search and smart urban planning.

Finally, a direction-based spatial skyline query (DSQ) returns all objects that are not dominated by other objects in the same direction w.r.t. a given query location. To be useful, a DSQ query needs to be not only rotationally invariant, but also fair and stable. The DSQ queries can be used to retrieve objects surrounding a user from a spatial database. A DSQ query can be helpful for a mobile user to explore point-of-interests such as restaurants and parks surrounding their location.

The rest of the paper is organized as follows. Section 2 provides an overview of the NHQ and RNHQ queries, applications, query processing algorithms and future work on NHQ and RNHQ queries. Section 3 presents DSQ queries, applications, query processing algorithms and potential future work on surrounding objects retrieval systems. Finally, Sect. 4 concludes the paper.

2   Neighborhood Queries

This section presents nearest neighborhood and reverse nearest neighborhood queries, and their applications, variants and query processing algorithms.

2.1   Preliminaries

Definition 1. Neighborhood *[3]. Given a set of users U, a distance parameter ρ and a positive integer k, a neighborhood w.r.t. ρ and k denoted by $NH(\rho, k)$, is a ρ-radius circle enclosing at least k users in U.*

Definition 2. Nearest Neighborhood Query *[3]. Given a set of users U, a distance parameter ρ, a query location q and a positive integer k, a nearest neighborhood query finds the center of the nearest neighborhood $NH(\rho, k)$ to q. We use NHQ to denote a nearest neighborhood query in spatial databases.*

Facility	x	y
f_1	12	17
f_2	12	18
f_3	6	3
f_4	5	1
f_5	20	1
f_6	30	9

(a) Facilities, F

User	x	y
u_1	4	10
u_2	8	13
u_3	8	8
u_4	13	5
u_5	10	2
u_6	17	10
u_7	20	13
u_8	21	8
u_9	16	17
u_{10}	23	4
u_{11}	26	6
u_{12}	26	3

(b) Users, U

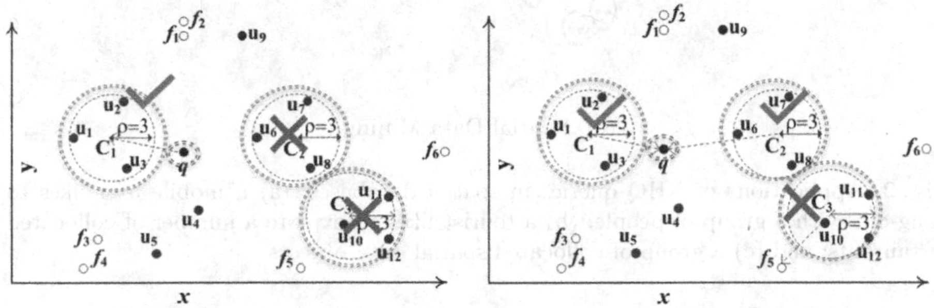

(c) NHQ Queries

(d) RNHQ Queries

Fig. 1. A toy dataset of (a) facilities (F); (b) users (U); (c) example of nearest neighborhood (NHQ) queries; and (d) reverse nearest neighborhood (RNHQ) queries

Definition 3. *Reverse Nearest Neighborhood Query* [5]. *Given a set of users U, a set of facilities F, a distance parameter ρ, a query location q and a positive integer k, a reverse nearest neighborhood query discovers the centers of all neighborhoods $NH(\rho, k)$ that finds q as the nearest facility among all facilities $f \in F$. We use RNHQ to denote the reverse nearest neighborhood query.*

Both nearest neighborhoods (NNHs) and reverse nearest neighborhoods (RNHs) are modeled by *nearest enclosing circles* (NECs) [3,5] - a circle which is pulled towards the query. The motivation for this is that a neighborhood is always pulled towards the query facility (service center) by it its special deals.

Example 1. Consider the datasets of facilities and users given in Fig. 1a and Fig. 1b. There are three neighborhoods of users in these datasets: C_1, C_2, and C_3 for radius constraint $\rho = 3$ and cardinality constraint $k = 3$. Although there are three neighborhoods, only C_1 is the nearest neighborhood of q as illustrated in Fig. 1c. This means that the distance between C_1 and the query q is smaller

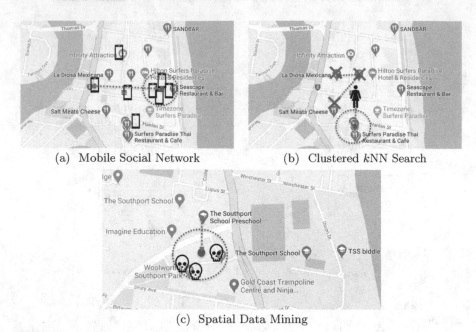

(a) Mobile Social Network   (b) Clustered kNN Search

(c) Spatial Data Mining

Fig. 2. Applications of NHQ queries in spatial databases: (a) a mobile user likes to hang-out with a group of people; (b) a tourist likes to explore a number of collocated restaurants; and (c) a group of collocated spatial data objects

than the distances between q and the other two neighborhoods C_2 and C_3, i.e., $d(q, C_1) < d(q, C_2)$ and $d(q, C_1) < d(d, C_3)$. Therefore, NHQ of the query facility q returns only C_1 as the answer. However, C_1 and C_2 find q nearer than any other facilities $f \in F$. The neighborhood C_3 finds f_5 nearer than the query q, i.e., $d(f_5, C_3) < d(q, C_3)$. Therefore, RNHQ of q returns C_1 and C_2 as the answer.

The main difference between NHQ and RNHQ queries is that we have to handle two datasets, namely, facility and user datasets in the case of RNHQ queries, whereas we only need to handle user dataset in the case of NHQ queries.

2.2 Applications

NHQ Query Applications. There are many potential applications of NHQ queries in spatial databases [3] as discussed below.

– **Mobile Social Network**: In mobile social network (MSN), the location-based mobile community can be formed by a group of mobile subscribers whose distances from each other are less than a threshold. By setting the threshold to be the radius parameter ρ, the NHQ query can be exploited to extract mobile communities nearby a user as illustrated in Fig. 2a.
– **Clustered kNN Search**: Consider a tourist is looking for a restaurant to dine as in Fig. 2b. The usual kNN search will return the k nearest restaurants

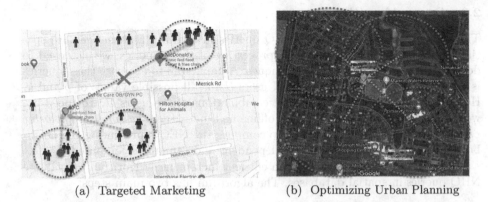

(a) Targeted Marketing   (b) Optimizing Urban Planning

Fig. 3. Applications of RNHQ queries in spatial databases: (a) a restaurant is planning to design a special deal to attract the nearest neighborhoods; and (b) optimizing the location selection of a children park fairly to serve the surrounding neighborhoods

to her location. If she is not satisfied with the nearest restaurant, she may need to travel a long distance to go to another restaurant. In this case, the best answer for her will be the nearest spot surrounded by clustered k restaurants. This can be easily answered by the NHQ query using a small ρ.

- **Spatial Data Mining**: Many works in spatial data mining aim to identify spatial clusters. In such works, it is needed to identify one or a few clusters in the proximity of a location of interest such as school, city hall, and museum. E.g., in order to determine danger zones nearby a school, it suffices to extract the clusters of crime locations that are nearest to the school rather than extracting all the clusters in the dataset as illustrated in Fig. 2c.

RNHQ Query Applications. Similar to NHQ queries, RNHQ queries [5] also have many important applications in spatial databases as discussed below.

- **Targeted Marketing**: Given a dataset of PoIs, such as restaurants, super-markets, gas stations etc., and a set of user locations, the RNHQ queries can be explored to discover the neighborhoods for a query PoI. The query PoI can then design special promotion plans or deals for the neighborhoods. As the users in a neighborhood are not far from each other geographically, the query PoI could minimize its travel cost to do the promotion as exemplified in Fig. 3a and therefore, might increase its profit.
- **Optimizing Urban Planning**: Consider a facility setup problem for the city council. The council can explore the RNHQ queries for optimizing suburb design and the distribution of the facilities it aims to provide such as town-halls, schools, train stations, parks etc. With the aim of the neighborhoods finding their own facilities as their nearest facilities as exemplified in Fig. 3b for the case of optimizing the location selection of a children's park. This is more viable than optimizing the urban planning for individuals.

2.3   Query Algorithms

The evaluations of NHQ and RNHQ queries in spatial databases require spatial data indexing. To expedite the processing of these queries, we also need to develop efficient data pruning techniques. A naïve way to evaluate these queries is to compute the neighborhoods of users U for all possible values of ρ and k. However, there are $\mathcal{O}(|U|^3)$ possible combinations of the users U. To speed up, we can discover these combinations offline and index them as *smallest enclosing circles*(SECs)[1]. However, we have to compute the NEC representing the neighborhood at run time as it is query dependent and cannot be computed offline.

Choi et al. [3] have developed an efficient incremental algorithm to evaluate NHQ queries in spatial databases. The algorithm has two main steps:

- **Step 1:** incremental retrieval of nearest neighbors by the best-first search after indexing the users U using the R-Tree; and
- **Step 2:** while incrementally visiting the next nearest user, keep track of SECs of users retrieved so far and thereby check whether these SECs can be covered by a circle of the given cardinality constraint k and radius ρ.

The authors [3] propose to transform the SECs into a Cartesian coordinate system, where an SEC is represented by two items: (a) its distance from q denoted by $C_i.d$ and (b) the angle range of its user points, which is denoted by $C_i[\theta_1, \theta_2]$. In this way, the algorithm is able to maintain and search the current SECs for the next nearest user. This can be implemented as 3-sided range search and can be solved in $\mathcal{O}(N + K)$ using the priority search tree. Finally, the authors have also developed some pruning techniques to speed up the algorithm. The authors found that the incremental evaluation of NHQ queries in the Cartesian coordinate system is much faster than the brute force method. The interested readers are referred to the original work [3] for the detail explanation of the NHQ query algorithms in spatial databases. Islam et al. [5] have proposed RNHQ query algorithms for spatial databases based on the idea of incremental evaluation of NHQ queries [3]. The steps are:

- **Discovering candidate RNH users:** given the datasets of existing facilities and users, this step discovers all candidate reverse nearest neighborhood (RNH) users of q; and
- **Incrementally constructing RNHs:** this step incrementally constructs all reverse nearest neighborhoods under the radius constraint ρ and cardinality constraint k from the candidate RNH users.

The authors [5] found that their bound, prune and refine algorithm (BPRA) performs better compared to the grid-based data indexing algorithm (GIBA). The performance of GIBA is also dependent on grid size. The interested readers are referred to the original work [5] for the detail explanation of the RNHQ query algorithms in spatial databases.

---

[1] A smallest enclosing circle of a given set of points P finds a circle that can enclose all points in P by minimising the radius.

2.4   Future Work

The authors in [5] have proposed a few variants of RNHQ queries in spatial databases such as top-l RNHQ queries (TlRNHQ) and min cover RNHQ queries (MCRNHQ). Although these queries are useful in selecting top l neighborhoods and searching for minimum cover for the reverse nearest neighborhood (RNH) users, there are many unexplored areas which can be investigated further. For example, both NHQ and RNHQ can be extended for spatio-textual databases.

To illustrate the importance of NHQ and RNHQ queries in spatio-textual data setting, assume that a restaurant owner wants to find the closest group of users which love "Sushi". After discovering the group, the owner would be able to design a special promotion plan for the users in the group. In the case of mobile social network, assume that a user only wants to hang out with the users of certain age group. These requirements can be embedded in the current NHQ and RNHQ queries and the current query algorithms can be investigated further to develop efficient query algorithms for these new variants.

The strict definition of neighborhoods (Definition 1), which models neighborhoods by circles [3,5], can be relaxed in the future works. For example, a few recent works on nearest neighborhood retrieval modeled neighborhoods based on the connectivity idea of density based clusters [1,2]. The work in [2] developed safe region based algorithms for moving RNHQ queries in peer-to-peer environments. Both NHQ and RNHQ queries can be extended further in the road networks where the road network distance is found to be more useful than the Euclidean-based distance measures.

3   Direction-Based Spatial Skyline Query

Consider a mobile user is searching for nearby restaurants surrounding her from the Cavil Avenue station (a tram stop in Gold Coast, Australia) as illustrated in Fig. 4. To fulfil the above information needs of a user, a direction-based spatial skyline query (DSQ) retrieves all objects from a spatial database that are not directionally dominated by other data objects w.r.t. a given query object. The DSQ query model proposed by Guo et al. [4] is given below.

Definition 4. DSQ Query Model [4]. *A data object p_i directionally dominates another data object p_j w.r.t. the query q, denoted by $p_i \prec p_j$, iff: (a) p_i and p_j are in the same direction w.r.t. q, i.e., $\angle p_i q p_j \leq \tau$, where τ is the user given acceptance angle; and (b) p_i is closer to q than p_j, i.e., if $d(q, p_i) \leq d(q, p_j)$, where $d(q, p_i)$ is the Euclidean distance between the query q and the object p_i.*

Consider the application example data given in Fig. 4 and user given angle threshold $\tau = 60°$, the DSQ query model proposed by Guo et al. [4] returns restaurants $\{r_4, r_5, r_6, r_9\}$, which are marked red in Fig. 4b. For $\tau = 45°$, the same query returns $\{r_2, r_4, r_5, r_6, r_8\}$. Clearly, we observe two issues in the DSQ query model proposed by Guo et al. [4]: (a) **missing result** issue and (b) **stability**. The missing result issue is caused by the phenomena where a non-resultant object

 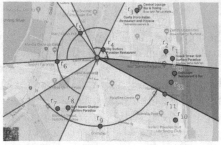

(a) Results of the DSQ Query Model [7]   (b) Results of the DSQ Query Model [4]

Fig. 4. Surrounding objects retrieval: (a) results of the DSQ query model [7]; and (b) results of DSQ query model [4] for $\tau = 60°$

can filter (cumulative domination) other data objects from the result set. This can observed by the huge gap that exists in between r_4 and r_9 as illustrated in Fig. 4b. The stability is caused by the sensitivity of the model to the settings of angel threshold. It would be hard for a user to come up with best value for it.

To address the issues in the DSQ query model [4], Shen et al. [7] proposed a new model of DSQ query based on the concept of directional zone.

Definition 5. *Directional Zone* [7]. *The directional zone of a data object p_i, denoted by $DZ(p_i)$ is defined according to the direction of object p_i w.r.t. the query object q. The direction of p_i w.r.t. q is represented by an imaginary ray $\overrightarrow{qp_i}$, which originates from q and passes through p_i. Now, if we rotate the ray $\overrightarrow{qp_i}$ from the object p_i (as the origin) by 45° both in clockwise and anticlockwise, we get two rotated rays: $\overrightarrow{p_ic}$ and $\overrightarrow{p_ia}$. The directional zone of a data object p_i formed by $\overrightarrow{p_ic}$ and $\overrightarrow{p_ia}$ as highlighted for p_2 in Fig. 5a.*

The DSQ query model [7] considers a spatial data object p_1 to be dominated by another spatial data object p_2 iff $p_1 \in DZ(p_2)$. The data object p_1 is also considered to be directionally similar to p_2 w.r.t. q iff $p_1 \in DZ(p_2)$. Clearly, the DSQ query model [7], which is defined based on directional zone, is rotationally invariant as the direction is query and data objects dependent. Unlike the model [4], this model is stable as there is no angle threshold dependency.

The DSQ query models [4,7] have been defined for point-based spatial data objects. These models do not work for arbitrary shaped data objects. Recently, Shen et al. [8] extended the DSQ query model for arbitrary shaped data objects. The authors extended the definition of the directional zone (Definition 5) for an arbitrary shaped data object p by three regions: $DZ(p) = D_q^-(p) \cup BL_q(p) \cup D_q^+(p)$, where $D_q^-(p)$, $D_q^+(p)$ and $BL_q(p)$ are called the upper dominance, lower dominance and blocking areas of p, respectively, w.r.t. the query q as illustrated in Fig. 5b. This definition is based on the idea of visible edges of the rectangular data object p w.r.t. the query location q. This can be further extended to arbitrary shaped objects. The interested readers are referred to the original work for the detail explanation [8].

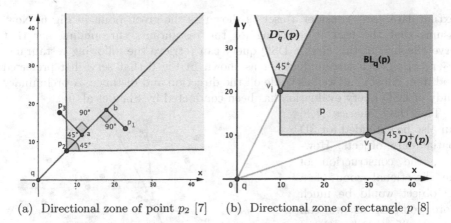

(a) Directional zone of point p_2 [7]   (b) Directional zone of rectangle p [8]

Fig. 5. Directional zones of: (a) a point obejct [7]; and (b) a rectangular object [8]

An important aspect of the DSQ query model proposed in [7,8] is the transitivity in directional dominance, which is defined as follows: if $p_i \prec p_j$ and $p_j \prec p_k$, then $p_i \prec p_k$ iff $p_k \in DZ(p_i)$. Finally, only the current skyline objects can filter other data objects in the DSQ query model proposed in [7,8]. This enables the DSQ queries [7,8] to retrieve objects surrounding a user fairly.

3.1   Query Algorithms

The query evaluation algorithms of the DSQ queries [7] first index spatial data objects into an R-Tree. Then, the algorithm incrementally retrieves the R-Tree objects based on their distances to the query object q and processes them to compute DSQ results. To do so, the algorithm inserts the children of the R-Tree root in a min heap $\mathcal{H}_q$ and initializes the result set $\mathcal{S}$ to $\emptyset$. Then, the algorithm repeatedly retrieves objects from $\mathcal{H}_q$ until the heap becomes empty: if the retrieved object is a data object and is not directionally dominated by any of the current resultant objects in the result set $\mathcal{S}$, it is added to $\mathcal{S}$, otherwise, the children nodes of the retrieved heap object (R-Tree node) is added to the min heap $\mathcal{H}_q$. The work in [7] proposed many data pruning techniques to speed up the above algorithm. The interested readers are referred to the original work.

The DSQ query evaluation of arbitrary shaped objects is much more complex than its evaluation for point-based spatial objects. The authors in [8] proposed to compute visible edges of the arbitrary objects and then apply slice and compare operations to establish dominance relationships between the arbitrary shaped objects. To understand the algorithm and the data pruning techniques, the interested readers are referred to the original work.

3.2   Future Work

The DSQ queries can be further investigated in spatio-textual databases for many practical applications. To motivate the need of DSQ queries for spatio-textual databases, consider a user as shown as the green point in Fig. 6. Now, assume that the user is searching for the restaurants surrounding her that serve "Sushi". In this case, a DSQ query can retrieve the following restaurants $\{r_2, r_3, r_4, r_5, r_6\}$ surrounding her as shown in Fig. 6 that serve her preferred food item "Sushi" as well as trade off the direction and distance. A preliminary study of DSQ query evaluation has been conducted by Shen et al. [6].

The DSQ queries [7,8] can also be extended for 3D spatial data objects. However, the construction of the directional zone of a 3D object would be much more complex as we can not simplify the directional zone for it by considering the extreme vertices only. We may need to model the directional zone of a 3D object in a tri-dimensional region where it will look like a funnel. The query algorithms need to be carefully designed as the dominance checking for the 3D objects needs to consider much more edges and vertices than 2D objects.

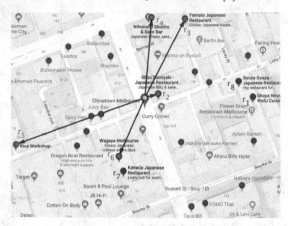

Fig. 6. Application example of DSQ queries for spatio-textual databases [6]

4   Conclusion

This paper has provided an overview of nearest neighbor, reverse nearest neighbor and direction-based spatial skyline queries. We have also presented potential applications and the processing algorithms of these queries in spatial databases. The proposed queries and their variants can be investigated further to develop many other useful applications in spatio-textual databases.

References

1. Allheeib, N., Islam, M.S., Taniar, D., Shao, Z., Cheema, M.A.: Density-based reverse nearest neighbourhood search in spatial databases. J. Ambient Intell. Human. Comput. 1–12 (2018)
2. Allheeib, N., Taniar, D., Al-Khalidi, H., Islam, M.S., Adhinugraha, K.M.: Safe regions for moving reverse neighbourhood queries in a peer-to-peer environment. IEEE Access **8**, 50285–50298 (2020)
3. Choi, D., Chung, C.: Nearest neighborhood search in spatial databases. In: ICDE, pp. 699–710. IEEE Computer Society (2015)
4. Guo, X., Zheng, B., Ishikawa, Y., Gao, Y.: Direction-based surrounder queries for mobile recommendations. VLDB J. **20**(5), 743–766 (2011)

5. Islam, M.S., Shen, B., Wang, C., Taniar, D., Wang, J.: Efficient processing of reverse nearest neighborhood queries in spatial databases. Inf. Syst. **92**, 101530 (2020)
6. Shen, B., Islam, M.S., Taniar, D., Wang, J.: Retrieving text-based surrounding objects in spatial databases. In: Barolli, L., Takizawa, M., Xhafa, F., Enokido, T. (eds.) AINA 2019. AISC, vol. 926, pp. 927–939. Springer, Cham (2020). https://doi.org/10.1007/978-3-030-15032-7_78
7. Shen, B., Islam, M.S., Taniar, D., Wang, J.: Direction-based spatial skyline for retrieving surrounding objects. World Wide Web **23**(1), 207–239 (2019). https://doi.org/10.1007/s11280-019-00694-w
8. Shen, B., Islam, S., Taniar, D.: Direction-based spatial skyline for retrieving arbitrary-shaped surrounding objects. Comput. J. **63**, 1668–1688 (2020)

Distributed Graph Processing: Techniques and Systems

Yanfeng Zhang[✉], Qiange Wang, and Shufeng Gong

Northeastern University, Shenyang, China
zhangyf@mail.neu.edu.cn, {wangqiange,gongsf}@stumail.neu.edu.cn

Abstract. During the past 10 years, there has been a surging interest in developing distributed graph processing systems. This tutorial provides a comprehensive review of existing distributed graph processing systems. We firstly review the programming models for distributed graph processing and then summarize the common optimization techniques for improving graph execution performance, including graph partitioning methods, communication mechanisms, parallel processing models, hardware-specific optimizations, and incremental graph processing. We also present an emerging hot topic, distributed Graph Neural Networks (GNN) frameworks, and review recent progress on this topic.

Keywords: Graph processing · Distributed systems · Parallel models

1 Introduction

Graphs have been widely used to abstract the relationships between entities for many applications such as social networks, website connections, collaboration networks, and co-purchase networks. Making sense of these relational data is critical for companies and organizations to make better business decisions and even bring convenience to our daily life. Recent advances in data mining, machine learning, and data analytics have led to a flurry of graph analytic techniques. With the magnitude of graph data growing rapidly, many distributed graph processing systems running on top of a cluster of commodity PCs have been proposed to perform data analytics and data mining on these massive graphs.

Graph Properties. Graphs are a common data structure to model relationships between data items. The graph data and the computations on graphs are usually endowed with the following properties:

- **Various Graph Representations**. Graphs can be represented by adjacency matrix, adjacency list, edge list, and so on. To leverage sparsity of graphs and support efficient access, graphs can be stored with CSR (compressed sparse row) format and CSC (compressed sparse column) format.
- **Complex Relationships**. Graphs are used to model the complex relationships between entities. There might be very complex connections between vertices, which can be used to mine the potential knowledge of graphs.

© Springer Nature Singapore Pte Ltd. 2021
Q. Chen and J. Li (Eds.): APWeb-WAIM 2020 Workshops, CCIS 1373, pp. 14–23, 2021.
https://doi.org/10.1007/978-981-16-0479-9_2

- **Power-law Characteristics**. In many real-world graphs, e.g., internet graphs, biological networks and social networks, the vertex degree distribution usually follows a power law, which implies that a small subset of the vertices connects to a large fraction of the graph.
- **Many Random Accesses**. Since a vertex can connect to any arbitrary vertex in a graph, graph algorithms usually show erratic access pattern and involve many random accesses to vertex state.
- **Iterative Computations**. Many graph mining algorithms require to traverse graph or perform information propagation, which leads to many iterations for refining graph state.

Challenges. The above summarized properties of massive graphs bring several big graph processing challenges.

- **Programming Variations**. Due to various graph representations, it is necessary to provide a general and intuitive programming interface for users to easily implement their graph algorithms.
- **Heavy Communication**. Graph data are assigned to many workers for distributed computation, each worker taking charge of a subset of vertices or edges, where the communication between workers can be very heavy.
- **Unbalanced Workload**. Due to the power-law degree distribution, it is difficult to partition the graph with evenly distributed workload.
- **Poor Locality**. Many random access including long jumps exhibit poor locality, which degrades performance.
- **Long Convergence Time**. Most of graph mining algorithms involve iterative computation. Given a big graph as input, the iterative computation may take pretty long running time for convergence.

To address these challenges, researchers have put great efforts on optimizing large-scale distributed graph processing. In this tutorial, we will briefly review the popular optimization techniques that are widely used in distributed graph processing systems and will introduce several representative systems. In addition, we will also present two emerging hot topics, incremental graph processing systems and distributed Graph Neural Networks (GNN) frameworks, and review recent works in these fields.

2   Optimization Techniques

2.1   Programming Models

As mentioned in Sect. 1, different graph representation options lead to the programming variations challenge. The graph programming models provide users unified interfaces to specify their graph algorithms and improve the usability of graph processing frameworks. Among the existing programming models, **vertex-centric** model is the most popular one. Users express their algorithms by "thinking like a vertex". Each vertex contains information about itself and all its outgoing edges, and the computation is expressed at the level of a single vertex.

The graph computation is defined as a sequence of message exchanges amongst vertices. A number of popular systems employ vertex-centric model, such as Pregel [24], PowerGraph [13], and GraphX [14]. On the other hand, X-Stream [29] leverages **edge-centric** model to obtain fully sequential access to edges (at the cost of random access to vertices), which greatly reduces the random I/O cost for querying specific vertices and is best for disk-based systems. PathGraph [47] employs **path-centric** model to maximize sequential access and minimize random access by clustering highly correlated paths together as tree based partitions. Blogel [44], Giraph++ [36], GRAPE [9] utilizes **block-centric** model that extends vertex-centric programming to blocks (i.e., a subgraph) and to exchange messages among blocks.

Besides, Pegasus [18] first proposes **Matrix-Vector Multiplication-based** programming model, which abstracts graph mining operations as a repeated matrix-vector multiplication. iMapReduce [53] relies on MapReduce interface (**MapReduce-based**) to implement a series of graph mining algorithms and provides iterative optimization for Hadoop MapReduce framework. Maiter [54] proposes **delta-based** graph computation, which abstracts the graph computation as an update accumulation process and can avoid invalid (zero-delta) updates to improve computation efficiency. SQLoop [10] leverages DBMS to implement graph iterative computations (**DBMS-based**) and extends standard SQL with efficient recursive aggregation support. Socialite [30], BigDatalog [32], and PowerLog [40] rely on Datalog language to express distributed graph algorithms (**Datalog-based**) and allow users to use very concise declarative programs to specify large-scale graph computations.

2.2   Graph Partitioning Methods

Graph partitioning is an essential yet challenging task for massive graph analysis in distributed computing. Offline methods [19] first load the complete graph into memory and then divide it into partitions, while streaming graph partitioning [27] operates online by ingesting the graph data as a stream. Graph can be partitioned by **edge-cut** [24,28], **vertex-cut** [13], or **hybrid-cut** [5] methods.

Edge-cut partitioning divides the vertices of a graph into equal-sized partitions and cuts edges, such as Metis [19] and PuLP [34]. While the vertex-cut partitioning divides edges of a graph into equal-sized clusters by making vertex replicas [7], such as SBV-Cut [20], Coordinated [13] and Neighbor Expansion (NE) [48]. The edge-cut partitioning usually results in replication of edges as well as imbalanced messages with high contention. The vertex-cut partitioning incurs high communication overhead among partitioned vertices and excessive memory consumption [5]. The hybrid-cut partitioning that integrates both edge-cut and vertex-cut address the major issues on skewed graphs, such as Ginger [5], Chunk-based partitioning [57] and Application-Driven partitioning [7].

All of the above partitioning methods are designed for synchronous distributed graph processing systems. They assume that, in each iteration, each vertex is only processed once and each edge only delivers one message. While in asynchronous frameworks, vertices can be processed at any time. The number of updates on each vertex and the number of messages passed through each edge are not consistent. Hotness balanced partitioning (HBP) [11, 12] is a novel graph partitioning method designed for prioritized iterative graph processing systems [52, 54]. HBP aims to balance the hotness values of vertices in each partition, minimizes the variance between hotness distributions of each partition and the original graph, and at the same time minimizes the communication cost between partitions.

In order to partition very large graphs that are not fit in main memory, the distributed graph partitioning methods or stream-based partitioning methods can offer solutions. The distributed graph partitioning algorithms first randomly divide graph data into several parts and assign them to distributed workers. Then they exchange edges/vertices between workers iteratively based on certain schemes. For example, Sheep [25] utilizes an elimination tree to partition the large graph distributively. Spinner [25] and XtraPuLP [35] employ label propagation to move vertices or edges iteratively. Although distributed graph partitioning algorithms are able to partition extremely large graphs, they suffer from performance issues since they may require multiple iterations to refine the partition results. Stream-based methods ingest the vertices or edges as a stream, and make partitioning decisions on the fly based on partial knowledge of the graph, such as Fennel [37], HDRF [27] and Pb-HBP [12]. Because only one pass of the graph data is needed, the stream-based partitioning methods are quite efficient. However, the quality of partitioning is sensitive to the stream order, and it is not able to take advantage of parallel partitioning.

2.3   Message Passing Models

Typical vertex-centric model relies on message passing to exchange intermediate results. **Push** and **pull** are two basic message passing operations, which are suitable for different scenarios [39, 42].

A number of popular systems [9, 24, 54] employ push based message passing model. Push-based model is flexible, since only the active vertices need to be processed. Furthermore, push-based model allow more powerful scheduling strategy to accelerate the convergence. PrIter [52] prioritizes message passing by distinguishing the important messages from the negligible messages and frequently transferring these important messages, so that the computation/update is more effective resulting in fast convergence. However, push-based model is not suitable for parallel processing, since the single-read-multi-write scheme will cause write-write conflict and may incur atomic overhead.

In contrast, PowerGraph [13] and Pregel+ [45] leverage pull-based model. With pull-based model, a vertex pull updates from its in-neighbours. Due to the multi-read-single-write updating scheme, pull-based can be parallel without atomic operations. However, pull-based model cannot achieve selective processing, all vertices have to be accessed no matter active or not. Therefore, redundant computation is inevitable when the active set is small.

Existing work demonstrates that, the size of active nodes set might be different in different stages, which implies that different stages may prefer different message passing strategies [33,39,57]. Ligra [33] proposed **hybrid push-pull** model for shared-memory system, which automatically switches between push and pull based on the size of active set, to reduce both redundant computation and atomic overhead. Gemini [57] extends the hybrid model to distributed environment and adopts similar approach. On the other hand, reducing redundant computation and atomic operation overhead is also critical for efficiently executing graph algorithm on massive parallel hardware, e.g., SEPgraph [39] extends hybrid push-pull model on GPUs and supports automatic push-pull model switch.

2.4   Parallel Processing Models

Graph computation usually exhibits iterative computing nature, where input data is computed iteratively until a convergence condition is reached. Synchronous parallel model requires all vertex updates completed before starting next iteration, while asynchronous parallel model does not have this requirement. With **synchronous** parallel processing [9,13,24,57], all workers keep the same pace The messages can be packed before being sent in order to reduce communication overhead (BSP model). Furthermore, synchronous programs are easy to write, tune and debug. However, the slowest worker will become the straggler and dominate the run time. With **asynchronous** parallel processing, workers do not need to keep consistent pace. Fast workers can perform more computations to accelerate the convergence [3,43,54]. Asynchronous parallel processing may incur irregular and redundant communications [40,43], and may lead to stale computation [8].

In order to avoid the shortcomings of both synchornous and asynchronous parallel models, **sync-async hybrid** parallel processing systems have emerged in the pass few years. PowerSwitch [43] proposes Hsync, which can automatically switch between synchronous model and asynchronous model. In PowerSwitch, in the same time period all workers in the cluster universally use the sync model or the async model. Grape+ [8] proposes Adaptive Asynchronous Parallel (AAP) processing, by monitoring the incoming message rate. AAP adaptively tunes the stale delay to achieve different parallel model (BSP, Staleness Parallel Processing, Asynchronous Parallel Processing). Different from PowerSwitch, in Grape+, the workers can use different parallel models, and each worker determines to choose its own parallel model. In addition, Grape+ is based on block-centric model, which can help combining messages and reduce communication. PowerLog [40] proposes that asynchronous parallel model under different message passing rates can result in different performance. PowerLog proposes a unified sync-async processing model by monitoring the local update frequency and can adaptively adjust the asynchronous degree to achieve better performance.

2.5   Hardware-Specific Optimizations

Hardware-specific optimizations are essential and emerging to provide the performance improvement significantly beyond those pure software optimizations can offer. GPU is adopted to pursue high performance of graph processing due to its data parallel capability. A number of graph processing systems with **GPUs** have been proposed for high-performance graph processing, such as Medusa [56], Gunrock [41], and SEP-Graph [39]. FPGA is an integrated circuit that enables designers to repeatedly configure digital logic in the fields after manufacturing, also called field-programmable. A number of existing works integrate **FPGAs** to support high-performance graph processing, such as CyGraph [2] and Fore-Graph [6]. Application-specific integrated circuit (ASIC) is usually fabricated on a wafer composed of silicon or other semiconductor materials that are customized for a particular use. Researchers follow vertex-centric model and form the **ASIC** circuit to support fast graph processing, e.g., Graphicionado [15].

On the other hand, graph processing can use disks, flashes or other external storage devices to store extremely large scale graphs. A number of studies aim to reduce the transmission cost of I/Os to improve performance. GraphChi [21] and GridGraph [58] are typical **out-of-core** solutions that reorganize the file storage structure of graph data to realize sequential disk file accesses and can process large graph in a single machine. There exist several studies using DRAM and **SSDs** to build hybrid graph system which stores vertex state in memory and edge lists on SSDs, such as MaiterStore [4], FlashGraph [55], and SMaiter [22]. There are also other studies that are optimized for communication networks. GraphRex [50] provides specific optimizations for high-performance network and under cross-rack cluster environment.

3   Emerging Applications

3.1   Incremental Graph Processing

With the continuously evolving nature of real-life graphs, the results of graph mining become stale and obsolete over time. Incremental processing graph [26, 31,38,51] is a promising approach for refreshing graph mining results. It utilizes previously saved states to avoid re-computation from scratch.

In order to process graph incrementally, i²MapReduce [51] uses MapReduce Bipartite Graph (MRBGraph) to model the data flow in MapReduce. Each vertex in the map task represents an individual map function. For the input delta graph, which contains the added/deleted edges and vertices, the i²MapReduce engine invokes the Map function for every record in the delta input. The Map function outputs the Delta MRBGraph that only contains the changes to the MRBGraph. Then i²MapReduce merges the preserved MRBGraph and the Delta MRBGraph, and obtains the updated MRBGraph. For each affected key in the updated MRBGraph, the merged list of values will be used to invoke the Reduce function to generate the updated final results.

Tornado [31] is an incremental iterative graph processing system that is built on top of Storm. Tornado contains a main loop and several branch loops. The main loop continuously gathers incoming data and approximates the results at the current instant, while the branch loops perform iterations over the snapshot that is taken when a result query is required. KickStarter [38] builds a set of dependency trees based on the dependency relationship between vertices. When an edge is deleted, KickStarter identifies the set of vertices impacted by the deleted edge. This can be done simply by finding the subtree rooted at the target vertex of the deleted edge. Then it resets the value of the impacted vertices and rebuilds the dependency tree by recomputing the values of the impacted vertices. GraphBolt [26] proposes a dependency graph for tracking dependency relationship between vertices. Vertices in the dependency graph maintain their intermediate values that are produced during the iterative computations. Edges in the dependency graph capture dependencies among intermediate values. As the graph changes, GraphBolt corrects the intermediate vertex states iteration-by-iteration according to the dependency graph.

3.2   Distributed GNN Training

Graph Neural Networks (GNNs) have been emerging as powerful learning tools for graph data. However, it is challenging to train a GNN for real-world large-scale graphs. Most of the existing popular deep learning frameworks run a single machine, which cannot offer much scalability. Therefore, building a scalable GNN training system for large-scale graphs is desirable [16,17,23,46,49].

A common GNN task contains the forward and backward propagation in standard deep learning and the iterative graph propagation in graph mining algorithms. These two distinct computing styles make it difficult to build high performance GNN systems in distributed environment. Neither existing graph processing systems nor deep learning systems can support GNN training well. An intuitive approach is completely partitioning the graph data to avoid communication between subgraphs (subtasks) and leverage the parameter server's data parallel model. Aligraph [46] relies on distributed Tensorflow's parameter server architecture. The graph data are stored in the server side. When training a K-layer GNN task, each worker pulls the training graph data of one batch (including its k-hop neighbours and their features) from the PS-server and locally performs the computation. Euler [1], AGL [49], PSGraph [17] adopt similar method. PSGraph builds the GNN training system on top of Hadoop and Spark ecosystems, which makes it easier to scale.

Acknowledgement. This work was supported by National Key R&D Program of China (2018YFB1003404), National Natural Science Foundation of China (62072082, 61672141, and U1811261) and Fundamental Research Funds for the Central Universities (N181605017 and N181604016), and Key R&D Program of Liaoning Province (2020JH 2/10100037).

References

1. Euler 2.0 (2020). https://github.com/alibaba/euler
2. Attia, O.G., Johnson, T., Townsend, K., Jones, P., Zambreno, J.: CyGraph: a reconfigurable architecture for parallel breadth-first search. Proc. IPDPS **2014**, 228–235 (2014)

3. Ben-Nun, T., Sutton, M., Pai, S., Pingali, K.: Groute: an asynchronous multi-GPU programming model for irregular computations. In: ACM SIGPLAN Notices, vol. 52, no. 8, pp. 235–248 (2017)
4. Chang, D., Zhang, Y., Yu, G.: MaiterStore: a hot-aware, high-performance key-value store for graph processing. In: Han, W.-S., Lee, M.L., Muliantara, A., Sanjaya, N.A., Thalheim, B., Zhou, S. (eds.) DASFAA 2014. LNCS, vol. 8505, pp. 117–131. Springer, Heidelberg (2014). https://doi.org/10.1007/978-3-662-43984-5_9
5. Chen, R., Shi, J., Chen, Y., Zang, B., Guan, H., Chen, H.: PowerLyra: differentiated graph computation and partitioning on skewed graphs. ACM Trans. Parallel Comput. (TOPC) **5**(3), 1–39 (2019)
6. Dai, G., Huang, T., Chi, Y., Xu, N., Wang, Y., Yang, H.: ForeGraph: exploring large-scale graph processing on multi-FPGA architecture. Proc. FPGA **2017**, 217–226 (2017)
7. Fan, W., et al.: Application driven graph partitioning. In: Proceedings of the 2020 ACM SIGMOD International Conference on Management of Data (SIGMOD 2020), pp. 1765–1779 (2020)
8. Fan, W., et al.: Adaptive asynchronous parallelization of graph algorithms. ACM Trans. Database Syst. (TODS) **45**(2), 1–45 (2020)
9. Fan, W., et al.: Parallelizing sequential graph computations. ACM Trans. Database Syst. (TODS) **43**(4), 1–39 (2018)
10. Floratos, S., Zhang, Y., Yuan, Y., Lee, R., Zhang, X.: SQLoop: high performance iterative processing in data management. In: Proceedings of ICDCS 2018, pp. 1039–1051 (2018)
11. Gong, S., Zhang, Y., Yu, G.: Accelerating large-scale prioritized graph computations by hotness balanced partition (online). IEEE Trans. Parallel Distrib. Syst. **32**, 746–759 (2020)
12. Gong, S., Zhang, Y., Yu, G.: HBP: hotness balanced partition for prioritized iterative graph computations. In: Proceedings of the 36th International Conference on Data Engineering (ICDE 2020), pp. 1942–1945 (2020)
13. Gonzalez, J.E., Low, Y., Gu, H., Bickson, D., Guestrin, C.: PowerGraph: distributed graph-parallel computation on natural graphs. In: Proceedings of OSDI 2012, pp. 17–30 (2012)
14. Gonzalez, J.E., Xin, R.S., Dave, A., Crankshaw, D., Franklin, M.J., Stoica, I.: GraphX: graph processing in a distributed dataflow framework. In: Proceedings of OSDI 2014, pp. 599–613 (2014)
15. Ham, T.J., Wu, L., Sundaram, N., Satish, N., Martonosi, M.: Graphicionado: a high-performance and energy-efficient accelerator for graph analytics. In: Proceedings of the 49th Annual IEEE/ACM International Symposium on Microarchitecture (MICRO 2016), pp. 1–13 (2016)
16. Jia, Z., Lin, S., Gao, M., Zaharia, M., Aiken, A.: Improving the accuracy, scalability, and performance of graph neural networks with ROC. In: Proceedings of Machine Learning and Systems (MLSys 2020), pp. 187–198 (2020)
17. Jiang, J., et al.: PSGraph: how Tencent trains extremely large-scale graphs with spark? In: Proceedings of ICDE 2020, pp. 1549–1557 (2020)
18. Kang, U., Tsourakakis, C.E., Faloutsos, C.: PEGASUS: a peta-scale graph mining system implementation and observations. In: Proceedings of ICDM 2009, pp. 229–238 (2009)
19. Karypis, G., Kumar, V.: METIS: a software package for partitioning unstructured graphs. Partitioning Meshes, and Computing Fill-Reducing Orderings of Sparse Matrices, Version 4(0) (1998)

20. Kim, M., Candan, K.S.: SBV-Cut: vertex-cut based graph partitioning using structural balance vertices. Data Knowl. Eng. **72**, 285–303 (2012)
21. Kyrola, A., Blelloch, G., Guestrin, C.: GraphChi: large-scale graph computation on just a PC. In: Proceedings of OSDI 2012, pp. 31–46 (2012)
22. Li, J., Zhang, Y., Gong, S., Yu, G., Gao, L.: Streamlined asynchronous graph processing framework. J. Softw. **3**, 528–544 (2018)
23. Ma, L., Yang, Z., Miao, Y., Xue, J., Wu, M., Zhou, L., Dai, Y.: NeuGraph: parallel deep neural network computation on large graphs. In: Proceedings of USENIX ATC 2019, pp. 443–458 (2019)
24. Malewicz, G., et al.: Pregel: a system for large-scale graph processing. In: Proceedings of SIGMOD 2010, pp. 135–146 (2010)
25. Margo, D., Seltzer, M.: A scalable distributed graph partitioner. Proc. VLDB Endow. **8**(12), 1478–1489 (2015)
26. Mariappan, M., Vora, K.: GraphBolt: dependency-driven synchronous processing of streaming graphs. In: Proceedings of EuroSys 2019, pp. 1–16 (2019)
27. Petroni, F., Querzoni, L., Daudjee, K., Kamali, S., Iacoboni, G.: HDRF: stream-based partitioning for power-law graphs. In: Proceedings of CIKM 2015, pp. 243–252 (2015)
28. Reittu, H., Norros, I., Rty, T., Bolla, M., Bazsó, F.: Regular decomposition of large graphs: foundation of a sampling approach to stochastic block model fitting. Data Sci. Eng. **4**(1), 44–60 (2019)
29. Roy, A., Mihailovic, I., Zwaenepoel, W.: X-Stream: edge-centric graph processing using streaming partitions. In: Proceedings of SOSP 2013, pp. 472–488 (2013)
30. Seo, J., Park, J., Shin, J., Lam, M.S.: Distributed socialite: a datalog-based language for large-scale graph analysis. Proc. VLDB Endow. **6**(14), 1906–1917 (2013)
31. Shi, X., Cui, B., Shao, Y., Tong, Y.: Tornado: a system for real-time iterative analysis over evolving data. In: Proceedings of SIGMOD 2016, pp. 417–430 (2016)
32. Shkapsky, A., Yang, M., Interlandi, M., Chiu, H., Condie, T., Zaniolo, C.: Big data analytics with datalog queries on spark. In: Proceedings of the 2016 International Conference on Management of Data (SIGMOD 2016), pp. 1135–1149 (2016)
33. Shun, J., Blelloch, G.E.: Ligra: a lightweight graph processing framework for shared memory. In: Proceedings of PPoPP 2013, pp. 135–146 (2013)
34. Slota, G.M., Madduri, K., Rajamanickam, S.: PuLP: scalable multi-objective multi-constraint partitioning for small-world networks. In: Proceedings of 2014 IEEE International Conference on Big Data, pp. 481–490 (2014)
35. Slota, G.M., Rajamanickam, S., Devine, K., Madduri, K.: Partitioning trillion-edge graphs in minutes. In: Proceedings of 2017 IEEE International Parallel and Distributed Processing Symposium (IPDPS 2017), pp. 646–655. IEEE (2017)
36. Tian, Y., Balmin, A., Corsten, S.A., Tatikonda, S., McPherson, J.: From "think like a vertex" to "think like a graph". Proc. VLDB Endow. **7**(3), 193–204 (2013)
37. Tsourakakis, C., Gkantsidis, C., Radunovic, B., Vojnovic, M.: FENNEL: streaming graph partitioning for massive scale graphs. In: Proceedings of WSDM 2014, pp. 333–342 (2014)
38. Vora, K., Gupta, R., Xu, G.: KickStarter: fast and accurate computations on streaming graphs via trimmed approximations. In: Proceedings of ASPLOS 2017, pp. 237–251 (2017)
39. Wang, H., Geng, L., Lee, R., Hou, K., Zhang, Y., Zhang, X.: SEP-graph: finding shortest execution paths for graph processing under a hybrid framework on GPU. In: Proceedings of PPoPP 2019, pp. 38–52 (2019)

40. Wang, Q., et al.: Automating incremental and asynchronous evaluation for recursive aggregate data processing. In: Proceedings of SIGMOD 2020, pp. 2439–2454 (2020)

41. Wang, Y., Davidson, A., Pan, Y., Wu, Y., Riffel, A., Owens, J.D.: Gunrock: a high-performance graph processing library on the GPU. In: Proceedings of PPoPP 2016, pp. 1–12 (2016)

42. Wang, Z., Gu, Y., Bao, Y., Yu, G., Yu, J.X.: Hybrid pulling/pushing for i/o-efficient distributed and iterative graph computing. In: Proceedings of SIGMOD 2016, pp. 479–494 (2016)

43. Xie, C., Chen, R., Guan, H., Zang, B., Chen, H.: SYNC or ASYNC: time to fuse for distributed graph-parallel computation. In: ACM SIGPLAN Notices, vol. 50, no. 8, pp. 194–204 (2015)

44. Yan, D., Cheng, J., Lu, Y., Ng, W.: Blogel: a block-centric framework for distributed computation on real-world graphs. Proc. VLDB Endow. 7(14), 1981–1992 (2014)

45. Yan, D., Cheng, J., Lu, Y., Ng, W.: Effective techniques for message reduction and load balancing in distributed graph computation. In: Proceedings of WWW 2015, WWW 2015, pp. 1307–1317 (2015)

46. Yang, H.: AliGraph: a comprehensive graph neural network platform. In: Proceedings of KDD 2019, pp. 3165–3166 (2019)

47. Yuan, P., Xie, C., Liu, L., Jin, H.: PathGraph: a path centric graph processing system. IEEE Trans. Parallel Distrib. Syst. 27(10), 2998–3012 (2016)

48. Zhang, C., Wei, F., Liu, Q., Tang, Z.G., Li, Z.: Graph edge partitioning via neighborhood heuristic. In: Proceedings of the 23rd ACM SIGKDD International Conference on Knowledge Discovery and Data Mining (KDD 2017), pp. 605–614 (2017)

49. Zhang, D., et al.: AGL: a scalable system for industrial-purpose graph machine learning. arXiv preprint arXiv:2003.02454 (2020)

50. Zhang, Q., et al.: Optimizing declarative graph queries at large scale. In: Proceedings of SIGMOD 2019, pp. 1411–1428 (2019)

51. Zhang, Y., Chen, S., Wang, Q., Yu, G.: i^2MapReduce: incremental mapreduce for mining evolving big data. IEEE Trans. Knowl. Data Eng. 27(7), 1906–1919 (2015)

52. Zhang, Y., Gao, Q., Gao, L., Wang, C.: Priter: a distributed framework for prioritized iterative computations. In: Proceedings of SOCC 2011, pp. 1–14 (2011)

53. Zhang, Y., Gao, Q., Gao, L., Wang, C.: iMapReduce: a distributed computing framework for iterative computation. J. Grid Comput. 10(1), 47–68 (2012)

54. Zhang, Y., Gao, Q., Gao, L., Wang, C.: Maiter: an asynchronous graph processing framework for delta-based accumulative iterative computation. IEEE Trans. Parallel Distrib. Syst. 25(8), 2091–2100 (2013)

55. Zheng, D., Mhembere, D., Burns, R., Vogelstein, J., Priebe, C.E., Szalay, A.S.: FlashGraph: processing billion-node graphs on an array of commodity SSDs. In: Proceedings of FAST 2015, pp. 45–58 (2015)

56. Zhong, J., He, B.: Medusa: a parallel graph processing system on graphics processors. ACM SIGMOD Rec. 43(2), 35–40 (2014)

57. Zhu, X., Chen, W., Zheng, W., Ma, X.: Gemini: a computation-centric distributed graph processing system. In: Proceedings of OSDI 2016, pp. 301–316 (2016)

58. Zhu, X., Han, W., Chen, W.: GridGraph: large-scale graph processing on a single machine using 2-level hierarchical partitioning. In: Proceedings of USENIX ATC 2015, pp. 375–386 (2015)

The Third International Workshop on Knowledge Graph Management and Applications

Method for Re-finding Mobile Phone Documents Based on Feature Knowledge Graph

Jing Zhang[1], Yukun Li[1,2(✉)], Yan Zhang[1], and Yunbo Ye[1]

[1] Tianjin University of Technology, Tianjin 300384, China
[2] Tianjin Key Laboratory of Intelligence Computing and Novel Software Technology, Tianjin, China

Abstract. People often need to find documents that previously saved on their mobile phones. When searching a document, sometimes people cannot recall the exact name of it, but can remember some objects in it, such as the figures, tables or formulas in the documents, the source of the documents, or related topics. And the existing mobile phone document management software cannot associate the content of the document with itself. Therefore, how to extract document information into attributes tags to associate them with documents and how to re-find the expected documents based on these tags are practical and valuable. This paper proposes a method for re-finding mobile phone documents based on feature knowledge graph. First, we use four features to describe the documents and extract tags to form attributes. Then we link the attributes with the documents to form the document knowledge graph and propose a calculation algorithm of the four tags' weight. Finally, we propose the sorting and re-finding method based on the feature knowledge graph. By using personal mobile phones data, the experiment results verify the effectiveness and efficiency of this method.

Keywords: Re-finding · Mobile phone documents · Feature knowledge graph

1 Introduction

With the rapid development of mobile Internet technology, more and more people have started to use mobile devices for work and study, such as mobile phones and tablets. With the accelerated spread and the exponential growth of information in the data age, more and more personal information is stored in mobile phones. According to the global mobile economy report [1] released by the GSMA in 2019, the total number of independent mobile users will reach 5.1 billion by the end of 2018, accounting for about two thirds of the global population. Relying on the mobile Internet, mobile office also has a breakthrough development in 2016. The international well-known data company IDC [2], their survey shows that 82% of Chinese employees use their mobile phones for work. With the accumulation of time, files stored in the mobile phones are increasing. How to effectively manage mobile files and how to quickly and efficiently find files become a big problem.

© Springer Nature Singapore Pte Ltd. 2021
Q. Chen and J. Li (Eds.): APWeb-WAIM 2020 Workshops, CCIS 1373, pp. 27–40, 2021.
https://doi.org/10.1007/978-981-16-0479-9_3

Studies have shown that most of the access to desktop information is to re-find the existing and visited information [3]. In the field of mobile devices such as mobile phones, files are saved through application software. Users cannot choose the proper path to store it on phones as easy as what they do on computers. Because the mobile phone files have application isolation, the documents downloaded by different applications will be saved in different folders. Besides, when people use the mobile phone, a large amount of redundant and irrelevant information will be generated. This information makes it difficult for users to quickly find the information they need.

But users often encounter the situations similar to the following: (1) when searching for a document, the user cannot remember the name of this document, but can only remember the topic of a picture in the document. For example, a user want to find a document he/she wrote a year before, but he/she can only remember a picture is about neural network in the document. (2) When users searching for a document, they can only remember where they get. For example, a user want to find a file, he/she can only remember that he/she got this file from WeChat, but as time went, the chat records are deleted by users (Because for Android phones, more and more chat records may make our phone slow, many users may clear their App data after a while) So he/she can't re-find the document with searching contents by App itself. (3) The user wants to find a document related to one topic, and can only remember a vague opened time. For example, when a user wants to find a file about big data, what he/she remembers is that he/she has opened the file a week ago.

It can be seen from the above examples that users often establish a relationship between document attributes and document titles in their minds, which is similar with knowledge graph structure. The knowledge graph can be used to establish the connection between attributes and documents. Knowledge graph is to describe knowledge resources and their carriers with visual technology, mining, analyzing, constructing, drawing and displaying knowledge and their interconnections. It can describe the connection between different entities concisely and intuitively, reduce the influence of invalid information, and integrate seemingly unrelated fragmented information to form a related graph. Knowledge graphs are widely used in management science, military science, medicine, economics and other fields. However, these applications are mainly concentrated in enterprises or academia, and there are relatively few applications in the field of personal information management. This paper applies the knowledge graph to the field of personal information management, and proposes the method for re-finding mobile phone documents based on feature knowledge graph.

The first section of the paper is the introduction, which puts forward the research of mobile phone documents and describes the discovered problems. The second section introduces the related works about re-find of desktops and mobile phones, the application of knowledge graph. The section three introduces the concepts model of feature knowledge graph and theoretical basis of them. The section four proposes feature-based weight assignment and search algorithms. The section five describes the experimental process and analyzes the results. The section six summarizes the contribution of this paper: by comparing the proposed sorting method with traditional methods such as mobile phone file management software, the method proposed in this article can re-locate the searched documents more efficiently and accurately, and finally introduced the future work direction.

2 Related Work

As far as the author knows, there is less work related to re-find documents in the field of mobile phones information management. Mobile file management applications are often used as classification. But when people can't remember the correct file name, this software loses its advantage.

In the field of computer desktop re-finding, there are two aspects. The first is based on browsing history information. Trien V. Do and Roy A. Ruddle [4] propose a tool which describe the user's interest in web pages by recording residence time, frequency of visits, number of recent visits and so on. The second is based on the user recall context for re-finding. Tangjian, D., Liang, Z. et al. [5] developed a context-based method of information reflection. They proposed to store it in a cluster method. When re-finding, they can access these relationships and positioning to the required information.

Xuan Luo [6] takes personal notes as a starting point and uses natural language processing technology to intelligently analyze the content of the notes. It is proposed to automatically extract attributes and make associations based on the relationships between attributes to construct a knowledge graph about notes. Yan Liang [7] proposed to manage fragmented knowledge based on knowledge graph technology. By constructing the associations between knowledge points, the fragmented learning resources are developed around each knowledge point, forming a learner's personal knowledge system.

Although there is some mobile phone file management applications, few people pay attention to the role of prominent descriptions of file content in mobile phone files re-finding. Re-finding tools for desktop files already have mature studies. However, these studies are not fully applied to mobile phone re-finding. One reason is the structure of mobile phones and computers is different, and the directory of documents is also different. Another reason is the most existing studies in PC need to interact with users to make sure the precision rate. But due to the limitation of the mobile phones screen, our re-finding will be limited without interacting with users. Based on above reasons, this paper uses the knowledge graph to connect the documents and its' attributes. Each document is marked with tags extracted by the algorithm, and these tags represent the relevant attributes of the documents. When a document has a certain tag, a connection between the document and the attributes is established. Based on this relationship, all documents in the mobile phones can be aggregated to form a graph of association relationships between documents. Perform qualitative and quantitative analysis on the document information in the mobile phones, and construct the "entity-attribute-attribute value" triples about the documents. Then the users can re-find the documents quickly with the method proposed in the paper.

3 Concept Model of Feature Knowledge Graph

In order to solve the problem of re-finding without keywords, the paper proposes the concept model of feature knowledge graph. The process of people's search activities is:

first of all, search for keywords with their mind. These keywords are not limited to the name of the document, but may be a word or a sentence appearing in the document, or a picture, table or mathematical formula referenced by the document [8]. The method proposed in reference [5] and [8] is to classify the attributes, which is not automatically tagged, and can only be applied to the computer. Different from reference [5] and [8], the paper proposes a method of quantifying tags. We propose four features. They are resource feature, time feature, user memory feature, location feature, and their corresponding tags are: topics, last opened time, references and sources. After tagged the document, we mainly use knowledge graphs to show the relationship between document content attributes.

3.1 Resource Feature

Resource feature reflect the content of a document as a whole. The resource feature can describe the characteristic of data distribution, such as the words frequency, the part of speech and the topics. In this paper, we use topics to describe the resource feature. Because every document has one or some topics and these usually make us impressive. Another reason is it can fully reflect the information of the documents and can highly summarize the content of the documents.

3.2 Time Feature

The time feature is described by the last opened time of the document. We interview 30 mobile phone users with different careers for interval time of re-finding the documents by phone, all of them use mobile phones to work. The survey results show 80% of the interviewees thought the last time he opened the document is no more than one month. Only 20% of them show they can sometimes re-finding documents beyond three months.

As time goes on, we will forget what we remembered. According to the forgetting curve (Fig. 1) proposed by the German psychologist Ebbinghaus [9]: The law of forgetting is not to forget the content of a fixed length in a fixed time, but to forget quickly and then slowly.

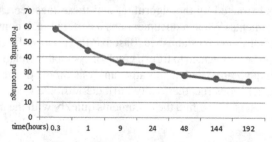

Fig. 1. Ebbinghaus forgetting curve

It can be seen from Fig. 1 that after the 6th day (the 144th hour), the forgetting curve started to be smooth. The user can only remember less than 30% of the documents opened six days ago. According to the Ebbinghaus Forgetting Curve as the theoretical basis, we took six days as a period named last opened time of documents to tag the time feature.

3.3 User Memory Feature

This feature describes the memory of users. Users are most likely to recall some fragments such as pictures, tables, mathematical formulas, etc. We use the above three factors to describe the user memory feature called references tag. Studies have pointed out in most cases, people always remember pictures better than words, which is called PSE (the picture superiority effect) [10]. It is because of the high compatibility between pictures rendering and visual space template.

3.4 Location Feature

The location feature refers to which applications the documents are downloaded by. Due to the isolation between different applications in the phone, taking WeChat and QQ application as an example, although both are Tencent's applications, the location of the data file is not the same. The files downloaded by WeChat are stored in the "tencent/MicroMsg/Download" directory under the internal storage file directory of the phone, and the files downloaded by QQ are stored in the "tencent/QQfile_recv" directory. DingTalk is the software which the 80% of mobile office enterprises choose. Its downloaded files are stored in the Dingtalk directory. For users who can-not clearly find the file directory, re-finding the documents from these applications is hard. Based on the above situation, we use source tag to describe the location feature of documents.

We have surveyed 141 enterprises which include varieties of industries to know the usage of DingTalk, WeChat and QQ. The result is shown in Fig. 2.

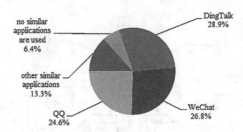

Fig. 2. The usage of DingTalk, WeChat and QQ

From Fig. 2, we can see the total proportion of DingTalk, WeChat and QQ applications is 80.3%. And from the questionnaire, we found more than 50% enterprises use these three applications to share the files. So we use WeChat, QQ, and DingTalk to classify the source tag.

3.5 Feature Knowledge Graph

The corresponding tags extracted from each document describe the relevant attributes of the document, and the knowledge graph is constructed by combining the documents and tags. Two kinds of nodes are provided in the knowledge graph constructed in this paper, namely document nodes and tag nodes. The document node records the relevant information of the document, including information such as title and content. The tag node records the relevant attributes of the document node, such as topic, source, last opened time, and references contained in the document. When a document has a certain tag, a connection between the document node and the tag node is established. Based on this basic relationship, all documents in a user's mobile phone are aggregated to construct a knowledge graph of the associations between personal mobile phone documents. Figure 3 describes the relationships between several entities. The nodes represent entities, and edges represent relationships between entities.

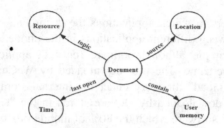

Fig. 3. The relationships between entities

Take the following three documents as an example. Figure 4 shows part of the knowledge graph. The graph diverges around these three documents and shows the connections between the three documents.

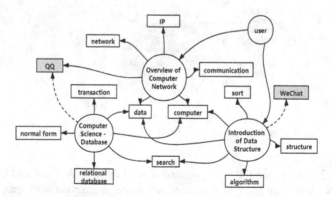

Fig. 4. The part of the knowledge graph

The round node represents the "document" entity, the white rectangular node represents the "resource" entity, the gray rectangular node represents the "location" entity, the solid arrow represents the relationship of "resource-topic tag-document", and the dashed arrow represents the relationship of "document- Source-location" relationship.

4 Re-finding Method Based on Feature Tags

We use four-tuple $D_i(L_i, T_i, M_i, R_i)$ to represent the four feature tags. Among them D_i means the ith document, L_i means the topic of D_i, T_i means the last opened time of D_i, M_i means a reference to D_i, R_i means the source of the D_i, For example, D_1 (Big data, 20191005, Table, WeChat)'s meaning is the topic of D_1 is "Big data", the latest opened time is "October 5, 2019", the reference contains "Table", and the document's source is "WeChat".

4.1 The Weight Assignment Algorithm of Feature Tags

Different users have different memory points when searching. For example, user A and user B search for the same document, user A remembers a table in the document, and user B remembers the source of the document. Obviously user A and user B have different focus on the tag. So considering the above situation, it is necessary to propose the weight distribution algorithm to adjust the weight of each feature for different user memories.

Resource Feature—Determine the Topic. We first use the TF_IDF to count the frequency of words, and second use LDA based on part of speech to select highly summarized topic.

The method used to count the word frequency is TF_IDF (term frequency–inverse document frequency), TF is the word frequency, IDF is the reverse file frequency, and the TF_IDF is the product of TF and IDF. However, after getting the TF_IDF values, the words with the highest TF_IDF value cannot be a topic of the document, because we cannot determine the distribution of these high-frequency words in the document. This situation may occur: The distribution of a high-frequency word is scattered in the document. And the scattered words are not enough to express the topic of the document. Therefore, we use the LDA topic model based on part of speech to determine the distribution of high-frequency words through TF_IDF statistics.

The LDA (Latent Dirichlet Allocation) topic model selects multiple groups of words. It is a Bag-of-word. It is most widely used in the field of text clustering and classification [11]. The traditional LDA topic model has the disadvantages of polysemy, blindness and semantic degradation. So we use POS_LDA model (a LDA topic model based on Part of Speech) to avoid the shortcomings of traditional model.

After removing "stop words", we build the POS_LDA model to calculate the probability of the words with parts of speech. We use a standard annotation set-ICTCLAS. The partial ICTCLAS comparison table is shown in Table 1.

By counting the parts of speech before segmentation, as shown in Fig. 5, we found the coverage of nouns and verbs reached 100%, and the coverage of adjectives reached 99.5%. After removing "stop words", the preserved parts of speech are nouns, verbs adjectives, distinguish words and place name. It was found that the accumulative proportion of nouns, verbs and adjectives accounted for more than 98%, while the remaining 10 parts of speech accounted for less than 2%. Therefore, we use nouns, verbs, and adjectives to represent document topics.

Table 1. Partial ICTCLAS comparison table

Part of speech	Meaning	Part of speech	Meaning
a	Adjective	n	Noun
b	Distinguish word	v	Verb
c	Conjunction	nh	Person name
d	Adverb	ns	Place name

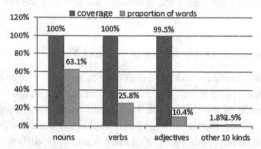

Fig. 5. Distribution of part of speech

The Weight Assignment Algorithm. We propose a dynamic weight algorithm for attributes with user priority based on information gain. Before the feature tags are added, the document has the original information entropy. After adding feature tags, the conditional information entropy is generated [12]. The information entropy calculation is as formula (1).

$$H(x_i) = -\sum_{i=1}^{n} p(x_i)logp(x_i) \qquad (1)$$

In this paper, we use the difference between the original information entropy and the conditional information entropy named information gain for weight allocating. Each document ensure the attribute tags selected by D_i corresponds to four variables of tags, they are x_1, x_2, x_3, x_4. The information gain algorithm of the four tags attributes is shown in Algorithm 1. k is the number of attributes contained in each tag and C_{x_i} is attribute variable in each tag.

Algorithm 1 Information Gain Algorithm of the Four Tags Attributes

---

Input: D_i document set

Output: IG of the four tags attributes

1: **for** each D_i **do**

2:    calculate the original information entropy with formula (1):

3:    $H(d_i) = -\sum_{k=1}^{n} p(x_k) \, logp(x_k);$

4:    calculate the conditional information entropy with formula (2) & (3):

5:    $H(d_i|x_i = c_{x_i}) = -\sum p(d|x_i = c_{x_i}) logp(d|x = c_{x_i})$ (2)

6:    $H(d|x_i) = \sum p(x_i = c_{x_i}) H(d_i|x_i = c_{x_i})$ (3)

7:    calculate the information gain with formula (4):

8:    $IG(x_i) = H(d_i) - H(d|x_i)$ (4)

9: **return** $IG(x_i)$

10: **end for**

After obtaining the information gain of each tag, formula (5) is used to calculate the weight corresponding to each attribute. W_t is the weight of four tags. The weight obtained here represents the importance of each attribute to the document.

$$W_t = \frac{IG(x_i)}{\sum_{i=1}^{n} IG(x_i)} (t = 1, 2, 3, 4) \tag{5}$$

4.2 Sorting and Re-finding Method Based on Feature Tags

The documents of most third-party file management applications are sorted by type or file size or time. This sorting method cannot effectively reduce the user's re-finding time, moreover, the traditional search methods did not personally optimize the search for each user's personal characteristics, nor did they show the relationship between the document and the content. Traditional search methods are often out of touch between the external and internal features of the document. The knowledge graph introduced in this paper establishes a relationship between the external characteristics of the document and the internal characteristics including the user characteristics, thereby turning the document and the user into an interconnected whole.

The subjective factor that affects the efficiency of document re-finding is the similarity between the keywords formed in the memory and the contents of the documents. The objective factors affect the re-finding efficiency are the classification and ordering rules of the documents. We propose a sorting re-finding algorithm to reduce the negative influences of subjective factors.

We have two assumes. The first one: the users are not affected by subjective memory when they are re-finding, which means they have a vague memory of some features of documents. When you ask them if they remember a table referenced in a document or where they get the document, they will tell you "I can't remember". So, we need to provide users with a sorting rule that minimizes the scope of the re-finding. Another assumption is users are affected by subjective memory when they are re-finding.

They know what keywords they are looking for. For example, user A needs to find a document. He clearly remembered there is a table in this document, but he has no impression of the document's name. For this situation, when A chose the references tags, the weight of references tag is changed, the ranking results are also changed. In this condition, in order to interact with users, we showed them the contents of four tags and asked them to select the tag closest to their remembered keyword. We dynamically adjust the weight of the tags by adding the user priority value (u_i), u_i is determined according to the connection between the user and the document in the personal knowledge graph. For example, the connection between the document D_1 and the user u_1 is that the user u_1 opened the document D_1 three days ago, and the corresponding tag is last opened time. The knowledge graph establishes a connection between users and attributes through documents, and then u_i can be calculated by formula (6). It means the percentage of the user's memory keyword (p_j) in the total number of tag's attributes it belongs to.

$$u_i = \frac{\sum_{j=1}^{m} p_j}{\sum_{k=1}^{n} x_k} \tag{6}$$

In order to ensure the attribute tags selected by users will not be ignored due to the small number of attribute tag values, the following calculation method is proposed to increase the weight of the attribute with a small attribute value.

$$IG'(x_i) = H(d_i) - (1 - u_i) * H(dlx_i), \quad WU_t = \frac{IG'(x_i)}{\sum_{i=1}^{n} IG'(x_i)} \quad (t = 1, 2, 3, 4) \tag{7}$$

When the value of u_1 is larger, the value of $IG'(x_i)$ is larger. And then, we use Algorithm 2 given below to get initial rank of documents for re-finding.

Algorithm 2 The Sorting Algorithm of Re-finding Documents

Input: the weight of documents W_t

Output: the rank of documents

1: **for** each re-finding tasks **do**

2:    **if** user have keywords in their memory **then:**

3:        calculate the weight with formula (7) by adding user priority value;

4:    **else**

5:        calculate the weight with formula (5);

6:    **end if**

7:    construct the attribute quantization matrix $A(a_{ij})_{n*m}$;

8:    construct weight matrix $W(w_t)_{m*1}$;

9:    calculate $S_{n*1} = A(a_{ij})_{n*m} * W(w_t)_{m*1}$;

10: **return** S_{n*1}

11: **end for**

In Algorithm 2, a_{ij} in $A(a_{ij})_{n*m}$ is the proportion of a certain attribute to the total attributes under each tag. The document corresponding to the first value in the S_{n*1}

matrix obtained in Algorithm 2 is most similar to the user's expectations. However, the following situation will occur: some documents similar to the user's expectations will be ranked in the lower position. In order to prevent the above situation, this paper uses the Common Neighbors algorithm to calculate the document similarity in the order of the matrix S_{n*1} by formula (8). $N(x)$ and $N(y)$ are two document nodes, the formula calculates the number of nodes shared between them.

$$CN_{sim(x,y)} = |N(x) \cap N(y)| \tag{8}$$

After obtain the document similarity, then uses the formula (9) to normalize the calculated number of nodes. The max is the maximum value of the sample data, and the min is the minimum value of the sample data.

$$S_i = \frac{CN_{sim(x,y)} - min}{max - min} \tag{9}$$

5 Experiment Evaluation

This paper studies the re-finding of the personal mobile phone documents. A big challenge is there is no public data set, and the data in personal mobile phones has a wide range of fields and diverse contents. Therefore, the data set of this experiment is constructed by collecting data of users' mobile phones.

5.1 Experiment Data Set and Preprocessing

Due to the privacy of the documents in the personal mobile phones, the experimental data were collected from personal data of mobile phone users. To make the data as comprehensive as possible, the users selected for the experiment cover different industries, including computers, electricity, education, and the economy. The experimental training set is 1680. To evaluate the efficiency of the proposed method, we selected 352 mobile phones data from real users in the last six months as test sets, and the details of the test set are shown in Table 2.

Table 2. Test set

Test set	Involved field	Number of documents
Test1	Economy	74
Test2	Computer	88
Test3	Finance	69
Test4	Mechanical	70
Test5	Electricity	51

5.2   Experiment Evaluation

We use search time to evaluate the experimental results. We find eight volunteers to help complete the experiment. The experiment is performed in two parts and takes two weeks. First, give the mobile phone with the test set to the volunteers, and require them to be as familiar with the content of the test set as possible for a week. Then give some re-finding tasks to the volunteers. Then we use the method proposed in this paper to compare with the file management applications and traditional directory method. Finally, the less time it takes, the higher the re-finding efficiency is. The description of ten tasks is shown in Table 3.

Table 3.   Test tasks

Task number	Re-finding mission details	User subjective memory factor
1	A document about computer	Document was last opened five days ago
2	A document about a school recruitment requirements	Contain a table about career
3	A document about the role of party members	Document is from WeChat
4	A document	Topic is about computer networks
5	A document about English translation	None
6	A document about a thermoelectric accident	Contain pictures about machine, document is from WeChat
7	A test question about Internet applications	Last opened a week ago and the document is from QQ
8	A document	Topic is educational and from WeChat
9	A document about the financial crisis	The document was last opened two weeks ago with a table
10	A document	Topic is about computer database and contains mathematical formulas

5.3   Analysis of Results

First, according to the method described in Sect. 3, all documents in the test set are tagged with the four feature tags to form the four-tuple. And the weights are calculated with method proposed in Sect. 4. The weight without user priority matrix is $W(w_t)_{m*1} = (0.361, 0.182, 0.257, 0.188)^T$ (three decimal places). So we have a basic rank of documents based on $W(w_t)_{m*1}$.

From the results of volunteer experiments we observe: (1) in task 2 the method proposed in this paper takes longer than the other two methods. After analysis, we find there are two main reasons: First, because the name of the document corresponding to task 2 starts with a number, it leads to the front position when using the file management applications. Since there is no need to scroll down when searching, the volunteers quickly found it. Second, volunteers have a deep memory of the document, which also results in shorter time. This situation is where we need to improve in the future. (2) From other tasks, it can be seen that the search time using the method proposed in this paper is shortened compared with the other two methods. Figure 6 shows the average search time of these three methods.

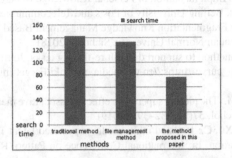

Fig. 6. The average search time of three methods

From Fig. 6, we obtain the following conclusions: (1) compared with the other two methods, the traditional search takes longer. The method proposed in this paper takes the least time and is generally shortened by about one-half compared with the traditional method. (2) When the users use the traditional mobile phone search function, time is mainly wasted between switching the parent and son directory of the folder. (3) The method proposed in this paper shortens the scope for users' re-finding and is efficient. It can dynamically sort according to the user's memory contents.

6 Conclusion

By analyzing the behavior and memory characteristics of mobile phones re-finding, this paper proposed to tag the mobile phone documents with four features and construct a knowledge graph. Then we proposed the quantitative calculation method of tags and sorting which was verified by experiments. The results showed that the method proposed in this paper took less time for re-finding and was an efficient method. But this is only a preliminary study. In future research, we will continue to improve the method with optimizing the value of the weights and improve the sorting method.

References

1. Stryjak, J., Sivakumaran, M.: The Mobile Economy 2019. GSMA Intelligence, Barcelona (2019)
2. 2016 Mobile Office Panorama Report (in Chinese). Mobile Information Researching Center, China (2016)

3. Tauscher, L., Greenberg, S.: Revisitation patterns in world wide web navigation. In: CHI97: ACM Conference on Human Factors & Computing Systems, pp. 3–10. Association for Computing Machinery, New York (1997)
4. Do, T.V., Ruddle, R.A.: The design of a visual history tool to help users refind information within a website. In: Baeza-Yates, R., et al. (eds.) ECIR 2012. LNCS, vol. 7224, pp. 459–462. Springer, Heidelberg (2012). https://doi.org/10.1007/978-3-642-28997-2_41
5. Tangjian, D., Liang, Z., et al.: ReFinder: a context-based information refinding system. IEEE Trans. Knowl. Data Eng. **25**, 2119–2132 (2013)
6. Xuan, L.: Design and Implementation of Personal Knowledge Management Platform Based on Knowledge Graph. Beijing University of Posts and Telecommunications, Beijing (2018)
7. Yan, L.: Study on the Fragmentation Knowledge Management Based on Knowledge Map in Mobile Learning. Sichuan Normal University, Sichuan (2018)
8. Liu, G., Feng, L.: A method to support difficult re-finding tasks. Journal **02**, 15–19 (2016)
9. Wikipedia Forgetting_curve. https://en.wikipedia.org/wiki/Forgetting_curve. Accessed 15 May 2020
10. Baadte, C., Bozana, M.: The picture superiority effect in associative memory: a developmental study. Br. J. Dev. Psychol. **37**(3), 382–395 (2019)
11. Qian, S., Zhang, T., Xu, C.: Boosted multi-modal supervised latent Dirichlet allocation for social event classification. In: International Conference on Pattern Recognition, pp. 1999–2004. IEEE (2014)
12. GuoYin, W., Hong, Y., DaChun, Y.: Decision table reduction based on conditional information entropy. J. Comput. Chin. Ed. **25**(07), 759–766 (2007)

Knowledge Graph Embedding
with Relation Constraint

Chunming Yang[1,4]([✉]), Xinghao Song[3], Hui Zhang[2], and Bo Li[1]

[1] School of Computer Science and Technology, Southwest University of Science
and Technology, Mianyang 621010, Sichuan, China
yangchunming@swust.edu.cn
[2] School of Science, Southwest University of Science and Technology,
Mianyang 621010, Sichuan, China
[3] Sichuan Branch of China Telecom Co., Ltd., Chengdu 610015, Sichuan, China
[4] Sichuan Big Data and Intelligent System Engineering Technology Research Center,
Mianyang 621010, Sichuan, China

Abstract. Knowledge graph (KG) is structure representations of the
real-world facts by triples, and embedding entities and relations of a KG
into continuous vector spaces is proven to be effective in many applications. Schema-based KG also has rich prior information about entities
and relations, such as entity constraints for relations which define the
semantic role of relations. In this paper, we propose TransRC (Translation model with Relation Constraint) model, which use relation constraint as a part of score function to extend the TransE. Experimental
results from multiple benchmarks knowledge graph datasets show that
the TransRC benefits from relation constraint information, and it is better than other methods on link prediction and triple classification.

Keywords: Knowledge graph embedding · Relation constraint · Link
prediction · Triple classification

1 Introduction

Knowledge graphs (KGs) are collections of triples, where each triple represents
a fact, and stored in the form of the directed graph. A fact triple is represented
as (h, r, t), where h is head entity, t is tail entity and r is the relation directed
from h to t. Each node represents an entity and each edge represents the relation
between entities in graph. Knowledge graphs such as WordNet [18], Freebase [1]
are extremely useful resources for many AI tasks, such as recommender system [4],
question-answering [5], search engine [17], information extraction [29], etc.

A typical KGs contain millions of entities and billions of relational facts,
the underlying symbolic character of such triples makes KGs hard to efficiently
compute. Knowledge graph embedding (KGE) [2,12,24] has been proposed to
learning low-dimensional vector spaces representations of entities and relations.
These methods have been shown to be scalable and effective, and can benefit a
board range of downstream applications [27,30].

© Springer Nature Singapore Pte Ltd. 2021
Q. Chen and J. Li (Eds.): APWeb-WAIM 2020 Workshops, CCIS 1373, pp. 41–51, 2021.
https://doi.org/10.1007/978-981-16-0479-9_4

Most of the existing KGE approaches to use a score function $f(h, r, t)$ describing the possibility of a candidate triple (h, r, t). The goal of the optimization is usually to score the true triple higher than corrupted false triple (h, r, t') or (h', r, t). It means that only considering the existing triples in KGs but not the implicit information. In addition to storing the observed facts, schema-based KGs also provide some prior information such as class hierarchies of entities and entity constraints for relations which define the semantic role of relations. These prior informations on relation provides semantic information, e.g. that the *isFatherOf* relation should relate only entities of class *Man*. In some previous work [13,14], it has been shown that the benefits greatly from the prior information about the semantic of relation for link predict and relation extraction task.

In this paper, we propose such an approach called TransRC by adding the relation constraint prior information to the score function for knowledge graph embedding. The score function of model can be divided into two parts, one part score for the relation constraint, the other for the candidate triple (h, r, t) in KGs. TransRC limits the relative position of relations and entities, and performs very well empirical despite its simplicity. We evaluate the TransRC on five knowledge graph benchmarks datasets including FB15K [2], FB15K237 [23], WN11 [22], WN18 [2], WN18RR [6]. Experimental results indicate that TransRC is simple yet surprising effective, achieving significant improvements over competitive baseline.

2   Related Work

The KGE is to embed entities and relations of a KG into continuous vector spaces by defines a scoring function on each fact to measure its plausibility. We categorize such embedding methods of three groups: translation-based model, bilinear model and other.

Translation-based models regarding the relation r as a translation from h to t for a triple, and measure the plausibility of a fact as the distance between the two entities. TransE [2] is the first translation-based model, which the relationship between two entities corresponds to a translation between the embeddings of entities, and represents both entities and relations as vectors in the same space. It was pointed in many researches that TransE has problems when modeling 1-N, N-1 and N-N relations. TransH [25] attempts to solve these problems by models a relation as a hyper plane together with a translation operation on it. TransR & CTransR [15] attempts to alleviate the problem of TransE and TransH that relations and entities are completed different objects, it may be not capable to embedding them in a common space. TransD [10] constructs a dynamic mapping matrix for each entity-relation pair by considering the diversity of entities and relations simultaneously. Compared with TransR/CTransR, TransD has fewer parameters and has no matrix vector multiplication. There are many other translation-based models, such as TransM [7] leverages the structure of the knowledge graph via pre-calculating the distinct weight for each training triplet according to its relational mapping property. TransF [8] regards relation as translation between head entity vector and tail entity vector with flexible magnitude, ManifoldE [26] propose a manifold-based embedding principle which could be treated as a well-posed algebraic system that expands point-wise modeling in current models to manifold-wise modeling, TranSpare [11] replaces the projection matrix in TransR by adaptive matrix. Bilinear models measure plausibility of facts by similarity-based scoring functions, they match latent semantics of entities and relations embodied in their vector space. RESCAl [20] uses vectors to capture the latent semantics of entities and each relation is represented as a matrix. They can be seen as an extension of low-rank matrix factorization method. DistMul [28] can be seen as a special case of RESCAL with a diagonal matrix for each relation, so it has the same number of parameters as TransE. Because the relation matrix of DistMult is a diagonal matrix, it can be seen as a vector. DistMult makes the model easy to train and eliminate the redundancy. However, it scores of $f(h, r, t)$ and $f(t, r, h)$ are same. ComplEx [24] uses complex vectors instead of real vectors and complex vectors can effectively capture anti-symmetric relations. Analogy [16] uses the real normal matrix to capture the symmetric, anti-symmetric and invertible relations. And Analogy simplifies the normal matrix with a 2×2 blocks in $\boldsymbol{B}_r$, where $\boldsymbol{B}_r$ represents the almost diagonal matrix. SimplE [12] is a bilinear model based on Canonical Polyadic decomposition. It learns two independent embedding vectors for each relation, one is for the normal relation and other is for the inverse relation.

Other model like R-GCN [21] uses graph convolutional networks(GCNs) to deal with the highly multi-relational data characteristic of realistic knowledge bases. ConvE [6] applies 2D convolution directly on embeddings to prevent overfitting due to over-parametrization. ConvKB [19] represents each triple to a 3-column matrix and fed to a convolution layer to generate different feature maps, and archives better link prediction performance links in knowledge graphs. KBGAN [3] uses generative adversarial networks(GANs) to generate negative facts to assist the training, it can be improved the training of a wide range of KGE models. These models focus on using different neural networks to embedding KGs.

Most of the previous works only consider the existing triples in KGs but not the implicit information, e.g., relation constraint, entity types, textual descriptions which define the class of linked entity. e.g. that the *marriedTo* relation should link only entities of the class *Person*, and *isFatherOf* relation should relate only entities of class *Man*. In this work we will demonstrate how to consider relation constraint prior information to the score function, and propose a model of knowledge graph embedding.

3   TransRC Model

3.1   Problem Definition

For a given knowledge graph, let $\mathcal{E}$ denote the set of all entities, $\mathcal{R}$ the set of all relations, and Δ denote the set of ground truth triples present in the knowledge graph. In general, a knowledge graph embedding (KGE) model learns vectors $\boldsymbol{h}, \boldsymbol{t} \in \mathbb{R}^{d_e}$ for $h, t \in \mathcal{E}$, and $\boldsymbol{r} \in \mathbb{R}^{d_r}$ for $r \in \mathcal{R}$. Some models also learn projection matrices $M_r \in \mathbb{R}^{d_r \times d_e}$ for relations. The ground truth triples is evaluated using a model specific score function $f(h,r,t) : \mathcal{E} \times \mathcal{R} \times \mathcal{E} \to R$. For learning the embeddings, a loss function $\mathcal{L}(\Delta, \Delta', \Theta)$, define over a set of positive triples Δ, set of negative triples Δ', and the parameters Θ is optimized.

3.2   Model Description

Some class hierarchies of entities and type-constraints for relations which define the semantic role of relations in schema-based KGs. The relation constraint prior information is used to represent constraints on relational by defining the classes or types of entities they should related to. In TransE, it maps both entities and relations into the same continuous low-dimensional vector space, and regarding the relation r as a translation from h to t for a triple (h,r,t). TransE presumes that the embedding vectors of the triple should satisfy $h + r \approx t$. So, t should be the nearest neighbor of $h + r$, as shown in Fig. 1(a), and the score function is

$$f(h,r,t) = -\|h + r - t\|_p \tag{1}$$

TransE uses score function calculate the possibility of a triple (h,r,t) by only the existing triples in KGs but not relation constraint information.

The relation constraint defines the class of linked entities, such as the *isFatherOf* relation should linked only entities of class Man. So, the entities related to special relation surround the relation in the embedding vector rather than randomly distributed in the Embedding space, as shown in Fig. 1(b), it limits the relative position of relations and entities. So, the score function of model can be divided into two parts, one part score for the relation constraint, the other for the candidate triple (h,r,t) in KGs.

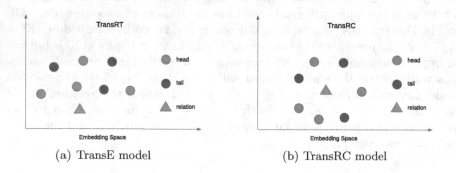

(a) TransE model   (b) TransRC model

Fig. 1. Comparison of TransE and TransRC

Here we define a relation constraint score function as following:

$$f_1(h,r) = -tanh(\|h - r\|_p - \varepsilon) \tag{2}$$

where ε is the distance parameter between h and r, we hope the entities sur-rounds the relation with ε, and tanh function is used for reducing limitation of relation constraint score function. If don't reduce the relation constraint score function, it would make $h \approx r \approx t$, this situation can make the model worse.

For a candidate triple (h, r, t) in KGs, we use the classic 2-norm score function from TransE, it has been proven simple and powerful. So, the candidate triple score function is defined as:

$$f_2(h, r, t) = -\|h + r - t\|_p \tag{3}$$

We combine the relation constraint score function with candidate triple score function as our final score function for the model:

$$f(h, r, t) = f_1(h, r) + f_2(h, r, t) \tag{4}$$

3.3 Model Learning

To learn a TransRC model, we use negative sampling and the Margin Ranking Loss define as follow:

$$\mathcal{L} = \sum_{(h,r,t)\in\Delta\cup(h',r,t')\in\Delta'} max(0, \gamma + f(h, r, t) - f(h', r, t')) \tag{5}$$

where Δ and Δ' are used to describe the positive triple set and negative triple set.

For a positive triple $(h, r, t) \in \Delta$, the model randomly decide to corrupt the head or tail. If the head is selected, replace h in the triple with an entity h' randomly chosen from $\mathcal{E} - \{h\}$ and make the corrupted triple $(h', r, t) \in \Delta'$. If the tail is selected, replace t in triple with an entity in the triple with an entity t' randomly chosen from $\mathcal{E} - \{t\}$ and make the corrupt triple $(h, r, t') \in \Delta'$.

4   Experiments and Results

4.1   Datasets

In this paper, we evaluate our model on five standard benchmarks. The statistics of these datasets are summarized in Table 1.

FB15K [2] is a subset of Freebase. The selected entities in FB15K that are also present in the Wikilinks datasets and that also have at least 100 mentions in Freebase.

FB15K237 [23] was created from FB15K by removing the inverse of many relations that are present in training set from validation and test set.

WN11 [22] is a subset of WordNet. It filters out triples from the testing set if either or both of their two entities also appear in the training set in different relation or oder.

Table 1. Number of entities, relations, and the Dataset partition.

Dataset	Rel	Ent	Train	Test	Valid
FB15K	1,345	14,952	483,142	59,071	50,000
FB15K237	237	14,541	272,115	20,466	17,535
WN11	11	38,588	112,581	10,544	2,609
WN18	18	40,934	141,442	5,000	5,000
WN18RR	11	40,934	86,835	3,134	3,034

WN18 [2] is a subset of WordNet.

WN18RR [6] was created from WN18 by removing the inverse relations from validation and test sets.

4.2   Evaluation Metrics

Link Prediction aims to predict the missing h or t for a relation fact triple (h, r, t), and use the filtered *MRR* and *Hit@N* for evaluating. For each test triple (h, r, t) we compute the score of (h', r, t) and (h, r, t') triples for all $h', t' \in E$ that $(h', r, t), (h, r, t') \notin train \cup test \cup valid$ with the score function and calculate the ranking R_h and R_t. Then we compute the *mean reciprocal rank (MRR)* of these as the mean of the inverse of rankings:

$$MRR = \frac{1}{2n_{test}} \sum_{(h,r,t)\in test} \frac{1}{R_h} + \frac{1}{R_t} \qquad (6)$$

The *Hit@N* for a model is computed as the percentage of test triples which ranking is less than or equal N.

Triple classification aims to judge whether a given triple (h, r, t) is correct or not, use accuracy to evaluate the performance. We set a threshold δ_r for every relation, for a given test triple, if its score function is smaller than δ_r, it will be classified as positive, otherwise negative. δ_r is optimized by maximizing classification accuracies on the validation set.

4.3   Experiment Setting

We implement TransRC model in OpenKE framework, and train the model using Adam and set the batch size $b = n_{train}/100$, the base train epochs $e = 1000$. During the training, evaluate the model with validation set every 100 epochs and save the best model for testing. If the best result is in the last 100 epochs, add 500 epochs on the base epochs to retrain the model. For FB15K and WN18, set embedding dimensions $d = 150$. For FB15K-237 and WN18RR, embedding dimensions $d = 200$. We use dropout to control overfitting and improve predictions, and the learning rate from 0.1, 0.01, 0.001, 0.0001, norm p form 1, 2, margin λ from (0.6, 0.7, 0.8, 0.9, 1.0), ε from (0.001, 0.002, 0.005, 0.01, 0.02, 0.05, 0.1) and dropout from (0, 0.1, 0.2, 0.3, 0.4).

4.4   Link Prediction Result

Table 2. The link prediction result on FB15K and WN18.

Model	FB15K		WN18	
	MRR	Hit@10	MRR	Hit@10
TransE [2]	–	.471	–	.892
TransH [25]	–	.644	–	.867
TransD [10]	–	.773	–	.925
TransR [15]	–	.702	–	.923
TranSpare [11]	–	.799	–	.939
DistMult [28]	.350	.577	**.890**	.942
TransRC	**.603**	**.834**	.591	**.945**

Table 3. The link prediction result on FB15K237 and WN18RR. Result marked with * are produced by running OpenKE [9] with its default parameters. All other baseline result are copied from their original papers

Model	FB15K237		WN18RR	
	MRR	Hit@10	MRR	Hit@10
TransE*	.292	.471	.176	.403
TransH*	.287	.457	.042	.073
ConvE [6]	**.316**	.491	**.460**	.480
DistMult*	.235	.400	.366	.380
ComplEx [24]*	.201	.388	.365	.377
R-GCN [21]	.249	.577	–	–
TransRC	.298	**.495**	.212	**.490**

Link prediction results of four datasets are shown in Table 2 and 3. Overall, TransRC outperforms previous models on most metrics across four datasets (apart from MRR on FB15K237, WN18 and WN18RR where DistMult and ConvE do better). TransRC effect is not best on MRR, which means that translation-based model can rank the correct candidate to top ten but will be lower than other models. However,other results show that this simple relation constraint leads to very good performance. Results achieved by TransRC are not only better than those of other translation-based models, such as TransE, TransR and TranSpares, but also better than the results of bilinear and neural network models, e.g. DistMult, R-GCN and ConvE. We believe the relation constraint information is a key property of the success of TransRC.

4.5 Triple Classification

Table 4. The triple classification results. All the results are produced by running OpenKE with its default parameters.

	FB15K	FB15K237	WN11	WN18	WN18RR
TransE	0.8867	0.7645	0.6328	0.9246	0.7643
TransH	0.8744	0.7539	0.6038	0.7958	0.652
TransD	0.8921	0.7579	0.6145	0.9658	0.6652
DistMult	0.9029	0.7231	0.5590	0.9681	0.7303
ComplEx	0.8963	0.7217	0.5582	0.9678	0.7168
Analogy [16]	0.8937	0.7184	0.5551	0.9691	0.7153
TrnasRC	**0.9033**	**0.7827**	**0.7242**	**0.9721**	**0.8286**

Evaluation results on the triple classification are shown in Table 4. From Table 4 we observe that: (1) On all five datasets TransRC significantly outperforms all baselines; this shows our model can better distinguish between true and false triples, the score function of TransRC has a bigger margin between true and false. (2) On WN11, FB15K237 and WN18RR translation-based model performs well than bilinear model. The result may correlate with the characteristics of datasets: There are few relations in these datasets, and there are no inverse relations. (3) The simple models like TransE, DistMult are good enough on triple classification, sometimes the more complicated it does not mean the powerful.

5 Conclusion and Future Work

In this work, we introduce TransRC, a translation-based model for knowledge graph embedding based on relation constraint, which achieves good results on five standard knowledge graph datasets. TransRC's number of parameters grows linearly with respect to embedding dimension as the number of entities or relations in a knowledge graph. We also show that improvements have been made through simple relation constraint on the translation-based model. Future work might include exploring the solutions of 1-N and N-1 relations problems for translation-based model and incorporate the relation constraint prior information into the bilinear model.

References

1. Bollacker, K.D., Evans, C., Paritosh, P., Sturge, T., Taylor, J.: Freebase: a collaboratively created graph database for structuring human knowledge. In: Proceedings of the ACM SIGMOD International Conference on Management of Data, SIGMOD 2008, Vancouver, BC, Canada, 10–12 June 2008, pp. 1247–1250 (2008). https://doi.org/10.1145/1376616.1376746

2. Bordes, A., Usunier, N., García-Durán, A., Weston, J., Yakhnenko, O.: Translating embeddings for modeling multi-relational data. In: Advances in Neural Information Processing Systems 26: 27th Annual Conference on Neural Information Processing Systems 2013. Proceedings of a Meeting held 5–8 December 2013, Lake Tahoe, Nevada, USA, pp. 2787–2795 (2013)
3. Cai, L., Wang, W.Y.: KBGAN: adversarial learning for knowledge graph embeddings. In: Proceedings of the 2018 Conference of the North American Chapter of the Association for Computational Linguistics: Human Language Technologies, NAACL-HLT 2018, New Orleans, Louisiana, USA, 1–6 June 2018, vol. 1 (Long Papers), pp. 1470–1480 (2018). https://www.aclweb.org/anthology/N18-1133/
4. Catherine, R., Cohen, W.W.: Personalized recommendations using knowledge graphs: a probabilistic logic programming approach. In: Proceedings of the 10th ACM Conference on Recommender Systems, Boston, MA, USA, 15–19 September 2016, pp. 325–332 (2016). https://doi.org/10.1145/2959100.2959131
5. Cui, W., Xiao, Y., Wang, H., Song, Y., Hwang, S., Wang, W.: KBQA: learning question answering over QA corpora and knowledge bases. PVLDB 10(5), 565–576 (2017). https://doi.org/10.14778/3055540.3055549
6. Dettmers, T., Minervini, P., Stenetorp, P., Riedel, S.: Convolutional 2D knowledge graph embeddings. In: Proceedings of the Thirty-Second AAAI Conference on Artificial Intelligence, (AAAI-2018), the 30th Innovative Applications of Artificial Intelligence (IAAI-2018), and the 8th AAAI Symposium on Educational Advances in Artificial Intelligence (EAAI-2018), New Orleans, Louisiana, USA, 2–7 February 2018, pp. 1811–1818 (2018)
7. Fan, M., Zhou, Q., Chang, E., Zheng, T.F.: Transition-based knowledge graph embedding with relational mapping properties. In: Proceedings of the 28th Pacific Asia Conference on Language, Information and Computation, PACLIC 28, Cape Panwa Hotel, Phuket, Thailand, 12–14 December 2014, pp. 328–337 (2014)
8. Feng, J., Huang, M., Wang, M., Zhou, M., Hao, Y., Zhu, X.: Knowledge graph embedding by flexible translation. In: Principles of Knowledge Representation and Reasoning: Proceedings of the Fifteenth International Conference, KR 2016, Cape Town, South Africa, 25–29 April 2016, pp. 557–560 (2016)
9. Han, X., Cao, S., Lv, X., Lin, Y., Liu, Z., Sun, M., Li, J.: OpenKE: an open toolkit for knowledge embedding. In: Proceedings of the 2018 Conference on Empirical Methods in Natural Language Processing, EMNLP 2018: System Demonstrations, Brussels, Belgium, 31 October–4 November 2018, pp. 139–144 (2018)
10. Ji, G., He, S., Xu, L., Liu, K., Zhao, J.: Knowledge graph embedding via dynamic mapping matrix. In: Proceedings of the 53rd Annual Meeting of the Association for Computational Linguistics and the 7th International Joint Conference on Natural Language Processing of the Asian Federation of Natural Language Processing, ACL 2015, 26–31 July 2015, Beijing, China, vol. 1: Long Papers, pp. 687–696 (2015)
11. Ji, G., Liu, K., He, S., Zhao, J.: Knowledge graph completion with adaptive sparse transfer matrix. In: Proceedings of the Thirtieth AAAI Conference on Artificial Intelligence, Phoenix, Arizona, USA, 12–17 February 2016, pp. 985–991 (2016)
12. Kazemi, S.M., Poole, D.: Simple embedding for link prediction in knowledge graphs. In: Advances in Neural Information Processing Systems 31: Annual Conference on Neural Information Processing Systems 2018, NeurIPS 2018, Montréal, Canada, 3–8 December 2018, pp. 4289–4300 (2018)
13. Krompaß, D., Baier, S., Tresp, V.: Type-constrained representation learning in knowledge graphs. In: Arenas, M., et al. (eds.) ISWC 2015. LNCS, vol. 9366, pp. 640–655. Springer, Cham (2015). https://doi.org/10.1007/978-3-319-25007-6_37

14. Krompaß, D., Nickel, M., Tresp, V.: Large-scale factorization of type-constrained multi-relational data. In: International Conference on Data Science and Advanced Analytics, DSAA 2014, Shanghai, China, 30 October–1 November 2014, pp. 18–24 (2014). https://doi.org/10.1109/DSAA.2014.7058046
15. Lin, Y., Liu, Z., Sun, M., Liu, Y., Zhu, X.: Learning entity and relation embeddings for knowledge graph completion. In: Proceedings of the Twenty-Ninth AAAI Conference on Artificial Intelligence, Austin, Texas, USA, 25–30 January 2015, pp. 2181–2187 (2015)
16. Liu, H., Wu, Y., Yang, Y.: Analogical inference for multi-relational embeddings. In: Proceedings of the 34th International Conference on Machine Learning, ICML 2017, Sydney, NSW, Australia, 6–11 August 2017, pp. 2168–2178 (2017)
17. Mai, G., Janowicz, K., Yan, B.: Combining text embedding and knowledge graph embedding techniques for academic search engines. In: Joint proceedings of the 4th Workshop on Semantic Deep Learning (SemDeep-4) and NLIWoD4: Natural Language Interfaces for the Web of Data (NLIWOD-4) and 9th Question Answering over Linked Data challenge (QALD-9) co-located with 17th International Semantic Web Conference (ISWC 2018), Monterey, California, USA, 8–9 October 2018, pp. 77–88 (2018), http://ceur-ws.org/Vol-2241/paper-08.pdf
18. Miller, G.A.: WordNet: a lexical database for English. Commun. ACM **38**(11), 39–41 (1995). https://doi.org/10.1145/219717.219748
19. Nguyen, D.Q., Nguyen, T.D., Nguyen, D.Q., Phung, D.Q.: A novel embedding model for knowledge base completion based on convolutional neural network. In: Proceedings of the 2018 Conference of the North American Chapter of the Association for Computational Linguistics: Human Language Technologies, NAACL-HLT, New Orleans, Louisiana, USA, 1–6 June 2018, vol. 2 (Short Papers), pp. 327–333 (2018). https://www.aclweb.org/anthology/N18-2053/
20. Nickel, M., Tresp, V., Kriegel, H.: A three-way model for collective learning on multi-relational data. In: Proceedings of the 28th International Conference on Machine Learning, ICML 2011, Bellevue, Washington, USA, 28 June–2 July 2011, pp. 809–816 (2011)
21. Schlichtkrull, M., Kipf, T.N., Bloem, P., van den Berg, R., Titov, I., Welling, M.: Modeling relational data with graph convolutional networks. In: Gangemi, A., et al. (eds.) ESWC 2018. LNCS, vol. 10843, pp. 593–607. Springer, Cham (2018). https://doi.org/10.1007/978-3-319-93417-4_38
22. Socher, R., Chen, D., Manning, C.D., Ng, A.Y.: Reasoning with neural tensor networks for knowledge base completion. In: Advances in Neural Information Processing Systems 26: 27th Annual Conference on Neural Information Processing Systems 2013. Proceedings of a meeting held 5–8 December 2013, Lake Tahoe, Nevada, USA, pp. 926–934 (2013)
23. Toutanova, K., Chen, D., Pantel, P., Poon, H., Choudhury, P., Gamon, M.: Representing text for joint embedding of text and knowledge bases. In: Proceedings of the 2015 Conference on Empirical Methods in Natural Language Processing, EMNLP 2015, Lisbon, Portugal, 17–21 September 2015, pp. 1499–1509 (2015)
24. Trouillon, T., Welbl, J., Riedel, S., Gaussier, É., Bouchard, G.: Complex embeddings for simple link prediction. In: Proceedings of the 33nd International Conference on Machine Learning, ICML 2016, New York City, NY, USA, 19–24 June 2016, pp. 2071–2080 (2016)
25. Wang, Z., Zhang, J., Feng, J., Chen, Z.: Knowledge graph embedding by translating on hyperplanes. In: Proceedings of the Twenty-Eighth AAAI Conference on Artificial Intelligence, Québec City, Québec, Canada, 27–31 July 2014, pp. 1112–1119 (2014)

26. Xiao, H., Huang, M., Zhu, X.: From one point to a manifold: knowledge graph embedding for precise link prediction. In: Proceedings of the Twenty-Fifth International Joint Conference on Artificial Intelligence, IJCAI 2016, New York, NY, USA, 9–15 July 2016, pp. 1315–1321 (2016)
27. Xiong, C., Power, R., Callan, J.: Explicit semantic ranking for academic search via knowledge graph embedding. In: Proceedings of the 26th International Conference on World Wide Web, WWW 2017, Perth, Australia, 3–7 April 2017, pp. 1271–1279 (2017). https://doi.org/10.1145/3038912.3052558
28. Yang, B., Yih, W., He, X., Gao, J., Deng, L.: Embedding entities and relations for learning and inference in knowledge bases. In: 3rd International Conference on Learning Representations, Conference Track Proceedings, ICLR 2015, San Diego, CA, USA, 7–9 May 2015 (2015)
29. Zhang, D., Mukherjee, S., Lockard, C., Dong, L., McCallum, A.: OpenKI: integrating open information extraction and knowledge bases with relation inference. In: Proceedings of the 2019 Conference of the North American Chapter of the Association for Computational Linguistics: Human Language Technologies, NAACL-HLT 2019, Minneapolis, MN, USA, 2–7 June 2019, vol. 1 (Long and Short Papers), pp. 762–772 (2019). https://aclweb.org/anthology/papers/N/N19/N19-1083/
30. Zhou, Z., et al.: Knowledge-based recommendation with hierarchical collaborative embedding. In: Phung, D., Tseng, V.S., Webb, G.I., Ho, B., Ganji, M., Rashidi, L. (eds.) PAKDD 2018. LNCS (LNAI), vol. 10938, pp. 222–234. Springer, Cham (2018). https://doi.org/10.1007/978-3-319-93037-4_18

Knowledge-Driven Multi-dimensional Dialogue Rewriting Model

Xiangwei Guo[1], Yongli Wang[1(✉)], Gang Xiao[2], and Feifei Ma[3]

[1] Nanjing University of Science and Technology, Nanjing 210094, China
{118106021967,yongliwang}@njust.edu.cn
[2] Science and Technology on Coplex Systems Simulation Laboratory, Nanjing, China
[3] Nanjing Power Supply Branch of State Grid Jiangsu Electric Power Co., Ltd.,
Nanjing 210000, China

Abstract. Traditional multiround dialogue systems have problems such as colloquial expression, co-referential resolution, and information default. These problems lead to misunderstandings of human intentions by the system and poor dialogue quality. In order to improve the quality of dialogue, this paper proposes a knowledge-driven entity rewriting model (ERM) at the entity level and proposes a multi-dimensional dialog rewriting model (multi-dimensional dialog rewrite model, MDRM). The model first uses the common sense knowledge graph for entity disambiguation to rewrite the entities in the historical and current dialogue texts to remove the ambiguity spoken expression; Then, it models the historical dialogue, rewrites the current dialogue, and solves the common reference resolution and information default problems of the current dialogue. The comparative experiment shows that the model can effectively improve the quality of dialogue, which verifies the feasibility and effectiveness of the model.

Keywords: Knowledge graph · Entity rewriting · Dialogue rewriting · Dialogue system

1 Introduction

With the rapid development of information technology, various types of text data show explosive growth. How to obtain effective information from massive data has become an important research topic. Traditional search engines perform searches based on keywords and keyword combinations, and there are many drawbacks. In response to the problems in traditional search engines, question answering systems have become one of the research hotspots in natural language processing tasks. Q&A systems are divided into single-talk dialogue systems and multi-round dialogue systems. Due to the strong limitations of single-round dialogue, single-round dialogue scenarios are rare. In contrast, multi-round dialogue scenarios are very common. Through the analysis of 4000 Chinese dialogue texts on the Internet, it is found that about 80% of the texts have the following situations: entity ambiguity, entity expression diversification, common reference,

© Springer Nature Singapore Pte Ltd. 2021
Q. Chen and J. Li (Eds.): APWeb-WAIM 2020 Workshops, CCIS 1373, pp. 52–65, 2021.
https://doi.org/10.1007/978-981-16-0479-9_5

information omission, etc. Therefore, how to improve the quality of multiple rounds of dialogue is a top priority.

Two typical dialogue scenarios are shown in Table 1.

Table 1. Typical dialog scenarios.

Scene name	Dialogue information	Real dialogue	A rewritten dialogue
Scene 1	Historical Dialogue 1	How was King James yesterday	How was James yesterday
	Historical Dialogue 2	Good. Kobe's playing well, too	Good. Kobe's playing well, too
	Current Dialog 3	Haha, I like both of them	Haha, I like both James and Kobe
Scene 2	Historical Dialogue 1	Has Xiaomi released any new models recently	Has Xiaomi mobile phone released any new models recently
	Historical Dialogue 2	Yes, the latest one is mi 10	Yes, the latest is the Xiaomi mobile phone 10
	Current Dialog 3	Wow, I'll take one	Wow, I'll buy a Mi 10 then

As shown in the table, in scene 1, "King James" is only a colloquial expression, not a normalized expression. Some people may think it is a certain emperor. This phenomenon is mainly a multi-word expression Ambiguity caused by an entity. "Xiaomi" in scenario 2 has two meanings, one is Xiaomi mobile phone, and the other is crop. This situation is caused by one word representing multiple meanings, which is an ambiguity at the entity level. In the current dialogue 3 of scene 1, "the two of them" has a co-referential relationship with "King James" and "Kobe" in the historical dialogue, while in the current dialogue 3 of scene 2, "one" is omitted from "Xiaomi". The key information of "Mobile 10" is a common reference and information default at the sentence level. Due to the above problems, the dialogue system may have a wrong understanding of people's true intentions and eventually produce wrong answers.

In order to solve the above problems, in this paper, we first propose to use the knowledge graph to rewrite the entities in the dialogue, so as to complete the tasks of entity disambiguation and entity normalization; Then the processed text is divided into historical dialogue and current dialogue according to the time sequence of occurrence, and then the current dialogue is rewritten by modeling the historical dialogue to solve the problems of common reference and information default.

2 Related Work

2.1 Entity Disambiguation and Entity Normalization

At present, many methods have been proposed for entity disambiguation. According to the differences of models, entity disambiguation methods can be divided into methods based on machine learning and methods based on deep learning.

The core of the entity disambiguation method based on machine learning is to calculate the similarity between entities, and then select the target entity mentioned by the pending entity on this basis. Literature [12] proposed a method to disambiguate target entities by using entity statistics and name statistics. Literature [10] uses encyclopedia data as background knowledge to assist disambiguation through encyclopedia knowledge. In addition, the literature [1] combined features such as entity popularity and semantic relevance, and used the maxi-mum interval algorithm to calculate the weight of each feature, and then realized entity disambiguation through the sorting algorithm.

The core of entity disambiguation based on deep learning is to construct a unified representation of multi-type, multi-modal context and knowledge, and to model the relationship between multi-source information and multi-source text. Literature [9] improves entity disambiguation by adding a convolutional neural network model to the original neural network language model. Literature [4] proposed a multi-source heterogeneous evidence vector representation learning method, which represents the knowledge in the knowledge base from differ-ent sources in a unified space, and finally completes the entity disambiguation. Literature [15] proposed to use Skip-Gram model to train word vectors, and then calculate similarity through word vectors to realize entity disambiguation.

In view of the need for a large number of corpus annotations in the above methods, to solve the shortcomings of entity disambiguation considering the local characteristics of the entity, this paper proposes an entity rewriting model based on the knowledge graph, which uses the knowledge graph to rewrite the entities in the text. So as to disambiguate and normalize the entity.

2.2 Co-reference Resolution and Information Default

Co-reference resolution aims to identify different expressions pointing to the same entity, and has a wide range of applications in text translation, machine translation, automatic question answering, and knowledge graphs. Currently, the more popular common reference resolution methods are mainly based on machine learning, deep learning, and knowledge base.

Literature [11] proposed a Bayesian generative model with hierarchical distance dependence to achieve coreference resolution. In the literature [6], the semantic correlation function is proposed to discover events, and then clustering algorithms are used to mine the co-referential relationship in the text. Literature [8] proposed a method of selectively expressing sentence semantics based on event trigger words to resolve the co-referential relationship of events in short texts. Literature [13] studied a new two-stage method to discover and improve the structure of sub-events to reduce the difficulty of coreference resolution. Literature [17] proposed an improved LED-ER model, which uses the LED model to achieve coreference resolution.

Due to the strong generalization ability of the deep learning model, the performance of the deep learning-based coreference resolution model has been greatly improved. Wiseman et al. [18] used the Recurrent Neural Model (RNN) to better capture the global features of the coreference resolution model based on the presentation ranking model. Literature [14] proposed a new neural language model ENTITYNLM, which adds additional random variables to each word based on the neural language model to represent the relationship be-tween the word and the entity expression, and adds it at the time point The new variable update rules have improved the performance of the coreference resolution model.

Literature [3] proposed a crowdsourcing-based coreference resolution method, which effectively uses crowdsourcing knowledge to supplement the traditional coreference resolution model. In [2], the performance of the basic coreference resolution model is improved by extracting knowledge from encyclopedia data. In [5], the coreference resolution model was improved by combining knowledge base and semantic feature extraction.

The above-mentioned methods have disadvantages such as high manual labeling cost and small data set size, which makes the accuracy of the model not high. Aiming at the two problems of co-reference resolution and information default, the literature [16] proposed a method of using pointer network to rewrite the dialogue to solve the above problems. This method is very creative to use the corpus of historical dialogues to conduct the current dialogue. However, it ignores the impact of the entity level on the dialogue system, so there is still room for improvement. This paper proposes a knowledge-driven multi-dimensional dialogue rewriting model, which solves the above problems at the entity and dialogue levels.

3   Model

In order to solve the problem of ambiguity and normalization at the entity level and the problem of co-referencing and information default at the sentence level, this paper proposes to implement system functions by constructing an entity rewriting model and a multi-dimensional dialogue rewriting model.

The architecture of the knowledge-driven multi-dimensional dialogue rewriting model is shown in Fig. 1.

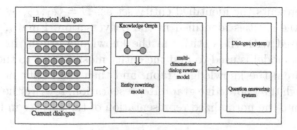

Fig. 1. System architecture diagram.

3.1   Entity Rewriting Model

Entities are a basic work in natural language processing. This work is very critical for upstream natural language processing tasks. However, due to the diverse development of daily expressions and languages, a word is polysemous and polymorphic. Circumstances, this situation makes the correct intention analysis difficult in the dialogue system, so this paper proposes the idea of rewriting it at the entity level to reduce uncertainties.

In this model, a common sense knowledge graph (DCKG) for entity disambiguation is constructed based on the information of Baidu Encyclopedia. Using DCKG, the target entity can be found through the entity link, and the entity description and the normalized representation of the entity can be obtained at the same time. The entity description and the normalized representation of the entity retrieved through the knowledge graph are shown in Fig. 2.

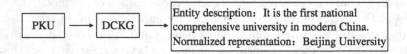

Fig. 2. System architecture diagram.

The entity description adopts the introduction of Baidu Baike corresponding to this paper, and the entity normalized expression represents the standardized expression of the entity (for example: entity: Peking University, entity normalized expression: Peking University).

In the entity rewriting model, all dialogue texts are firstly identified as named entities. In this step, this paper spliced the historical dialogue into a piece of text and completed the task of Chinese named entity recognition through the mainstream Bi-LSTM + CRF. In the implementation process, $S = (s_1, s_2, \ldots, s_n)$ represents the historical dialogue text, n represents the number of sentences in the historical dialogue, and the spliced text is expressed as $W = (w_1, w_2, \ldots, w_m)$, where m represents the total number of words in the dialogue text, and then the named entity is identified by Bi-LSTM + CRF. This paper represents the identified entity set as: $E = \{e_1, e_2, \cdots, e_p\}$, where p represents all the entities identified in the conversation. Finally, the identified entities are linked with the entities in the knowledge graph. In this step, the entity rewriting model is used to find the entity most similar to the entity in the dialogue text from the knowledge graph, and then the entity normalization is obtained through the knowledge graph Representation, rewrite the entities in the dialogue text into the normalized representation of the entities in the knowledge graph.

The block diagram of entity rewrite model is shown in Fig. 3.

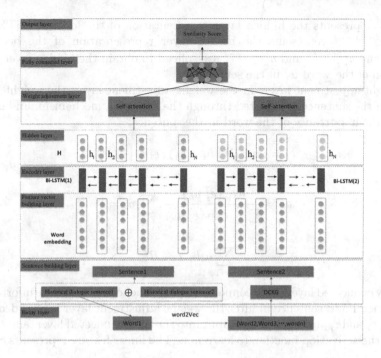

Fig. 3. Block diagram of entity rewrite model.

Entity layer: In the entity rewriting model, the entity to be rewritten is first identified from the historical dialogue text as $Word_1$, and the similar entity set of $Word_1$ is found through Word2vec as $\{Word_2, Word_3, \cdots, Word_n\}$, find the most similar entities from the set in turn.

Sentence building layer: At the sentence building layer, this model will splicing the historical context dialogue of $Word_1$ into sentence 1, which represents the context of $Word_1$, and then select $Word_m, (2 \leqslant m \leqslant n)$ from the set of similar entities. After the knowledge graph link, find the entity description of $Word_m$ in the knowledge graph (DCKG) and record it as sentence m, and use sentence 1 and sentence m as input for similarity comparison.

Feature vector building layer: In the feature vector building layer, all words of sentence 1 and sentence m are mapped to a low-dimensional vector space, the vector space is denoted as R_E, E is the dimension of the feature vector.

Encoder layer: In the Encoder layer, the feature vector is learned through the Bi-LSTM model. The Bi-LSTM model is composed of a forward LSTM model and a backward LSTM model. The forward LSTM model is used to obtain the above information, and the backward LSTM model is used to obtain the following information, and the hidden layer information h_i of the word w_i in the sentence can be obtained through Bi-LSTM:

$$h_i = h_i^{\text{forward}} + h_i^{\text{backward}} \tag{1}$$

$h_i^{forward}$ represents the hidden layer representation of the forward LSTM network, $h_i^{backward}$ represents the hidden layer representation of the backward LSTM, and $h_i^{forward}$ and $h_i^{backward}$ are spliced to obtain the hidden layer representation of the word w_i in the sentence.

Weight adjustment layer: In the weight adjustment layer, the weight of the words in the sentence is adjusted through the attention mechanism, and a_i represents the importance of the word in the sentence.

$$e_i = \tanh\left(W_h h_i + b_h\right), e_i \in [-1, 1] \tag{2}$$

$$a_i = \frac{\exp\left(e_i^T u_h\right)}{\sum_{t=1}^{T} \exp\left(e_i^T u_h\right)}, \sum_{i=1}^{T} a_i = 1 \tag{3}$$

$$r = \sum_{i=1}^{T} a_i h_i, r \in R^{2L} \tag{4}$$

Fully connected layer (fully connected layer): The semantic feature information of sentence 1 and sentence m after the weight adjustment layer is recorded as r_1 and r_m, r_1 and r_m are spliced and input into the fully connected layer, and $tanh$ is used as the activation function to learn non- The linear feature represents c.

$$r = r_1 \| r_m, r \in R^{4L} \tag{5}$$

$$c = \tanh\left(W_c^r + b_c\right) \tag{6}$$

Output layer: The output layer uses SVM as a classifier, and the probability of output $[0,1]$ is used to measure the similarity of words.

Through the entity rewriting model, we can find the most similar entity of $Word_1$ in the historical dialogue. Since the normalized expression of the entity is recorded in the knowledge graph, it can be rewritten later according to the normalized expression.

The entity rewriting model transforms the similarity analysis of entities into sentence similarity analysis through the knowledge graph, and the semantics are strengthened. At the same time, the normalized expression of the entities can be obtained through the knowledge graph to complete the rewriting of the entities. For example: the entity "Apple", through the entity rewriting model, will determine its normalized expression as "Apple mobile phone", this paper will rewrite the entity "Apple" in the historical dialogue text, "Apple" = "iPhone".

3.2   Multi-dimensional Dialog Rewriting Model

Through the entity rewriting model, the problem of entity disambiguation and entity normalization is solved, but in dialogue scenarios, common reference and information default situations often occur. In order to solve this problem, this paper draws on the multi-round dialogue rewriting model [16], and performs referential disambiguation and information supplementation on the current dialogue. At the same time, it combines with the entity rewriting model proposed above to process the multi-dimensional dialogue rewriting model., After the multi-dimensional dialogue rewriting model is processed, the text is more accurate and the quality is better.

First, the text of the historical multiple rounds of dialogue is expressed as $H(U_1, U_2, \cdots, U_{n-1})$, which represents the $n-1$ sentence dialogue of the history, U_n is the current round of dialogue, this paper will entity H rewrite, the processed text is expressed as $H'(U'_1, U'_2, \cdots, U'_{n-1})$, H' round information is modeled and rewritten Current dialogue U_n, restore the reference and missing information of the current dialogue, the current dialogue after rewriting is denoted as R, and this process is denoted as $(H, U_n \rightarrow R)$. By labeling the training text, the dialogue rewriting model will learn Find a correct mapping function, which is expressed as $p(R|(H, U_n))$.

The framework diagram of the multi-dimensional dialogue rewriting model is shown in Fig. 4.

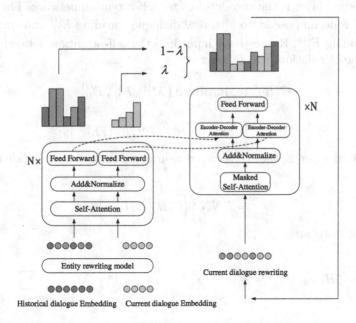

Fig. 4. Framework diagram of multi-dimensional dialogue rewriting model.

As shown in the figure, the model consists of an encoder and a decoder. In the encoder part, the historical dialogue and the current dia-logue are taken as input, and the word embedding is expressed as:

$$I(w_i) = WE(w_i) + PE(w_i) + TE(w_i) \tag{7}$$

$WE(w_i)$ is represented as word embedding, $PE(w_i)$ is represented as position embedding, and $TE(w_i)$ represents which dialogue the word currently belongs to.

After obtaining the vector representation of the word, input it into the encoder of the L layer to obtain the encoding representation. Each encoder contains self-attention and feedforward neural network FNN:

$$E^0 = [I(w_1), I(w_2), \ldots, I(w_m)] \tag{8}$$

$$E^l = FNN\left(\text{MultiHead}\left(E^{(l-1)}, E^{(l-1)}, E^{(l-1)}\right)\right) \tag{9}$$

Through the above formula, the output E^l of the encoder is obtained.

In the decoder part, the decoder is mainly composed of three layers, the first layer of multi-head self-attention network:

$$M^l = \text{MultiHead}\left(D^{(l-1)}, D^{(l-1)}, D^{(l-1)}\right) \tag{10}$$

D represents the text formed by combining historical dialogue H and current dialogue U_n according to the weight λ.

The second layer is the encoder-decoder self-attention network. The encoder output E^l is decomposed into historical dialogue encoding $E_H^{(l)}$ and current dialogue encoding $E_{U_n}^{(l)}$. Respectively input into the self-attention network for processing, the calculation is as follows:

$$C(H)^l = \text{MultiHead}\left(M^{(l)}, E_H^{(l)}, E_H^{(l)}\right) \tag{11}$$

$$C(U_n)^l = \text{MultiHead}\left(M^{(l)}, E_{U_n}^{(l)}, E_{U_n}^{(l)}\right) \tag{12}$$

The third layer is the feedforward neural network, which is calculated as follows:

$$D^{(l)} = FNN\left(\left[C(H)^l C(U_n)^l\right]\right) \tag{13}$$

Output distribution:

$$p(R_t = w \mid H, U_n, R_{<t}) = \lambda \sum_{i:(w_i=w)\wedge(w_i\in H)} a_{t,i} + (1-\lambda) \sum_{j:(w_j=w)\wedge(w_j\in U_n)} a'_{t,i} \tag{14}$$

$$a = \text{Attention}\left(M^{(L)}, E_{U_n}^{(L)}\right) \tag{15}$$

$$a' = \text{Attention}\left(M^{(L)}, E_H^{(L)}\right) \tag{16}$$

$$\lambda = \sigma\left(w_d^\top D_t^L + w_H^\top C(H)_t^L + w_U^\top C(U_n)_t^L\right) \tag{17}$$

In the above formula, a and a' represent the attention distribution of words in the historical dialogue H and the current dialogue U_n, $w_d^\top$, $w_H^\top$, $w_U^\top$ are the learning parameters, σ is the sigmoid function, λ is the weight, and the word at the current position Is it extracted from the historical dialogue H or copied from the current dialogue U_n.

4 Experiment and Result Analysis

4.1 Construction of Common Sense Knowledge Graph for Entity Disambiguation

Introduction to the Common Sense Knowledge Graph (DCKG) for Entity Disambiguation: Mainly for the Chinese Encyclopedia website (Baidu Baike) after knowledge extraction, knowledge cleaning, and knowledge supplementation, the Chinese Common Sense Knowledge Graph for Entity Disambiguation is mainly used for entities. Including commonly used entities and entities that are prone to ambiguity, there are about 300,000 in total. The attributes of each entity have entity descriptions and entity normalization expressions for entity disambiguation and normalization. Figure 5 shows an example of an entity ambiguity common sense knowledge graph.

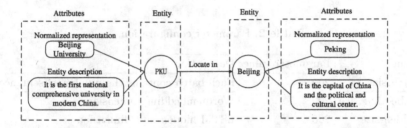

Fig. 5. Entity ambiguity common sense knowledge graph example.

When constructing DCKG, it mainly includes the following steps. Firstly, common entities and relationships are collected. After that, each entity adds the attributes of entity description and entity normalization. This is similar to constructing a common knowledge graph, but this paper focuses on each entity All have added special attributes (entity description, entity normalization representation).

4.2 Comparison Experiment of Entity Elimination and Normalization

In order to verify the feasibility and effectiveness of the entity rewriting model, this paper uses the "Chinese name disambiguation task" data set released in the CIPS-SIGHAN International Conference on Chinese Processing (CLP-2012) [7] as the test data set. The recall rate, accuracy rate, and F1 value of the four mainstream entity disambiguation methods are compared for experiments. A brief introduction of several entity disambiguation methods is as follows:

1. Wikify: The core idea of this model for entity disambiguation is to count the probability that a word is linked to the corresponding concept in the Wikipedia text, and the link with a higher probability will be confirmed as a candidate link.
2. Random Walk: The basic idea of this model for entity disambiguation is to define the calculation method of Wiki concept similarity based on the random walk algorithm, and use this method in the calculation of the similarity of entity referents and entity candidates.
3. Knowledge Base: The core idea of this model for entity disambiguation is to obtain prior knowledge from the knowledge base, and combine the acquired prior knowledge and a series of evidence information to perform entity disambiguation.
4. SCEW: A model for entity disambiguation based on semantic classification of entity linking methods. Its core idea is to train a word vector model, cluster entities to obtain category labels as features, and then predict the subject of the target entity through a multi-classification model Category features, combined with entity popularity features for entity disambiguation.

The parameters of this experiment are configured in the Table 2.

Table 2. Parameter configuration.

Name	Parameter value	Description
Batch_size	200	Each batch contains the number of sentences
Embedding_size	200	Word embedding dimension
Hidden-size	200	LSTM hidden unit dimension
Drop_out	0.5	Drop out probability
Max_len	150	Maximum sentence length
Epoch	100	Number of iterations

The results of the comparative experiment are shown in the Table 3.

Table 3. Comparison of experimental results.

Model	Recall rate	Accurate rate	F1 value
Wikify	63.2%	58.2%	60.5%
Random walk	68.2%	63.1%	65.6%
Knowledge base	66.5%	65.6%	66.0%
SCEW	72.1%	70.2%	71.3%
ERM	**73.8%**	**75.8%**	**74.8%**

As shown in Table 3, the accuracy, precision and F1 value of the entity rewrite model (ERM) are higher than those of several main-stream methods. The entity rewriting model transforms the similarity analysis of entities into the similarity analysis of sentences through the knowledge graph, and the semantics are strengthened. The entity is linked to the corresponding entities in the knowledge graph to complete the entity disambiguation. Experiments show that the effect is better.

4.3   Multidimensional Dialogue Rewriting Comparative Experiment

In order to verify the effectiveness of the knowledge-driven multi-dimensional dialogue rewriting model, this paper uses 20,000 data sets of the dialogue rewriter [16]. In order to enrich the dialogue scenarios of this data set, this paper organizes 5000 natural dialogue data. According to the format of the data set, it is supplemented for better training and verification of the overall model.

Examples of dialogue rewriting data are shown in Table 4.

Table 4. Example of dialogue rewriting some data.

Dialogue type	Example
Historical dialogue text	The Legend of Lu Xiaofeng
	Who is Lu Xiaofeng
Current dialog text	Have you seen this movie
Rewritten dialog text	Have you watched the legend of Lu Xiaofeng

Related comparative experiments are introduced as follows:

PRT: This model is to model historical dialogues and rewrite current dialogues to improve the quality of dialogues.

MDRM: The model in this paper firstly rewrites the dialogue content at the entity level through the knowledge graph, completes entity disambiguation and entity normalization, and then rewrites the current dialogue through the dialogue rewriting model, thus at a multi-dimensional level A model to improve the quality of dialogue.

The experimental results are shown in the Table 5.

Table 5. Experimental results.

Model	BLEU-1	BLEU-2	BLEU-4	ROUGE-1	ROUGE-2	ROUGE-L
PRT	73.65%	64.44%	49.86%	77.64%	59.67%	76.20%
MDRM	**74.20%**	64.32%	**51.40%**	**77.90%**	58.24%	**77.89%**

As shown in the above table, compared with the PRT model, the MDRM model not only pays attention to co-reference resolution and information loss at the dialogue level, but also uses the knowledge graph at the entity level to perform entity disambiguation and entity normalization. The dialog text quality is better.

5   Conclusion

In order to solve the text quality problem of multiple rounds of dialogue, this paper proposes a knowledge-driven multi-dimensional dialogue rewriting model, which provides a new way of thinking for dialogue systems and question answering systems. In order to verify the effectiveness of this model, this paper constructs a common sense knowledge graph DCKG for entity disambiguation. This is a very meaningful work. It is effective for entity disambiguation and entity normalization. Knowledge proposes an entity rewriting model. At the same time, this paper combines the dialogue-level rewriting method to use the historical dialogue text after entity rewriting as information to rewrite the current dialogue so that the current dialogue has enough correct information. Solve the problem of common reference and in-formation default. The model in this paper proves to be effective in real dialogue scenarios, but the model proposed in this paper also has certain limitations. For example, in the process of entity rewriting, words have new meanings with the development of language. It is also a big challenge to add a new meaning to the existing model, At the same time, the number of rounds of the dialogue is currently only three rounds. Whether the number of rounds has a greater impact on rewriting has not been explored yet. We will work hard in these directions in the next step.

References

1. Bosselut, A., Rashkin, H., Sap, M., Malaviya, C., Celikyilmaz, A., Choi, Y.: Comet: commonsense transformers for automatic knowledge graph construction. arXiv preprint arXiv:1906.05317 (2019)
2. Brill, E., Dumais, S., Banko, M.: An analysis of the AskMSR question-answering system. In: Proceedings of the 2002 Conference on Empirical Methods in Natural Language Processing (EMNLP 2002), pp. 257–264 (2002)
3. Cai, L., Wang, W.Y.: Kbgan: adversarial learning for knowledge graph embeddings. arXiv preprint arXiv:1711.04071 (2017)
4. Chen, P., Lu, Y., Zheng, V.W., Chen, X., Yang, B.: KnowEdu: a system to construct knowledge graph for education. IEEE Access **6**, 31553–31563 (2018)
5. Diefenbach, D., Both, A., Singh, K., Maret, P.: Towards a question answering system over the semantic web. Semant. Web (Preprint), 1–19 (2020)
6. Ding, B., Wang, Q., Wang, B., Guo, L.: Improving knowledge graph embedding using simple constraints. arXiv preprint arXiv:1805.02408 (2018)
7. Du, H., et al.: Research development on sustainable urban infrastructure from 1991 to 2017: a bibliometric analysis to inform future innovations. Earth's Future **7**(7), 718–733 (2019)

8. Lin, H., Liu, Y., Wang, W., Yue, Y., Lin, Z.: Learning entity and relation embeddings for knowledge resolution. Procedia Comput. Sci. **108**, 345–354 (2017)
9. Lin, X.V., Socher, R., Xiong, C.: Multi-hop knowledge graph reasoning with reward shaping. arXiv preprint arXiv:1808.10568 (2018)
10. Liu, W., et al.: K-bert: enabling language representation with knowledge graph. In: AAAI, pp. 2901–2908 (2020)
11. Luan, Y., He, L., Ostendorf, M., Hajishirzi, H.: Multi-task identification of entities, relations, and conference for scientific knowledge graph construction. arXiv preprint arXiv:1808.09602 (2018)
12. Mohamed, S.K., Nováček, V., Nounu, A.: Discovering protein drug targets using knowledge graph embeddings. Bioinformatics **36**(2), 603–610 (2020)
13. Paulheim, H.: Knowledge graph refinement: a survey of approaches and evaluation methods. Semant. web **8**(3), 489–508 (2017)
14. Shi, B., Weninger, T.: ProjE: embedding projection for knowledge graph completion. arXiv preprint arXiv:1611.05425 (2016)
15. Song, Q., Wu, Y., Lin, P., Dong, L.X., Sun, H.: Mining summaries for knowledge graph search. IEEE Trans. Knowl. Data Eng. **30**(10), 1887–1900 (2018)
16. Su, H., et al.: Improving multi-turn dialogue modelling with utterance rewriter. arXiv preprint arXiv:1906.07004 (2019)
17. Xiong, W., Hoang, T., Wang, W.Y.: DeepPath: a reinforcement learning method for knowledge graph reasoning. arXiv preprint arXiv:1707.06690 (2017)
18. Xu, J., Chen, K., Qiu, X., Huang, X.: Knowledge graph representation with jointly structural and textual encoding. arXiv preprint arXiv:1611.08661 (2016)

Towards Knowledge Graphs Federations: Issues and Technologies

Xiang Zhao[✉]

National Univerisity of Defense Technology, Changsha, China
xiangzhao@nudt.edu.cn

Abstract. In recent decades, knowledge graph plays an increasingly significant role in intelligent information services. However, for some domains, knowledge graphs are constructed for special purposes and disconnected with each other, which fails to take advantage of knowledge from different knowledge graphs. To this end, we are motivated to propose the concept of knowledge graph federation. In this keynote, we first discuss the issues about knowledge graph federation, and then we introduce two technologies of automatic knowledge graph construction, i.e., relation extraction and entity alignment. The issues in this keynote will provide guidelines for the development of knowledge graph technology.

Keywords: Knowledge graph federation · Relation extraction · Entity alignment

1 Introducing Knowledge Graph Federation

The initial concept of knowledge graph (KG) originates from the idea of semantic web which aims to use the WWW infrastructure to create a global, decentralized, weblike mesh of machine-processable knowledge [2]. From this point of view, the weblike mesh of machine-processable knowledge is exactly the KG. KG uses graph structures to model and record the relationships between all things in the world and deposit knowledge about all things, which provides a feasible solution for the association, integration and utilization of information. Currently, there have been a number of large-scale KGs, such as Wikidata [24], DBpedia [1], CN-DBpedia [28], and CN-Probase [5].

After nearly two decades of development, the related technologies of KGs have been widely used in many fields including search engines [18], intelligent question answering [33] and recommender system [40], and are recognized as the realization of cognitive intelligence, which is considered to be an important cornerstone of intelligent interconnection.

In modern enterprise information infrastructure, knowledge grows within information systems, and typically when an information system is equipped with a knowledge base, it becomes an expert system. Conventionally, an expert system is built by human experts, as shown in Fig. 1. Besides, human experts, who are under the assistance of knowledge engineers, create the knowledge base

© Springer Nature Singapore Pte Ltd. 2021
Q. Chen and J. Li (Eds.): APWeb-WAIM 2020 Workshops, CCIS 1373, pp. 66–79, 2021.
https://doi.org/10.1007/978-981-16-0479-9_6

which is central to the expert system. Using the knowledge base, the system can interact and infer with end users through intelligent question answering and recommender system.

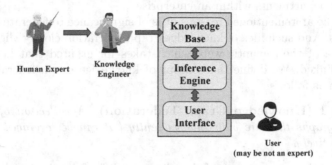

Fig. 1. A typical expert system.

However, there is a long-standing issue that tends to occur in most information systems, in particular the existing or legacy systems. Generally, information systems are built by every department without an enterprise-level or strategic plan, and hence, they are disconnected and may not work together smoothly. From an exterior perspective, these information systems inside an enterprise stand side by side like chimneys, which produce something for different purposes. And due to this reason, the isolation also happens to the knowledge bases thereof, which are again disconnected. And this hinders the use of knowledge across departments. In this connection, the power of knowledge has not been fully discovered and exploited.

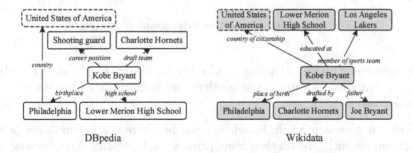

Fig. 2. Examples of different KGs.

Because a department mainly looks at a particular part of the enterprise, and the knowledge graph it constructs is usually extracted from a single data source, i.e., the data the department has in hand. And therefore, the knowledge graph is unlikely to reach full coverage of the domain. Example in Fig. 2 presents partial graphs concerning the entity `Kobe Bryant` from DBpedia and Wikidata, respectively. It can be seen from the example that for both graphs, the information is incomplete, and that these KGs contain information that the other KG does not contain. From this aspect, we are motivated to federate different KGs by different departments within an enterprise.

Due to the aforementioned reasons, it is of significance to federate the knowledge graphs. And such idea of knowledge graph federation closely align with the original idea of the semantic web, which takes for granted that knowledge is inherently linked. We define the concept of knowledge graph federation by its connotation as follows:

Definition 1 (Knowledge Graph Federation). *A collection of (domain) knowledge graphs that are built independently but can be leveraged to achieve a goal collectively.*

It is noted that the concept of federation may differ from the popular notion of federated learning in the machine learning community. As where we are standing, federated learning pays much attention to the privacy and security issues when conducting distributed machine learning. In fact, however, the word federation has no such implication with respect to privacy and security aspects.

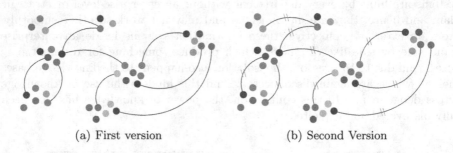

(a) First version   (b) Second Version

Fig. 3. Two streams of knowledge graph federations.

As mentioned above, according to whether knowledge can be shared without or with privacy and security considerations, we have two streams of knowledge graph federations:

- In the first version where knowledge can be shared across multiple parties without potential restriction from privacy and security, management and applications can be carried out across the federated knowledge graphs via direct data access. Such scenario is depicted by the Fig. 3(a). Some important issues in leveraging this knowledge graph federation mainly arise from the distribution of knowledge. For instance, we need to consider the overhead of moving knowledge during distributed learning, the communication cost, the alignment of overlapped knowledge, the amplification of each single knowledge graph by taking advantage of others, and etc. We hold the view that this version of federation exposes itself to the enterprises that have a strong/mandatory enforcement of relevant policies like information infrastructure and data sharing. For example, this can be applicable to governmental organs.

– In the second version as shown in Fig. 3(b), while the departments are expected to collaborate, they may have certain conflict of interest, and hence, data privacy and information security have to be taken into account. As a consequence, knowledge may not be shared directly across departments, and some methods have to be taken in pursuit of knowledge safety. For instance, homomorphic encryption may be executed to achieve encrypted knowledge sharing. That is, all those emerging technologies in the popular federated learning may be applicable in this scenario. In comparison with the previous version, this version of federation may be seen in a larger scale enterprises.

In this keynote, we are going to focus on the first version, and we will discuss some recent progress on the key technologies to knowledge graph federations.

2 Technologies for Constructing Knowledge Graph Federation

In this section, we will see how to better extract relations for domain knowledge graphs, and a comprehensive evaluation of state-of-the-art solutions to entity alignment across multiple knowledge graphs. We believe that these two technologies are essential to build an informed knowledge graph federation. The purpose of **relation extraction** is to amplify the information of the domain KGs, and the aim of **entity alignment** is to pinpoint those overlapped entities in order to fuse two knowledge graphs.

2.1 Domain Relation Extraction

Task Definition. Relation extraction (RE) is the task to determine the relation held between two entities, and subsequently, a triplet consisting of a relation and two entities can be formed to enrich existing KGs. Formally, we give the task definition as follow:

Definition 2 (Relation Extraction). *Given a sentence S with entity pair (h, t), relation extraction is to obtain a relation $r_i \in \mathbf{R}$ for (h, t), where $\mathbf{R} = \{r_1, r_2 \ldots r_n\}$, and n is the number of the candidate relations.*

When it comes to distant supervision data or noisy data, we can extend a sentence S to an instance bag B where B consists of all sentences mentioning the same entity pair (h, t).

Related Work. Recent development of deep learning leads to the interest of neural relation extraction models. Some work takes the raw text as input and employs different neural networks to embed the text. Zeng et al. first propose position embedding and employ convolutional neural network (CNN) to embed texts [35]. To capture structural information, piece-wise CNN (PCNN) segments a sentence into three parts based on two entities and apply piece-wise max-pooling over each part [34]. Another group of studies are based on dependency paths. Xu et al. argue that shortest dependency path (SDP) maintains most relevant information about the target relation and diminishes useless noise [30]. They utilize long short-term memory network (LSTM) to encode words along SDP, dependency relations between words, and linguistic information for extracting semantic features. Observing that associated predicate of an entity pair is always lost in SDP, recent work designs root augmented dependency path (RADP) to reserve the predicate [7]. As for distantly supervised RE or RE under noisy data, different granularity attention mechanisms are introduced to denoise at instance level [11,16] and word level [20].

Motivation. Previous work mainly focuses on general purpose KGs and establishes the neural model with enough training data. However, the text sparsity issue generally exists in domain texts and KGs, i.e., there might be few texts mentioning an entity pair or few entity pairs for a specific relation. In this connection, RE models based on sparse texts remain to be explored from two aspects:

- Selective attention aims at fitting a probability distribution over noisy sentences (or words). Nonetheless, when fed with limited training data, the text sparsity refrains selective attention from training a probability distribution.
- SDP based RE models aim to remove noisy words in each sentence, and retain key information that are related to entities. However, SDP is likely to drop associated predicates.

Therefore, we are motivated to revisit the two challenges in domain RE:

- **Denoising at sentence level:** To effectively remove the sentence-level noises, an entity-integrated attention mechanism is proposed to better assign weights to different instances. Besides, the integration of entity information enhances features derived from sparse domain texts.
- **Denoising at word level:** The purpose of word-level denoising is to remove trivial and misleading words from raw word sequence (RWS). Thus, we design a novel denoising structure, namely multiple dependency paths (MDP), to capture the predicate-argument and other key words.

Our Approach. In our method, we regard multiple dependency paths (MDP) as additional knowledge to be incorporated with raw word sequence (RWS), and the combination of RWS and MDP allows them to complement each other, resulting in more comprehensive features for RE. Specifically, we use two separate CNN layers to encode RWS and MDP respectively:

$$
\begin{aligned}
\mathbf{p}_x &= \text{CNN}(x_i), \\
\mathbf{p}_s &= \text{CNN}(s_i),
\end{aligned}
\tag{1}
$$

where CNN($\cdot$) is the CNN encoder, x_i and s_i denote RWS and MDP respectively. Afterwards, we fuse them by concatenation:

$$\mathbf{p} = [\mathbf{p}_x : \mathbf{p}_s], \tag{2}$$

For an instance bag B, we denote the feature vectors as $\{\mathbf{p}_1, \ldots, \mathbf{p}_m\}$ where m is the number of sentences in B. The bag-level feature vector is obtained by:

$$\mathbf{p} = \sum_{i=1}^{m} \alpha_i \mathbf{p}_i,$$

$$\alpha_i = \frac{\exp([\mathbf{p}_i : \mathbf{e}_1 : \mathbf{e}_2]\mathbf{Ar})}{\sum_k \exp([\mathbf{p}_k : \mathbf{e}_1 : \mathbf{e}_2]\mathbf{Ar})}, \tag{3}$$

where $\mathbf{A}$ is a weighted diagonal matrix, $\mathbf{r}$ is the query vector concerning the target relation r, $\mathbf{e}_1$ and $\mathbf{e}_2$ are word embeddings of two entities. Finally, we harness a softmax classifier to predict the relation type.

$$\mathbf{o} = \mathbf{U}[\mathbf{p} : \mathbf{e}_1^* : \mathbf{e}_2^*] + \mathbf{v},$$

$$p(r) = \frac{\exp(o_r)}{\sum_{j=1}^{n} \exp(o_j)}, \tag{4}$$

where $\mathbf{U}$ and $\mathbf{v}$ are parameters, $\mathbf{e}_1^*$ and $\mathbf{e}_2^*$ are obtained by projecting $\mathbf{e}_1$ and $\mathbf{e}_2$ linearly. $p(r)$ is the probability of a sentence S or an instance bag B associated to a relation type r.

Experimental Results. We selected several neural RE models as baselines and conducted experiments on two Chinese RE datasets, Wiki and Baike. The experimental results in Fig. 4 show that our model com-CNN outperforms all competing methods. More details and analysis can be seen in [19].

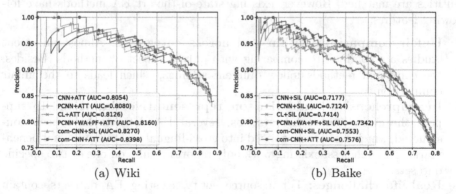

(a) Wiki   (b) Baike

Fig. 4. P-R curves.

2.2 Entity Alignment

Task Definition. The task of entity alignment (EA) aims to identify equivalent entities in different KGs, which facilitates the integration of knowledge from multiple sources. It is an effective method to obtain a more large-scale KG by integrating existing KGs. We give the task formulation of EA as follow:

Definition 3 (Entity Alignment). *A KG is usually represented as* $G = (E, R, A, V)$, *where E, R, A and V denote entities, relations, attributes and attribute values respectively. Given two KGs, G_1 and G_2, entity alignment aims to automatically mine new aligned entity pairs based on existing seed entity pairs* $S = \{(e_{i1}, e_{i2}) \mid e_{i1} \in G_1, e_{i2} \in G_2\}_{i=1}^{m}$.

Related Work. The task entity alignment (EA) comes from a more generic problem–identifying entity records referring to the same real-world entity from different data sources [13]. EA focuses on handling entity resolution with KG data, where we are given multiple KGs and required to find equivalent entities in the KGs [9]. At present, there are mainly three categories of EA models. The first group of studies merely harness the KG structure to align entities, and representative work includes [4,6,14]. The second category of methods iteratively label most likely aligned entity pairs as the additional training data and progressively enhance the alignment performance [22,41,42]. Although it is intuitive to leverage KG structures for aligning entities, KGs also contain rich semantic information, which is complementary for structural information. Models in the third category distinguish themselves by the use of literal information in addition to the structural information [21,31,38].

Motivation. Generally, current entity alignment (EA) methods assume that equivalent entities have similar neighboring structures, and hence have the similar vector representations. The pair-wise similarity of entities can be easily evaluated as their distance in the embedding space, which determines whether two entities are matched. However, existing state-of-the-art EA methods have following features:

- **Unfair comparison within and across categories:** Almost all recent studies are confined to comparing with only a subset of methods. Besides, the compared methods follow different settings, which leads to the unfair comparison.
- **Incomprehensive evaluation on representative datatsets:** To support the evaluation of EA systems, several EA datasets have been constructed, which can be categorized into cross-lingual and mono-lingual benchmarks. Nevertheless, existing work only reports results on one or two specific datasets.
- **Real-life challenges:** For a source entity, existing EA datasets contain exactly one corresponding target entity. However, in real-life scenario, KGs contain entities that the target KGs do not contain. In addition, real-life equivalent entities might not have similar names while different entities in KGs might possess the same name.

Consequently, we are motivated to provide an empirical evaluation of state-of-the-art EA approaches by giving a general EA framework and proposing a new benchmark dataset that mirrors pragmatic difficulties mentioned above.

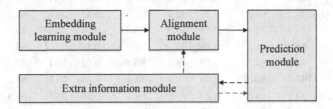

Fig. 5. A general EA framework.

Entity Alignment Framework. By carefully examining current EA solutions, we summarize a general EA framework into four components as shown in Fig. 5:

– **Embedding learning module:** This module is aimed at learning vector representations for entities in KG. In general, embedding learning methods can be categorized into two groups: KG representation based models, e.g. TransE [3], and graph neural network (GNN) based models, e.g., graph convolutional network (GCN) [12].
– **Alignment module:** This component is responsible for mapping entities in different KGs into a unified space. Some work harnesses the margin-based loss to enforce the seed entity pairs to be placed adjacently in the embedding space. Another group of studies focus on corpus fusion, which directly embeds entities in different KGs into the same vector space.
– **Prediction module:** Given entity embeddings in the unified space, the prediction module selects the most likely target entity for each source entity in the test set. The strategies of calculating similarities between entity pairs include the cosine similarity, the Euclidean distance, and the Manhattan distance.
– **Extra information module:** On top of three components mentioned above, some work resorts to extra information to further improve EA performance. Some models leverages bootstrapping (or self-training) strategy to regard confidently aligned entity pairs as additional training data, as black dashed lines shown in Fig. 5. Another practice is to take advantage of literal information, such as attribute and entity names, denoted by blue line in Fig. 5.

It is worth mentioning that the first three components are necessary for an EA system while extra information is not always available.

Experimental Results. We conducted experiments on three mainstream EA datasets, DBP15K, DWY100K, and SRPRS, for three groups of EA models. We provide the results on DBP15K in Table 1 and leave out the performance on the other two datasets in the interest of space, which can be found in [39].

Table 1. Experiment results on DBP15K.

Method	ZH-EN			JA-EN			FR-EN		
	Hits@1	Hits@10	MRR	Hits@1	Hits@10	MRR	Hits@1	Hits@10	MRR
MTransE [6]	20.9	51.2	0.31	25.0	57.2	0.36	24.7	57.7	0.36
JAPE-Stru [21]	37.2	68.9	0.48	32.9	63.8	0.43	29.3	61.7	0.40
GCN [25]	39.8	72.0	0.51	40.0	72.9	0.51	38.9	74.9	0.51
RSNs [8]	**58.0**	81.1	**0.66**	**57.4**	79.9	**0.65**	**61.2**	84.1	**0.69**
MuGNN [4]	47.0	83.5	0.59	48.3	**85.6**	0.61	49.1	**86.7**	0.62
KECG [15]	47.7	**83.6**	0.60	49.2	84.4	0.61	48.5	84.9	0.61
ITransE [41]	33.2	64.5	0.43	29.0	59.5	0.39	24.5	56.8	0.35
BootEA [22]*	61.4	84.1	0.69	57.3	82.9	0.66	58.5	84.5	0.68
NAEA [42]	38.5	63.5	0.47	35.3	61.3	0.44	30.8	59.6	0.40
TransEdge [23]	**75.3**	**92.4**	**0.81**	**74.6**	**92.4**	**0.81**	**77.0**	**94.2**	**0.83**
JAPE [21]	41.4	74.1	0.53	36.5	69.5	0.48	31.8	66.8	0.44
GCN-Align [25]	43.4	76.2	0.55	42.7	76.2	0.54	41.1	77.2	0.53
HMAN [32]	56.1	**85.9**	0.67	55.7	86.0	0.67	55.0	87.6	0.66
GM-Align [29]	59.5	77.9	0.66	63.5	83.0	0.71	79.2	93.6	0.85
RDGCN [26]	69.7	84.2	0.75	76.3	**89.7**	**0.81**	87.3	95.0	0.90
HGCN [27]	70.8	84.0	**0.76**	75.8	88.9	**0.81**	88.8	**95.9**	**0.91**
CEA [36]	**78.7**▲	–	–	**86.3**▲	–	–	**97.2**▲	–	–
Embed	**57.5**	**68.6**	**0.61**	**65.1**	**75.4**	**0.69**	**81.6**	**88.9**	**0.84**
Lev	7.0	8.9	0.08	6.6	8.8	0.07	78.1	87.4	0.81

Based on the experimental results in Table 1, we provide some guidelines and suggestions for users of EA approaches.

Guidelines for Practitioners. There are many factors that might influence the choice of EA models. We select four most common factors and give the following suggestions:

- **Input information.** If the inputs only contain KG structure information, one might have to choose from the methods in Groups I and II. Conversely, if there exist abundant side information, one might want to use methods from Group III to take full advantage of these features and provide more reliable signals for alignment.
- **The scale of data.** Some state-of-the-art methods have rather poor scalability. Therefore, the scale of data should be taken into consideration before making alignment decisions. For data of very large scale, one could use some simple but efficient models such as GCN-Align to reduce the computational overhead.
- **The objective of alignment.** If one only focuses on the alignment of entities, one might want to adopt GNN based models since they are usually more robust and scalable. Nevertheless, if there are additional tasks such as alignment of relations, one might want to use the KG representation based

methods since they intrinsically learn both entity and relation representations. Besides, several recent studies [23, 26] demonstrate that the relations can help the alignment of entities.

- **The trade-off in bootstrapping.** The bootstrapping process is effective, as it can progressively augment the training set and lead to increasingly better alignment results. Nevertheless, it suffers from the error propagation problem, which might introduce wrongly-matched entity pairs and amplify their negative effect on the alignment in the following rounds. Also, it can be time-consuming. Consequently, when deciding whether to use the bootstrapping strategy, one could estimate the difficulty of the datasets. If the datasets are relatively easy, e.g., with rich literal information and dense KG structures, exploiting the bootstrapping strategy might be a better choice. Otherwise, one should be careful when using such a strategy.

Suggestions for Future Research. We also discuss some open problems that are worthy of exploration in the future:

- **EA for long-tail entities.** In real-life KGs, only a few entities are densely connected to others, and the rest majority possess rather sparse neighborhood structure. The alignment of these long-tail entities is vital to the overall alignment performance, which, however, was largely neglected by current EA literature. A very recent study [37] leverages the side information to complement structural information for aligning entities in tail. It also proposes to reduce long-tail entities through augmenting relational structure via KG completion embedded into an iterative self-training process. Nevertheless, there is still much room for further improvement.
- **Multi-modal EA.** An entity could be associated with information in multiple modalities, such as texts, images, and even videos. To align such entities, the task of multi-modal entity alignment is worth further investigation [17].
- **EA in the open world.** Current EA solutions work under the closed-domain setting [10]; that is, they assume every entity in the source KG has an equivalent entity in the target KG. Nevertheless, in practical settings, there always exist unmatchable entities. Besides, the labeled data, which are required by the majority of state-of-the-art approaches, might be unavailable. Therefore, it is of significance to explore EA in the open-world settings.

More implementation details and experimental analysis can be seen in [39].

3 Closing Remarks

In this keynote, we introduce two versions of knowledge graph federations which provide a feasible method for multiple knowledge graphs to cooperate with each other. To construct knowledge graphs federations, we introduce two technologies, relation extraction and entity alignment. Specially, relation extraction is responsible for amplifying the triplets in domain knowledge graphs, while entity alignment is aimed at fusing multiple knowledge graphs. In the future, we need develop a unified version of knowledge graph federation which allows multiple knowledge graphs to complement each other under the premise of guaranteeing privacy and security.

Acknowledgement. The author was partially supported by NSFC under grants Nos. 61872446, 61902417, 71971212 and U19B2024, and NSF of Hunan Province under grant No. 2019JJ20024.

References

1. Auer, S., Bizer, C., Kobilarov, G., Lehmann, J., Cyganiak, R., Ives, Z.: DBpedia: a nucleus for a web of open data. In: Aberer, K., et al. (eds.) ASWC/ISWC -2007. LNCS, vol. 4825, pp. 722–735. Springer, Heidelberg (2007). https://doi.org/10.1007/978-3-540-76298-0_52
2. Berners-Lee, T., Hendler, J., Lassila, O.: The semantic web. Sci. Am. **284**(5), 34–43 (2001)
3. Bordes, A., Usunier, N., García-Durán, A., Weston, J., Yakhnenko, O.: Translating embeddings for modeling multi-relational data. In: Advances in Neural Information Processing Systems 26: 27th Annual Conference on Neural Information Processing Systems 2013. Proceedings of a Meeting Held 5–8 December 2013, Lake Tahoe, Nevada, United States, pp. 2787–2795 (2013)
4. Cao, Y., Liu, Z., Li, C., Liu, Z., Li, J., Chua, T.: Multi-channel graph neural network for entity alignment. In: Proceedings of the 57th Conference of the Association for Computational Linguistics, ACL 2019, Volume 1: Long Papers, Florence, Italy, 28 July–2 August 2019, pp. 1452–1461 (2019)
5. Chen, J., et al.: CN-Probase: a data-driven approach for large-scale Chinese taxonomy construction. In: 2019 IEEE 35th International Conference on Data Engineering (ICDE), pp. 1706–1709. IEEE (2019)
6. Chen, M., Tian, Y., Yang, M., Zaniolo, C.: Multilingual knowledge graph embeddings for cross-lingual knowledge alignment. In: Proceedings of the Twenty-Sixth International Joint Conference on Artificial Intelligence, IJCAI 2017, Melbourne, Australia, 19–25 August 2017, pp. 1511–1517 (2017)
7. Fan, Y., Wang, C., He, X.: Exploratory neural relation classification for domain knowledge acquisition. In: Proceedings of the 27th International Conference on Computational Linguistics, COLING 2018, Santa Fe, New Mexico, USA, 20–26 August 2018, pp. 2265–2276 (2018)
8. Guo, L., Sun, Z., Hu, W.: Learning to exploit long-term relational dependencies in knowledge graphs. In: ICML, pp. 2505–2514 (2019)
9. Hao, Y., Zhang, Y., He, S., Liu, K., Zhao, J.: A joint embedding method for entity alignment of knowledge bases. In: Chen, H., Ji, H., Sun, L., Wang, H., Qian, T., Ruan, T. (eds.) CCKS 2016. CCIS, vol. 650, pp. 3–14. Springer, Singapore (2016). https://doi.org/10.1007/978-981-10-3168-7_1
10. Hertling, S., Paulheim, H.: The knowledge graph track at OAEI. In: Harth, A., et al. (eds.) ESWC 2020. LNCS, vol. 12123, pp. 343–359. Springer, Cham (2020). https://doi.org/10.1007/978-3-030-49461-2_20
11. Ji, G., Liu, K., He, S., Zhao, J.: Distant supervision for relation extraction with sentence-level attention and entity descriptions. In: Proceedings of the Thirty-First AAAI Conference on Artificial Intelligence, San Francisco, California, USA, 4–9 February 2017, pp. 3060–3066 (2017)

12. Kipf, T.N., Welling, M.: Semi-supervised classification with graph convolutional networks. In: 5th International Conference on Learning Representations, ICLR 2017, Conference Track Proceedings, Toulon, France, 24–26 April 2017 (2017)
13. Konda, P., et al.: Magellan: toward building entity matching management systems. Proc. VLDB Endow. **9**(12), 1197–1208 (2016)
14. Li, C., Cao, Y., Hou, L., Shi, J., Li, J., Chua, T.: Semi-supervised entity alignment via joint knowledge embedding model and cross-graph model. In: Proceedings of the 2019 Conference on Empirical Methods in Natural Language Processing and the 9th International Joint Conference on Natural Language Processing, EMNLP-IJCNLP 2019, Hong Kong, China, 3–7 November 2019, pp. 2723–2732 (2019)
15. Li, C., Cao, Y., Hou, L., Shi, J., Li, J., Chua, T.S.: Semi-supervised entity alignment via joint knowledge embedding model and cross-graph model. In: EMNLP, pp. 2723–2732 (2019)
16. Lin, Y., Shen, S., Liu, Z., Luan, H., Sun, M.: Neural relation extraction with selective attention over instances. In: Proceedings of the 54th Annual Meeting of the Association for Computational Linguistics, ACL 2016, Volume 1: Long Papers, Berlin, Germany, 7–12 August 2016 (2016)
17. Liu, Y., Li, H., Garcia-Duran, A., Niepert, M., Onoro-Rubio, D., Rosenblum, D.S.: MMKG: multi-modal knowledge graphs. In: Hitzler, P., et al. (eds.) ESWC 2019. LNCS, vol. 11503, pp. 459–474. Springer, Cham (2019). https://doi.org/10.1007/978-3-030-21348-0_30
18. Mai, G., Janowicz, K., Yan, B.: Combining text embedding and knowledge graph embedding techniques for academic search engines. In: Semdeep/NLIWoD@ ISWC, pp. 77–88 (2018)
19. Pang, N., Tan, Z., Zhao, X., Zeng, W., Xiao, W.: Domain relation extraction from noisy Chinese texts. Neurocomputing **418**, 21–35 (2020). https://doi.org/10.1016/j.neucom.2020.07.077
20. Qu, J., Ouyang, D., Hua, W., Ye, Y., Li, X.: Distant supervision for neural relation extraction integrated with word attention and property features. Neural Netw. **100**, 59–69 (2018)
21. Sun, Z., Hu, W., Li, C.: Cross-lingual entity alignment via joint attribute-preserving embedding. In: d'Amato, C., et al. (eds.) ISWC 2017. LNCS, vol. 10587, pp. 628–644. Springer, Cham (2017). https://doi.org/10.1007/978-3-319-68288-4_37
22. Sun, Z., Hu, W., Zhang, Q., Qu, Y.: Bootstrapping entity alignment with knowledge graph embedding. In: Proceedings of the Twenty-Seventh International Joint Conference on Artificial Intelligence, IJCAI 2018, Stockholm, Sweden, 13–19 July 2018, pp. 4396–4402 (2018)
23. Sun, Z., Huang, J., Hu, W., Chen, M., Guo, L., Qu, Y.: TransEdge: translating relation-contextualized embeddings for knowledge graphs. In: Ghidini, C., et al. (eds.) ISWC 2019. LNCS, vol. 11778, pp. 612–629. Springer, Cham (2019). https://doi.org/10.1007/978-3-030-30793-6_35
24. Vrandečić, D., Krötzsch, M.: Wikidata: a free collaborative knowledgebase. Commun. ACM **57**(10), 78–85 (2014)
25. Wang, Z., Lv, Q., Lan, X., Zhang, Y.: Cross-lingual knowledge graph alignment via graph convolutional networks. In: EMNLP, pp. 349–357 (2018)
26. Wu, Y., Liu, X., Feng, Y., Wang, Z., Yan, R., Zhao, D.: Relation-aware entity alignment for heterogeneous knowledge graphs. In: IJCAI, pp. 5278–5284 (2019)
27. Wu, Y., Liu, X., Feng, Y., Wang, Z., Zhao, D.: Jointly learning entity and relation representations for entity alignment. In: EMNLP, pp. 240–249 (2019)

28. Xu, B., et al.: CN-DBpedia: a never-ending Chinese knowledge extraction system. In: Benferhat, S., Tabia, K., Ali, M. (eds.) IEA/AIE 2017. LNCS (LNAI), vol. 10351, pp. 428–438. Springer, Cham (2017). https://doi.org/10.1007/978-3-319-60045-1_44

29. Xu, K., et al.: Cross-lingual knowledge graph alignment via graph matching neural network. In: ACL, pp. 3156–3161 (2019)

30. Xu, Y., Mou, L., Li, G., Chen, Y., Peng, H., Jin, Z.: Classifying relations via long short term memory networks along shortest dependency paths. In: Proceedings of the 2015 Conference on Empirical Methods in Natural Language Processing, EMNLP 2015, Lisbon, Portugal, 17–21 September 2015, pp. 1785–1794 (2015)

31. Yang, H., Zou, Y., Shi, P., Lu, W., Lin, J., Sun, X.: Aligning cross-lingual entities with multi-aspect information. In: Proceedings of the 2019 Conference on Empirical Methods in Natural Language Processing and the 9th International Joint Conference on Natural Language Processing, EMNLP-IJCNLP 2019, Hong Kong, China, 3–7 November 2019, pp. 4430–4440 (2019)

32. Yang, H.W., Zou, Y., Shi, P., Lu, W., Lin, J., Xu, S.: Aligning cross-lingual entities with multi-aspect information. In: EMNLP, pp. 4422–4432 (2019)

33. Yin, J., Jiang, X., Lu, Z., Shang, L., Li, H., Li, X.: Neural generative question answering. In: Proceedings of the Twenty-Fifth International Joint Conference on Artificial Intelligence, IJCAI 2016, New York, NY, USA, 9–15 July 2016, pp. 2972–2978 (2016)

34. Zeng, D., Liu, K., Chen, Y., Zhao, J.: Distant supervision for relation extraction via piecewise convolutional neural networks. In: Proceedings of the 2015 Conference on Empirical Methods in Natural Language Processing, EMNLP 2015, Lisbon, Portugal, 17–21 September 2015, pp. 1753–1762 (2015)

35. Zeng, D., Liu, K., Lai, S., Zhou, G., Zhao, J.: Relation classification via convolutional deep neural network. In: 25th International Conference on Computational Linguistics, Proceedings of the Conference: Technical Papers, COLING 2014, Dublin, Ireland, 23–29 August 2014, pp. 2335–2344 (2014)

36. Zeng, W., Zhao, X., Tang, J., Lin, X.: Collective entity alignment via adaptive features. In: ICDE, pp. 1870–1873. IEEE (2020)

37. Zeng, W., Zhao, X., Wang, W., Tang, J., Tan, Z.: Degree-aware alignment for entities in tail. In: SIGIR, pp. 811–820. ACM (2020)

38. Zhang, Q., Sun, Z., Hu, W., Chen, M., Guo, L., Qu, Y.: Multi-view knowledge graph embedding for entity alignment. In: Proceedings of the Twenty-Eighth International Joint Conference on Artificial Intelligence, IJCAI 2019, Macao, China, 10–16 August 2019, pp. 5429–5435 (2019)

39. Zhao, X., Zeng, W., Tang, J., Wang, W., Suchanek, F.: An experimental study of state-of-the-art entity alignment approaches. IEEE Trans. Knowl. Data Eng. 1 (2020). https://doi.org/10.1109/TKDE.2020.3018741

40. Zhou, K., Zhao, W.X., Bian, S., Zhou, Y., Wen, J.R., Yu, J.: Improving conversational recommender systems via knowledge graph based semantic fusion. In: Proceedings of the 26th ACM SIGKDD International Conference on Knowledge Discovery & Data Mining, pp. 1006–1014 (2020)

41. Zhu, H., Xie, R., Liu, Z., Sun, M.: Iterative entity alignment via joint knowledge embeddings. In: Proceedings of the Twenty-Sixth International Joint Conference on Artificial Intelligence, IJCAI 2017, Melbourne, Australia, 19–25 August 2017, pp. 4258–4264 (2017)
42. Zhu, Q., Zhou, X., Wu, J., Tan, J., Guo, L.: Neighborhood-aware attentional representation for multilingual knowledge graphs. In: Proceedings of the Twenty-Eighth International Joint Conference on Artificial Intelligence, IJCAI 2019, Macao, China, 10–16 August 2019, pp. 1943–1949 (2019)

The Second International Workshop on Semi-structured Big Data Management and Applications

A Learning Interests Oriented Model for Cold Start Recommendation

Yuefeng Du[1], Tuoyu Yan[1], Xiaoli Li[1(✉)], Jiafan Zhou[1], Yang Wang[2], and Jing Shan[3]

[1] Information College, Liaoning University, Shenyang 110036, China
duyuefeng@lnu.edu.cn, xlli7396@sohu.com
[2] Information Technology Department, China Securities Co., Ltd., Beijing 100009, China
[3] Information and Control Engineering School,
Shenyang Jianzhu University, Shenyang 110168, China

Abstract. In recent years, with the increasing importance of education and the development of technology such as the internet and big data, more and more researchers have applied big data research to the field of education. Although big data contains high value, it can easily lead to information overload. Therefore, researchers have developed an education recommendation system that combines education with big data to find valuable information from massive data. Based on the user's historical behavior, the recommendation system can find out the user's interest characteristics, analyze the user's needs and interests, and thereby recommend content that the user is interested in. But when it comes to new users or new products, the recommendation system can not find information about their preferences, which can easily cause data sparseness and cold start problem. In this paper, we propose a cold-start recommendation model for interests, which can enhance the usability of user-related data. The model first uses the Pearson coefficient to calculate the learning interest perception relationship between users with temporal context. Second, based on this model, we use neural network to analyze the semantics of relevant data. In order to find suitable relevant data for recommendation, we use the KNN algorithm by reducing the number of neural network outputs. Finally, the experimental results are proved from the real data of Douban book, experiments show that cold-start recommendation model for learning interests solves the problem of data sparseness and cold start to a certain extent that is compared with the traditional recommendation model based on collaborative filtering algorithm.

Keywords: Learning interest · Recommendation system · Neural network · Cold start

1 Introduction

In recent years, with the increasing investment in education and the rapid development of Internet, big data, cloud computing and other technologies, the amount of data has exploded worldwide. Although the value of big data is of great value, but at the same time, it also leads to information overload. Therefore, how to combine education with

Q. Chen and J. Li (Eds.): APWeb-WAIM 2020 Workshops, CCIS 1373, pp. 83–95, 2021.
https://doi.org/10.1007/978-981-16-0479-9_7

big data and find out the information we need from massive data is very important in the development of big data. This is why the education recommendation system has come into being in recent years. On the basis of the users' historical behavior, it is able to find out the users' interest characteristics and analyze the users' needs and interests so as to recommend the content that the user is interested in, and then to personalize the list of the result for uses. For example, social networking platforms such as Tencent QQ and WeChat recommend friends to users, and video apps such as iQiyi and Youku recommend videos to users. After more than 20 years of research and application, the recommendation system has almost formed a complete theoretical system and application framework, which is playing an increasingly important role in the rapid development of the Internet today and has become an indispensable tool for Internet websites and users. Among them, the recommendation algorithm works as the core of the recommendation system, where currently the most successful application lies in a collaborative filtering algorithm that has been widely used in many fields such as personalized websites. What is more, this algorithm is mainly used to calculate the similarity between users and users and between items and items based on historical feedback of users, and then to recommend the most similar items to users.

Taking the educational big data recommendation system as an example, with the explosive growth of educational information and data and the rapid growth of the number of users, collaborative filtering recommendation algorithms still face some challenges, including severe data sparseness and cold start. In other words, this means when the user feedback data is too sparse, the quality and accuracy of educational recommendations will be greatly reduced, especially the rapid development of today's network applications, making these problems more serious. Therefore, how to reduce data sparseness and cold start has become a research hotspot in the recommendation field. In response to the above problems, researchers have proposed a large number of solutions, such as knowing that Dangdang and other educational platforms have added book review and other functions, and established user-to-user relationships to solve the problem. Data sparseness and cold start have started to a certain extent. Moreover, this relationship is of great help in improving the performance of the recommendation system. However, in real life, people keep making new friends, so you are affected by the accuracy of your recommendations. At the same time, in such a huge educational network, this is a good way to solve the cold start problem, which can help users accurately select the content they need most, and temporarily discard those unimportant friends.

In summary, this article propose a learning interests oriented model for cold start recommendation, which is based on the user-based collaborative filtering algorithm and temporal context to model, effectively solving the problem of data sparseness and improving the quality of recommendations. On the other hand, we use the KNN algorithm to leave only the recommended results you need, solving the cold start problem caused by the sparse data resulted from the large space of the neural network.

The main contributions of our research are summarized as follows.

1. Aiming at the problem of data sparseness, this paper uses the Pearson correlation coefficient to calculate the similarity between users and users, but need to be adjusted based on the recognition time.

2. Based on this, a neural network matrix is established. This article adjusts the weight of the neural network according to the similarity between users and users, and then obtains more accurate results.
3. Finally, we use the KNN algorithm to find the TOP-K recommendation with the highest similarity to this user, reduce the neural network, and propose a new solution to the problem of cold start caused by data sparseness.
4. We have conducted extensive experiments on the Douban Book Website data set, and have obtained the results that show that our recommendation algorithm can well solve the problems of data sparseness and cold start.

The rest of this article is organized as follows. Brief commentary on work related to Sect. 2. In Sect. 3, we introduced the use of the improved Pearson coefficient to calculate similarities between users. In Sect. 4, we introduce Pearson coefficients to the neural network matrix and use the KNN algorithm for recommendation. We then show the experimental results in Sect. 5. Section 6 concluded.

2 Related Work

Due to the great success of the education recommendation systems, more and more scholars have begun to study recommendation algorithms, in particular, the most important and most used-widely coordinated filtering algorithm (CF). At present, the CF algorithm is mainly divided into three categories: User-based coordinated filtering, item-based coordinated filtering, and model-based coordinated filtering. Additionally, they have been widely used in e-commerce and various large-scale websites. However, with the increasing number of users and the system as well as larger and larger scale of the Internet, it is imperative for the collaborative filtering algorithm to deal with serious data sparseness and the problem of the cold start. Especially in recent years, with the booming development of Internet applications, these two issues have worse effects, so how to effectively solving them becomes a research hotspot of recommendation algorithms.

When it comes to solving the problem of data sparseness, [2] proposed a graph recommendation algorithm *AttentionRank*$^+$ based on attention relationships and multi-user behavior. Its main idea is to establish "user-item" feedback graph on the basis of user feedback, calculate the similarity between the user node and each node and then converge to a certain value on it, and finally, the value is recommended to the user as an item recommendation list. The data sparseness problem has been mitigated to some extent, but the algorithm cannot connect the similarity between users and users. [3] established a social Bayesian personalized ranking (SBPR). In terms of the influence of friends' purchase on user preferences, it assigned users to a higher level to the items their friends like and proved that friendships can not only improve the recommendation performance, but also can solve the problem of cold start to a certain extent through evaluation by real four datasets. However, this article does not use the KNN algorithm for processing, which may cause too many recommendations. [4] proposed a position-based advertising recommendation model, which is an extension of the coordinated filtering algorithm, using the GA method for context-aware collaborative filtering and creating a context-aware recommendation model (CACF-GA) in traditional CF, is created, which are helpful to settle data sparseness to a certain extent, but it has no good effect on the cold start problem. The cold start is caused by the sparseness. The education recommendation system analyzes the rating matrix between the user and the item to infer the user's interest and recommend the products that the user may be interested in. However, in reality, because of the large number of users and products as well as increasing websites and users, especially with the development of e-commerce websites, the cold start problem arises. The cold start problem consists of two categories: user cold-start problems and product cold-start problems. The former refers to the fact that users have not evaluated any products when they first entered the system, so the system fails to dig out the interests and preferences of new users or find new users who have similar interests, so it is impossible for the traditional recommendation system to make recommendations to new users. The latter actually is similar to the former. [6] proposed a multifaceted collaborative filtering model and finded user characteristic values with high similarity to users When a new product first enters the system, no user has evaluated the product, so the system cannot find neighbors similar to the product and recommend it. In addition, different students may have different learning interests, and even one student will have multiple learning interests. [8] used the KNN algorithm has been proven to be a good solution for learning interest [9, 10]. At the same time, [13] proposed social networks and KNN algorithms can effectively solve the problem of recommended cold start [14, 15]. [19] used HIN to model the side information, and at the same time designed an effective algorithm framework in order to obtain better recommendations. Through HIN and mega-graph, a variety of side information is perfectly unified into a framework, that is "MF + FM", It simply puts that it is to perform matrix decomposition on several matrices with similarity to obtain a number of implicit features of users and products, and then stitch all the features together that would be trained and predicted in score by factorization machine. However, this algorithm does not effectively solve the problem of cold start. [20] proposed a joint personal and social potential factor (PSLF) model, which combined collaborative filtering algorithms and network modeling methods for social recommendation, and played a key role in solving the problem of data sparseness, but the model does not take into account the issue of trust between different users.

In summary, this paper proposes a cold-start recommendation model based on recognition time. As we all know, existing recommendation algorithms only calculate the similarity between users and users through simple collaborative filtering, without considering the potential impact time on users. At the same time, this paper uses the KNN algorithm based on the neural network matrix to reduce the range of the neural network and find the required one through matrix calculations, alleviating the cold start problem caused by sparse data.

3 Discovering Learners' Similarity

In this section, we introduce the Pearson correlation coefficient, which is used to reflect the degree of linear correlation between two random variables. Pearson algorithm attaches great importance to the integrity of the data set when calculating the similarity, which can increase the depth of recommendation. Therefore, we calculate the similarity between users based on the Pearson coefficient of the temporal context.

3.1 Pearson with Learning Interests

For the problems of sparse data and cold start, this section first uses the Pearson correlation coefficient to calculate the similarity between users and users, but in the calculation process, this article will get an adjusted Pearson coefficient based on the recognition time.

Use the Pearson correlation coefficient defined by the following equation to calculate the similarity between friends and friends:

$$S_{a.u} = \frac{\sum_i (r_{a.i} - \overline{r_a}) * (r_{u.i} - \overline{r_u})}{\sqrt{\sum_i (r_{a.i} - \overline{r_a})^2} * \sqrt{\sum_i (r_{u.i} - \overline{r_u})^2}} (-1 \leq S_{a.u} \leq 1) \tag{1}$$

Among them $S_{a.u}$ is the similarity between friend a and u. The higher the similarity, the more they like to rate the items together, i represents the item index owned by two users, $r_{a.i}$ refers to the rating of item i by friend and, $\overline{r_a}$ represents his average rating, $r_{u.i}$ is the rating of item i by friend u, and $\overline{r_u}$ refers to his average rating.

Although this traditional recommendation algorithm gains very good results in network recommendations of many applications, it may not be enough to only take the relationship between friends and friends into consideration, because different users have different degrees of trust on friends. So the temporal context-based neural network model comes into being. When calculating the similarity and satisfaction between friends, we take into account the length of time that friends know each other to define a similarity matrix of temporal context. When figuring out its similarity, we employ the adjusted Pearson coefficient to change the formula for calculating the similarity between friends and friends to the following equation:

$$S'_{a.u} = S_{a.u} * w(a, b) \tag{2}$$

$$w(a, b) = \frac{1}{1 + e^{-x}} \tag{3}$$

According to the above formula, $S'_{a.u}$ represents the coefficient of the adjusted Pearson indicates that the trust between friends and friends will increase as the year increases when friends are familiar with each other. When two people have just met, $x = 0$, $w(a, b) = 0.5$. When the year increases, x will increase gradually, and so does $w(a, b)$.

The specific calculation is shown in the following Fig. 1, where in terms of the user and his value of trust, we default to 1, and then we start to calculate that of different users via formula.

3.2 Temporal Context Similarity

The performance of the algorithm is continuously optimized by adjusting the Pearson coefficient. When calculating the similarity between friends, $S'_{a.u}$ is used as a comprehensive consideration of the proportion of the similarity between users. But the coefficient will change with the increase of the recognition time. The longer the recognition time, the value of $S'_{a.u}$ will continue to increase and be infinitely close to 1.

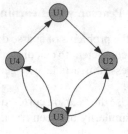

context	U1	U2	U3	U4
U1	1			$w(4,1)$
U2	$w(1,2)$	1	$w(3,2)$	
U3		$w(2,3)$	1	$w(4,3)$
U4			$w(3,4)$	1

(a) Friend-Friend Matrix   (b) Social Network Graph

Fig. 1. Calculation of temporal context similarity between friends

We divide the entire data set into five groups by time window (see Table 1). Each group of acquaintances is increased by one year, and the improved Pearson coefficient is calculated.

Table 1. Example for Temporal Context Similarity

Users	I	II	III	IV	V
Acquaintance	2019–11	2018–11	2017–11	2016–11	2015–11
Testing	2019–11	2019–11	2019–11	2019–11	2019–11
$W(a,b)$	0.5	0.73	0.88	0.95	0.99

4 Neural Network for Recommendation

In this section, we introduce how to introduce the improved Pearson coefficient into the neural network matrix and how to obtain accurate recommendation results using the KNN algorithm.

4.1 P.neural Network

A neural network is featured by a hierarchical structure that includes an input layer, a hidden layer (which consists of multiple layers), and an output layer. The input layer is used to receive signals, while the output layer is applied to output signals. The nodes of adjacent layers are fully connected, but different nodes have different weight ratios between connections. What is more, each connection will have a connection weight, but nodes in the same layer will not have connections.

For a new user, whether he can properly recommend the item he wants, the users' friends play a certain guiding role. For example, when the users' friend likes a certain type of item, and their relationship is very close, so such kind of recommendation will greatly solve the problem of accuracy and cold start. Therefore, we establish a P.neural network based on Pearson coefficients. In the above, we have calculated the similarity between different friends, introduced this value as a user preference into the neural network, and used it as the connection weight between nodes. Finally, the trust value between friends in the neural network will be added. The following formulas are used to work out the results from the input layer to the hidden layer and from the latter to the former.

$$y_j(p) = sigmoid\left[\sum_{i=1}^{n} x_{ij}(p) * \omega_{ij}(p)\right] \tag{4}$$

$$\omega_{ij} = \alpha * S_{a.u} * \delta_j(p) \tag{5}$$

$$\delta_j(p) = y_i(p) * \left[1 - y_i(p)\right] * \sum_{k=1}^{n} \delta_k(p) * \omega_{jk}(p) \tag{6}$$

The above process refers to the one from the input layer to the hidden layer, where p is the number of iterations, $y_j(p)$ is the output of the hidden layer, $x_{ij}(p)$ is the input value, $\omega_{ij}(p)$ is the weight vector, and $\delta_k(p)$ is the error gradient, α is the learning rate.

$$y_k(p) = sigmoid\left[\sum_{j=1}^{m} x_{jk}(p) * \omega_{jk}(p)\right] \tag{7}$$

$$\omega_{jk} = \alpha * S_{a.u} * \delta_k(p) \tag{8}$$

$$\delta_k(p) = y_k(p) * \left[1 - y_k(p)\right] * e_k(p) \tag{9}$$

Algorithm: Optimizing neural networks

Input: x
Output: y

1:     **Input** layer (p);
2:     **While** (p)
3:       **run:** $\quad y_j(p) = sigmoid[\sum_{i=1}^{n} x_{ij}(p) * \omega_{ij}(p)]$
4:       **run:** $\quad \omega_{jk} = \alpha * S_{a.u} * \delta_k(p)$
         run: $\quad \delta_j(p) = y_i(p) * [1 - y_i(p)] * \sum_{k=1}^{n} \delta_k(p) * \omega_{jk}(p)$
         Return hidden layer();
5:     **hidden** layer(p);
         While (p)
6:       **run:** $\quad y_k(p) = sigmoid[\sum_{j=1}^{m} x_{jk}(p) * \omega_{jk}(p)]$
7:       **run:** $\quad \omega_{jk} = \alpha * S_{a.u} * \delta_k(p)$
8:       **run:** $\quad \delta_k(p) = y_k(p) * [1 - y_k(p)] * e_k(p)$
9:     **Return** output layer();
10:     **End**

The above process is the one from the hidden layer to the output layer, which is similar to the course from the input layer to the hidden layer $e_k(p)$ is the error signal, and other symbols are the same as the previous process. The above neural network model calculates the similarity between users and users, and the features are layered to find out features suitable for the user that will be recommended, greatly reducing the sparseness of the entire matrix. Next, we make use of the KNN algorithm to optimize the neural network matrix to reduce the neural network and find a suitable range of neural networks and to reduce the problem of cold start caused by difficulty in finding.

4.2 KNN Method for Recommendation

After establishing the neural network matrix, in order to effectively solve the cold start problem, we use the KNN algorithm for TOP-K model recommendation.

The K in the KNN algorithm refers to the nearest neighbor, that is, the nearest neighbor, which means that each sample can be represented by its nearest K neighbors. As we all know, the traditional KNN algorithm determines that the K nearest neighbors is used to determine the category of the sample to be tested by voting method. The selection of K value has a great impact on the final classification result, so does the KNN algorithm. The core idea of the KNN algorithm is that if most of the K most adjacent samples of a sample in the feature space belong to a certain category, the sample also belongs to this category and has the same characteristics.

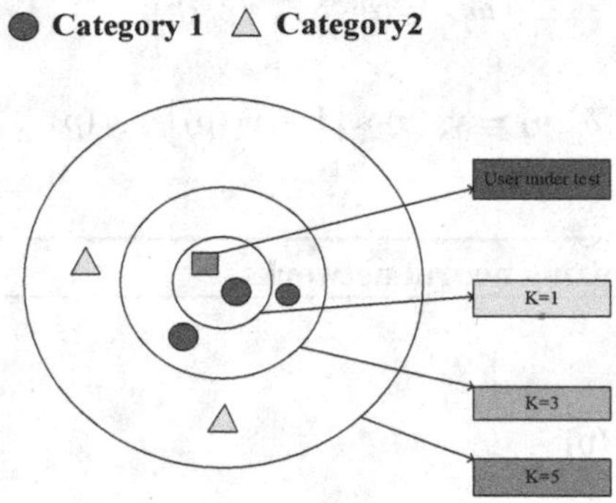

Fig. 2. Schematic diagram of KNN nearest neighbor classification

The schematic diagram of the K-nearest neighbor classifier shown in Fig. 2 can make us more directly find the effect of the K value on the classification result of the KNN algorithm. When the K value is 1, the test sample is identified as category one; when the K value is 3, the sample to be tested is identified as category 2; when the value of K is equal to 5, the result of the test sample is identified as category 3. Therefore, when the KNN algorithm with different values of K is used to classify the data in Fig. 1, its results change with the value of K. Generally speaking, the choice of K value in the KNN algorithm directly determines the range of the neural network. If the range is too large, there are too many items that meet the requirements, which will be negative to deal with the cold start problem. Nevertheless, if the range is too small, it will cause the item set too small, resulting in a worse accuracy of the recommendation.

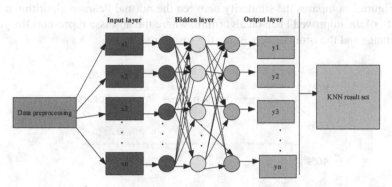

Fig. 3. Processing results using KNN

As shown in Fig. 3, we introduce the K value into the neural network. The basic idea is: first, the model uses Pearson correlation coefficients to calculate the similarity of the input data, then the results are input to the neural network, through the input layer, hidden layer, and output layer of the neural network, and finally the output results of the neural network are different using K values. The KNN algorithm works on the neural network dataset to find the best K value. In this way, not only can the most accurate recommendation result be obtained, but also the cold start problem caused by the excessive amount of data can be solved.

Next, we use experiments to select different K values (1, 3, 5, 7, 9) to verify this idea to ensure the accuracy of the algorithm.

5   Experiments

To evaluate the performance of the proposed model, we performed experiments on a real dataset.

5.1   Experimental Setting

There are 12 nodes in our experiment, including 2 management nodes, 4 data nodes, 4 processing nodes, 1 back up node, and 1 console node, which takes about four hours. In addition, all experiments will be performed on a Linux operating system.

In order to evaluate the accuracy and effectiveness of the algorithm, experiments will apply the Douban book dataset, which is from the well-known website Douban that is a community site, established by Yang Bo (with Net name "ABEI") on March 6, 2005. The website started with books and videos, and provides information about books, the film, music, and furthermore, whether described or commented is provided by the user (User-generated content, UGC), a unique website on the Web 2.0A. Additionally, it has been dedicated to helping urban people discover useful things in life. Our data set consists of 13075 books, 78450 records, as well as the title, listed time, price, rating, content introduction and book classification.

5.2 Effect of Adjusting Pearson Coefficient on Algorithm Correlation

Before conducting experiments, we first need to analyze the improved Pearson algorithm. Figure 3 compares the similarity between the normal Pearson algorithm and the similarity of the improved Pearson algorithm, where the abscissa represents the year of acquaintance and the ordinate represents the similarity.

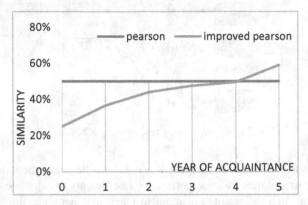

Fig. 4. Effect of adjusting Pearson coefficient on correlation

As shown in Fig. 4, as the year of acquaintance increases, the improved Pearson coefficient will be closer to the normal Pearson coefficient. It can be said that if two people have not known each other for a long time, the similarity of the normal Pearson coefficient calculation will be inaccurate, so add a parameter. When two people have known each other long enough, this parameter is infinitely close to 1, and the improved Pearson coefficient is infinitely close to the normal Pearson coefficient, so it has better effectiveness.

5.3 Comparison of Recommendation Accuracy

We have explained the KNN algorithm before, we have improved the problem of data sparseness by neural networks with Pearson coefficients, and we have used KNN to reduce the scope of the neural network to avoid the problem of cold start. In order to prove the contribution of this definition, we perform experiments by comparing the datasets from Douban Book, without the recommended cold-start solution by the KNN algorithm (no-KNN). The experimental results are as follows.

The results are shown in Fig. 5. We use different K values, and the accuracy of the recommendations is higher than that without KNN algorithm. In comparison, when K = 3, the algorithm has the highest recommendation accuracy and the best recommendation effect. We compare with the experiments of [14] and [17], and the experimental results are shown in the figure below.

The experimental results are shown in Fig. 6. Compared with [19] and [20], our recommendation results using K = 3 show that our algorithm is more accurate than the other two algorithms.

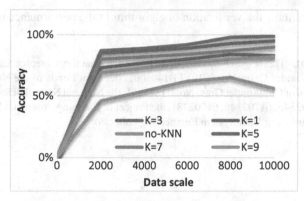

Fig. 5. Comparison of different K values

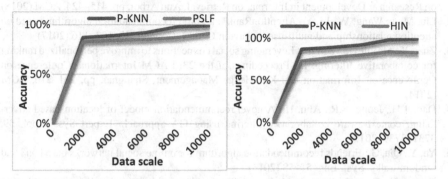

Fig. 6. Performance comparison of different recommendation algorithms

6   Conclusion

This paper proposes a learning interests oriented model for cold start recommendation on the basis of experiments. According to the real situation, this algorithm is to solve the problem of inaccurate recommendation and cold start due to data sparseness in big educational data era. In the neural network matrix, different weight calculations are performed for users with different recognition times, and the range of the neural network is reduced by the KNN algorithm to improve the accuracy of the recommendation and effectively solve the cold start problem. More than 13,000 books were selected from the Douban website taken as an experimental data set to analyze the performance of the algorithm. The experimental results show that the algorithm can effectively improve the performance of the recommendation, and solve the problem of cold start by calculating the friend relationship of the user with sparse behavior. In the future, I hope to design a more effective recommendation algorithm that can play an effective role not only in the relationship between users and users, but also in the relationship between users and items and items and items, making it into a more reasonable and larger neural network. In addition, we will spend more time in finding out larger scale and more diverse data on the website to make the verification of algorithm in the performance more accurate and reasonable.

Acknowledgement. This research was supported by the National Key Research and Development Program of China under Grant No. 2019YFB1406002, the Joint Funds of the National Natural Science Foundation of China under Grant No. U1811261, the National Natural Science Foundation of China No. 61702345, 61702346, 61702381, the Project of Liaoning Provincial Public Opinion and Network Security Big Data System Engineering Laboratory.

References

1. Rocio, C., Pablo, C.: Should I follow the crowd? A probabilistic analysis of the effectiveness of popularity in recommender systems. In: The 41st International ACM SIGIR Conference on Research & Development in Information Retrieval, Ann Arbor, pp. 415–424. ACM (2018)
2. Liu, M.-J., Wang, W., Li, Y.: AttentionRank$^+$: a graph recommendation algorithm based on attention relationship and multi-user behavior. Chin. J. Comput. **40**, 102–116 (2017)
3. Zhao, T., Mcauley, J., King, I.: Leveraging social connections to improve personalized ranking for collaborative filtering. In: Proceedings of the 23rd ACM International Conference on Conference on Information and Knowledge Management, Shanghai, pp. 261–270. ACM (2014)
4. Dao, T.H., Jeong, S.R., Ahn, H.: A novel recommendation model of location-based advertising: context-aware collaborative filtering using GA approach. Expert Syst. Appl. **39**, 3731–3739 (2012)
5. Yu, Y., Qiu, G.: Friends recommendation algorithm for online social networks based on local random walks. Syst. Eng. 51–58 (2013)
6. Koren, Y.: Factorization meets the neighborhood: a multifaceted collaborative filtering model. In: Proceedings of the 14th ACM SIGKDD International Conference on Knowledge Discovery and Data Mining, Nevada, pp. 426–434. ACM (2008)
7. Wang, H., Wang, N., Yeung, D.Y.: Collaborative deep learning for recommender systems. In: Proceedings of the 21th ACM SIGKDD International Conference on Knowledge Discovery and Data Mining, Sydney, pp. 261–270. ACM (2015)
8. Komai, Y., Sasaki, Y., Hara, T., Nishio, S.: A KNN query processing method in mobile ad hoc networks. IEEE Trans. Mob. Comput. **13**, 1090–1103 (2014)
9. Lu, D., Ning, M., Zang, J.: Improved KNN algorithm based on BP neural network decision. Comput. Appl. **37**, 65–68 (2017)
10. Lu, Y., Hong, L.: A recommendation system algorithm based on real value and topology neural networks in social networks. J. San Ming Univ. 36–42 (2018)
11. Feng, W., Zhu, Q., Zhuang, J., Yu, S.: An expert recommendation algorithm based on Pearson correlation coefficient and FP-growth. Clust. Comput. **22**(3), 7401–7412 (2018). https://doi.org/10.1007/s10586-017-1576-y
12. Chen, G., Wang, H.: Personalized recommendation algorithm based on improved Pearson correlation coefficient. J. Shandong Agric. Univ. (Nat. Sci. Edn.) 940–944 (2016)
13. Adamic, L., Adar, E.: How to search a social network. Soc. Netw. **27**, 187–203 (2005)
14. Guy, I., Ronen, I., Wilcox, E.: Do you know? Recommending people to invite into your social network. In: Proceedings of the 14th International Conference on Intelligent User Interfaces, Florida, pp. 77–86. ACM (2009)
15. Liben-Nowell, D., Kleinberg, J.: The link-prediction problem for social networks. J. Am. Soc. Inf. Sci. Technol. **58**, 1019–1031 (2007)

16. Cheng, L., Gao, M.: Recommendation algorithm based on deep neural network. Mod. Comput. (Prof. Ed.) 5–9 (2018)
17. Sun, J., Ma, J., Liu, Z.: Leveraging content and connections for scientific article recommendation in social computing contexts. Comput. J. **57**, 1331–1342 (2014)
18. Ma, H., Yang, H., Lyu, M.R.: SoRec: social recommendation using probabilistic matrix factorization. In: Proceedings of the 17th ACM Conference on Information and Knowledge Management, pp. 931–940. ACM (2008)
19. Zhao, H., Yao, Q., Li, J.: Meta-graph based recommendation fusion over heterogeneous information networks. In: Proceedings of the 23rd ACM SIGKDD International Conference on Knowledge Discovery and Data Mining, Halifax, pp. 635–644. ACM (2017)
20. Shen, Y., Jin, R.: Learning personal + social latent factor model for social recommendation. In: Proceedings of the 18th ACM SIGKDD International Conference on Knowledge Discovery and Data Mining, Beijing, pp. 1303–1311. ACM (2012)

A Composite Chain Structure Blockchain Storage Method Based on Blockchain Technology

Junlu Wang[1](✉), Su Li[1], and Wenyuan Ma[2]

[1] School of Information, Liaoning University, Shenyang 110036, China
wangjunlu@lnu.edu.cn
[2] School of International Education,
Beijing University of Chemical Technology, Beijing 100029, China

Abstract. Blockchain is an effective means to store data securely. Existing blockchain systems mostly adopt the equal mining mode, and all bookkeepers (entities) record ledger books on a single main chain, resulting in random data storage in the whole blockchain. Moreover, in complex or classification scenarios, data in a single main chain cannot be correlated or regularly stored, resulting in low storage efficiency. To solve these problems, this paper proposes a composite chain structure blockchain storage method based on blockchain technology. This method firstly proposes the blockchain model of composite chain structure, then constructs the private chain and alliance chain respectively, and finally realizes the adaptive data association storage in complex or classified scenarios. The experimental results show that a composite chain structure blockchain storage method based on blockchain technology proposed in this paper has great advantages in storage efficiency, storage overhead, security performance, availability and other aspects.

Keywords: Composite chain structure · Private chain · Alliance chain

1 Introduction

Blockchain [1] is a new computing paradigm [2] and collaboration model for establishing trust at low cost in an untrusted competitive environment. Due to its features such as high storage density [3], tamper-proof [4] and traceability, blockchain technology has been more and more widely applied. Blockchain stores data by adding blocks [5], and all data are stored on a single chain. However, with the expansion of time and transaction data, data inflation [6] may result in the reduction of storage efficiency. At the same time, single chain storage mode cannot realize associated storage or regular storage in complex or classified scenarios [7].

For example, in the blockchain system of financial activities, if all financial enterprises (entities) store data in the single chain mode in an equal manner [8], the transaction data of financial enterprises (entities) will be chaotic and random [9]. At the same time, according to the single mode to store all financial enterprises (entities) transaction

© Springer Nature Singapore Pte Ltd. 2021
Q. Chen and J. Li (Eds.): APWeb-WAIM 2020 Workshops, CCIS 1373, pp. 96–103, 2021.
https://doi.org/10.1007/978-981-16-0479-9_8

data, when the associated relationship between financial enterprises (entities), the headquarters and the branch of the financial enterprise, for example, when the total entity (headquarters) of a financial enterprise entity in legal cases has returned to the bad debts to the branch of the financial enterprise, cannot be achieved in a single storage mode to store their relationship. Therefore, how to establish an efficient blockchain storage method has always been a difficulty in the field of blockchain research.

In view of the above problems, this paper proposes a composite chain structure blockchain storage method based on blockchain technology. The main contributions are as follows:

- To solve the problem of low storage efficiency caused by single blockchain storage structure, a blockchain model with composite chain structure is proposed to realize adaptive data association storage in complex or classified scenarios.
- According to the characteristics of the entity data to be stored and the storage requirements of the entity itself, a private chain is built within each entity [10].
- On this basis, combined with the characteristics of different application modes of blockchain technology, the alliance chain is constructed among different entities [11], and the alliance chain and the private chain are combined to build the composite chain blockchain.

2 Related Work

At present, many scholars have conducted in-depth research on the blockchain storage method and achieved certain research results.

In the building of blockchain storage, literature [12] proposes a method of using blockchain to store data. This method proves that using blockchain to store data has the characteristics of high storage density, traceability and tamper-proof, which provides ideas for subsequent research in the storage field. Literature [13] gives a detailed introduction to the data storage mechanism used in the current popular blockchain system, and points out that due to the limitation of data storage mode, the existing blockchain system has the problems of simple query function and low query performance. Literature [4] proposes a method for storing data in blockchain structure of single chain mode. This method is simple and efficient, but it cannot accurately and completely reflect the association or implied relationship between nodes in complex application scenarios. Literature [14] proposed a method of building multi-fork chain block chain structure to store data. This method can store complex and huge data, but using multi-fork chain structure to store data reduces the efficiency of storage and query.

To sum up, existing methods in blockchain storage have problems such as low storage efficiency and complex storage structure. Therefore, considering the efficiency and accuracy of storage, this paper proposes a composite chain structure blockchain storage method based on blockchain technology.

3   The Model of Composite Chain Structure Blockchain

According to the data storage requirements in complex or classified scenarios, combined with the different application patterns of blockchain technology and the data characteristics of the entities that need to be stored, a model of composite chain structure blockchain is presented.

The composite chain structure model of blockchain is composed of private chain and alliance chain. The private chain is built inside the entity to represent the transaction information of the entity. Based on the private chain, the alliance chain between entities is constructed to form the composite chain structure blockchain model. The blockchain model of composite chain structure is shown in Fig. 1.

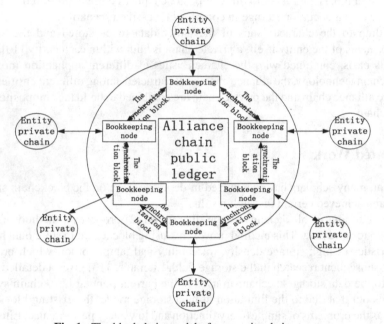

Fig. 1. The blockchain model of composite chain structure

4   The Construction of Composite Chain Structure Blockchain

Based on the composite chain blockchain model, according to different storage requirements, the private chain block structure based on Merkle tree and the alliance chain block structure based on Merkle Patricia tree were established respectively, and finally the composite chain structure of the block chain was constructed.

4.1   Private Chain Block Structure Based on Merkle Tree

The private chain introduces the ECDSA algorithm to generate two different keys (the public key and the private key), which encrypts the data and decrypts it with the public key when the transaction data needs to be verified. Each block consists of two parts of the head and the block body, head by last the block Hash value (Prev Hash), time stamps, random number (Nonce) and trade to the Root of the Hash (Root Hash), the "transaction type" index table, "suspicious transactions" index table, by adding block hash, root hash and random number information, the hash algorithm is used to generate the hash value of the current block, each block of the preceding block pointer links constitute the whole block link relations in time order. The private chain block header data is shown in Table 1.

Table 1. The private chain block header stores information

The property of the block header	Meaning
The Version number	The version number of the data block
Prev Hash	Hash value obtained by hashing data such as Merkle Root and timestamp of the previous block
The timestamp	the approximate time at which the block is generated
The random number	The random number of solutions to the current block consensus process
Merkle roots	The root of the Merkle tree for all transactions in the block body through a hash operation
Transaction type index table	Record the type of transaction to which the transaction for that block belongs
Suspicious transactions Index table	Record the Hash value of a suspicious transaction

The block body stores all the transaction information, and each transaction information is converted into a string of unique hash values through the hash function and stored on the leaf node of the Merkle tree. The hash value of the upper node is generated layer by layer through the hash function, and each data set corresponds to a unique hash root. If the underlying transaction record is tampered, the Merkle root value will also change.

Before the transaction data is stored in the block, all the transaction types carried out by the entity should be counted and numbered uniformly. When the transaction data is stored in the block, the transaction type information of the transaction should be added to the index table of "Transaction Types". Then suspicious transaction rules are formulated. When data is stored in the block, suspicious transaction rules are used to determine whether the transaction is a suspicious transaction. If so, after calculating the Hash value of the transaction, the Hash value is stored in the Merkle tree and the Hash value is also stored in the "suspicious Transaction" index table in the block head.

4.2 Alliance Chain Block Structure Based on Merkle Patricia Tree

As described in Sect. 4.1, each entity's private chain will serve as an account in the alliance chain. The contact between entities will be established in the form of signing contracts, and the alliance chain block structure based on Merkle Patricia tree will be established for data storage. The block structure diagram of the alliance chain is shown in Fig. 2.

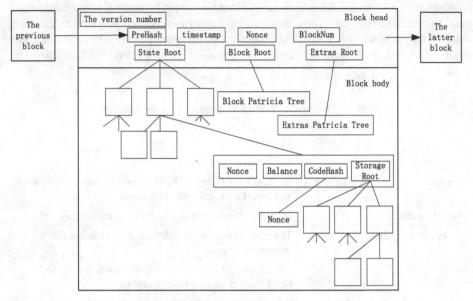

Fig. 2. Block structure of alliance chain

The alliance chain also introduces ECDSA algorithm to encrypt data. The block header consists of the Prev Hash, timestamp, random number (Nonce) of the previous block, and the root hashes of the three Merkle Patricia trees, which correspond to the state tree, the transaction tree, and the receipt tree respectively. The transaction information is stored in the block body. Three levelDB databases are established in the alliance chain, namely BlockDB, StateDB and ExtrasDB. BlockDB stores block headers and transaction records, StateDB stores entity status data, and ExtrasDB stores contract information signed between entities. Based on this, the underlying database of the alliance chain is built. Each block contains the root hash of the entire state tree, which is updated with period T.

5 Experiment and Analysis

The experimental data set is the data on the website of the Tonghuashun. The experiment selects the data from the Tonghuashun to calculate, and verifies the effectiveness of the block chain storage method based on the composite chain structure based on the block chain technology through the aspects of storage efficiency and cost respectively, and compares with the single chain structure and the multi-chain structure.

5.1 Storage Efficiency Analysis

The experiment simulates the efficiency comparison of the blockchain storage structure with the single chain storage structure and the multi-chain storage structure. The x-coordinate represents the storage entity data set, and the y-coordinate represents the storage time required. The experimental results are shown in Fig. 3.

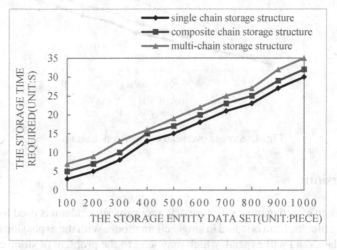

Fig. 3. Comparison of storage efficiency

It can be seen from Fig. 3 that the storage efficiency of the blockchain storage structure of the composite chain structure proposed in this paper is between the single chain structure and the multi-chain structure.

5.2 Storage Cost Analysis

The experiment simulates the cost comparison between the blockchain storage structure of composite chain structure, single chain storage structure and multi-chain storage structure. The x-coordinate represents the storage entity data set, and the y-coordinate represents the amount of space required for storage. The experimental results are shown in Fig. 4.

It can be seen from Fig. 4 that the storage cost of the blockchain storage structure of the composite chain structure proposed in this paper is between the single chain structure and the multi-chain structure.

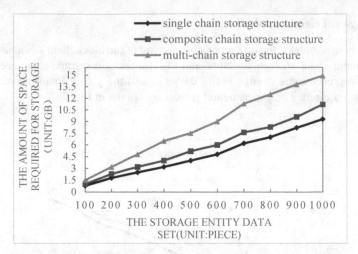

Fig. 4. Storage overhead comparison diagram

6   Conclusion

Blockchain is an effective means to store data securely. Blockchain is used for data storage by adding blocks. Data is stored in single chain mode. With the expansion of time and transaction data, data will expand, which may lead to the problem of storage efficiency reduction. At the same time, the single chain storage mode cannot realize the adaptive data association storage in complex or classified scenarios. To solve these problems, this paper makes an in-depth study of the block chain storage structure method, and proposes a composite chain structure blockchain storage method based on the blockchain technology. This method firstly proposes the blockchain model of composite chain structure, then constructs the private chain and alliance chain respectively, and finally realizes the adaptive data association storage in complex or classified scenarios.

References

1. Yuan, Y., Feiyue, W.: Development status and prospect of blockchain technology. J. Autom. **42**(4), 481–494 (2016). (in Chinese)
2. Bartoletti, M., Bracciali, A., Lande, S., et al.: A general framework for blockchain analytics. In: Proceedings of the 1st Workshop on Scalable and Resilient Infrastructures for Distributed Ledgers, Las Vegas, Nevada, pp. 11–15 (2017)
3. He, P., Yu, G., Zhang, Y.F., et al.: Prospective review of blockchain technology and application. Comput. Sci. **44**(4), 1–7 (2017). (in Chinese)
4. Iemieux, V.L.: Trusting records: is blockchain technology the answer. Rec. Manag. J. **2** (2016)
5. Wang, S., Dinh, T.A., Lin, Q., et al.: ForkBase: an efficient storage engine for blockchain and forkable applications. In: Proceedings of 44th International Conference on Very Large Data Bases, Rio de Janeiro, pp. 1137–1150 (2018)
6. Halpin, H., Piekarska, M.: Introduction to security and privacy on the blockchain. In: European Symposium on Security and Privacy Workshops (2017)

7. Lind, J., Naor, O., et al.: Teechain: reducing storage costs on the blockchain with offline payment channels. In: SYSTOR 2018, pp. 125–125 (2018)
8. Karlsson, K., Jiang, W., Wicker, S., et al.: Vegvisir: a partition-tolerant blockchain for the internet-of-things. In: International Conference on Distributed Computing Systems, pp. 1150–1158. IEEE Computer Society (2018)
9. Iuon-Chang, L., Tzu-Chun, L.: A survey of blockchain security issues and challenges. Int. J. Network Secur. **19**(5), 653–659 (2017)
10. Dannen, C.: Introducing Ethereum and Solidity: Foundations of Cryptocurrency and Blockchain Programming for Beginners. Apress, Berkeley (2017)
11. Dinh, T.T.A., Wang, J., Chen, G., et al.: BLOC- KBENCH: a framework for analyzing private blockchains. In: International Conference on Management of Data, pp. 1085–1100 (2017)
12. Shao, Q., Jin, C., Zhang, Z., Qian, W., Zhou, A.: Blockchain technology: architecture and progress. J. Comput. Sci. **05** (2018). (in Chinese)
13. Wang, Q., He, P., Nie, T., Derong, S., Yu, G.: Overview of data storage and query Technology of blockchain system. Comput. Sci. (2018). (in Chinese)
14. Jin, H., Dai, X., Xiao, J.: Towards a novel architecture for enabling interoperability amongst multiple blockchains. In: International Conference on Distributed Computing Systems, pp. 1203–1211. IEEE Computer Society (2018)

Curriculum-Oriented Multi-goal Agent for Adaptive Learning

Jieyue Ma[1], Xiaoli Li[1(✉)], Xin Zhang[1], Tingting Liu[1], Yuefeng Du[1], and Tie Li[2]

[1] School of Information, Liaoning University, Shenyang 110036, China
`zhangxin@lnu.edu.cn`
[2] Shenyang AeroTech Co. Ltd., Shenyang, China

Abstract. Adaptive learning is an important part of Intelligent Tutoring System (ITS). Given that students have different learning targets and knowledge concepts proficiency, a smart intelligent tutor should be able to provide personalized learning materials to them, and help students master target knowledge and skills with learning materials as less as possible. Reinforcement Learning (RL) algorithms are good at solving sequence decision problems, so they are widely used in learning material recommendation. However, the existing intelligent tutoring systems based on reinforcement learning usually consider only one learning target. Moreover, the agent needs to learn in the case of sparse rewards, resulting in inefficient learning. To this end, we propose a curriculum-oriented multi-goal reinforcement learning method, which combines an off-policy RL algorithm with Hindsight Experience Replay (HER) to enable the agent to learn from past failed experiences to alleviate the problem of sparse rewards. Besides, our method is applicable to the case of multi-goal learning, and the agent learns specific strategy for each goal. Additionally, according to different learning stages of the agent, we set different learning pseudo goals adaptively for it to accelerate learning speed.

Keywords: Adaptive learning · Curriculum learning · Multi-goal reinforcement learning

1 Introduction

Adaptive learning is a core part for ITS [1], which is different from traditional education style (e.g. learning in classroom and presenting same learning materials to all learners). It can provide personalized learning resources by offering suitable materials to different learners based on levels of knowledge and learning target. Nowadays, there exists a group of successful online learning platform, such as Khan Academy (Khan Academy.org) and Massive Open Online Course (MOOCs) [2]. The crucial step for building a successful ITS is the construction of

Supported by the National Natural Science Foundation of China (U1811261).

Q. Chen and J. Li (Eds.): APWeb-WAIM 2020 Workshops, CCIS 1373, pp. 104–115, 2021.
https://doi.org/10.1007/978-981-16-0479-9_9

recommendation system, which generates customized recommendation material in sequence and help each learner find suitable learning method.

To overcome sequential decision problem, reinforcement learning has been commonly utilized in recommendation of learning material [3]. Reinforcement learning is a goal-driven technology, the agent interacts with the environment with the goal of maximizing total reward, and the environment follows the setting of Markov Decision Process (MDP) [4]. The reward given by the environment is crucial for the agent. However, in learning material recommendation scenarios, the agent usually receive a positive reward only when the student achieves the learning target. This sparse rewards are difficult to guide the agent to learn effective recommendation strategies during the long learning process. Some of existing recommendation methods [6] used manually designed reward function to alleviate this problem. However, such reward shaping usually requires intensive learning expertise and specific domain knowledge. Moreover, in the recommendation of learning material, it is difficult to give the agent an exact reward or punishment based on the student's response.

Furthermore, different students may have different learning targets, or even a student will have multiple learning targets. It is necessary to train a multi-goal agent in the learning material recommendation. Curriculum learning for reinforcement learning [7] has been proven to be a good solution to multi-goal learning tasks [8,9], most of which are applied in multi-goal robotic arm manipulation and multi-goal navigation. In multi-goal learning material recommendation, training a multi-goal agent can obtain strategies to reach different goals.

In this paper, we propose a curriculum-oriented multi-goal agent to meet the challenges mentioned above. HER is a classic method for multi-goal tasks in curriculum learning for reinforcement learning [10]. It makes the agent learn from the failed experience by treating the achieved state in the failed experience as a pseudo goal under the premise that the pseudo goal will not affect the dynamics of the environment. HER can be combined with any off-policy RL algorithm to form an implicit curriculum for the agent to learn. However, not all failure experiences are equally useful for different stages of learning. In this regard, we improve the traditional HER method by gradually adjusting the sampling method of the replay goals to achieve the student's learning target. Inspired by [16], we use the distance between the pseudo goal and the real target as a measure of target difficulty. The agent learns how to reach some simple goals as soon as possible in early stage, and gradually increase the difficulty of the goal in the following learning process. The curriculum learning method can speed up the learning speed of the agent in difficult tasks. We conduct extensive experiments on a real-world e-learning dataset. Experimental results show the success rate of the proposed method over the state-of-the-art baselines in multi-goal learning material recommendation with sparse rewards.

2 Problem Formulation

2.1 Learning Material Recommendation

In the learning material recommendation, the intelligent tutor (agent) interacts with a learner $l \in L$ at discrete time step. At each time step t, the agent feeds an exercise e_t to the learner, where $e_t \in E$ is from the recommendable exercise set. Then learner gives the feedback f_t, where $f_t = \{0, 1\}$ corresponds to the student' score on the exercise e_t. The interaction process forms a sequence $X_t = \{l, e_1, f_1, \ldots, e_t, f_t\}$, which indicates student's learning path.

As one of indispensable modules in the adaptive learning, the Cognitive Diagnosis models (CDM) will measure mastery of knowledge concepts once the learner takes a learning action. It utilizes the response logs of students and delivers the diagnosis report $\phi(X) \rightarrow [0, 1]^{(1 \times K)}$, where $\phi(X)$ is a proficiency vector denotes the student's mastery of K knowledge concepts, as the basis in further recommendation. In the literature, massive efforts have been devoted for cognitive diagnosis, such as Deterministic Inputs, Noisy And gate model (DINA) [11], Item Response Theory (IRT) [12] and Neural Cognitive Diagnosis (NeuralCD) [13] etc. In this paper, we utilize NeuralCD to capture the knowledge level of students. Although not studied in this paper, it is assumed that the parameters of the cognitive diagnosis model in the simulations are well-calibrated by historical data.

With the aid of the cognitive diagnosis model, the learning flow of intelligent tutor in the learning material recommendation system can be represented in Fig. 1. Given current state s_t, the intelligent tutor recommends an exercise a_t to the student according to current policy. Then, student do this exercise for practice and leave the corresponding response log. With cognitive diagnosis method, the diagnostic report containing the student's proficiency on each knowledge concept is regarded as the next state s_{t+1} for the intelligent tutor. Finally, the achievement to the standard of knowledge proficiency judged from student's target is regarded as immediate reward r_t to feedback to the agent.

2.2 MDP for Learning Material Recommendation

In terms of RL, we can formulate the learning material recommendation problem as a MDP, in which the recommendation agent interacts with the environments $\mathcal{E}$ by sequentially recommending items to maximize the long-term cumulative rewards. More precisely, the MDP can be defined by $\mathcal{M} = \langle \mathcal{S}, \mathcal{A}, \mathcal{P}, \mathcal{R}, \gamma \rangle$, where $\mathcal{S}$ is the state space, $\mathcal{A}$ is the action space, $\mathcal{P} : \mathcal{S} \times \mathcal{A} \times \mathcal{S} \rightarrow \mathbb{R}$ is the transition function, $\mathcal{R} : \mathcal{S} \times \mathcal{A} \rightarrow \mathbb{R}$ is the reward function, and $\gamma \in [0, 1]$ is the discount factor. A policy $\pi : \mathcal{S} \times \mathcal{A} \rightarrow [0, 1]$ assigns each state $s \in \mathcal{S}$ a distribution over actions, where $a \in \mathcal{A}$ has probability $\pi(a|s)$. In learning material recommendation, $\langle \mathcal{S}, \mathcal{A}, \mathcal{P}, \mathcal{R} \rangle$ are set as follow:

- **State Space $\mathcal{S}$** is a set of states. We design the state at time step t as the current student's proficiency on each knowledge concept $s_t = \phi(X_t)$, which calculated by CDM.

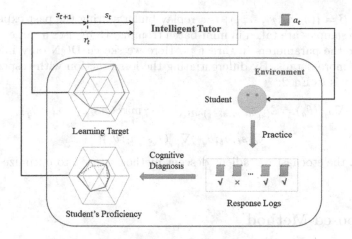

Fig. 1. The learning flow of intelligent tutor.

- **Action Space** $\mathcal{A}$ is a finite set of actions. The action a_t is the recommending exercise e_t.
- **Transition** $\mathcal{P}$ is the transition function with $p(s_{t+1}|s_t, a_t)$ being the probability of seeing state s_{t+1} after taking action a_t at s_t. In our case, the uncertainty comes from student's response (e.g. correct or wrong) w.r.t. a_t and s_t.
- **Reward** $\mathcal{R}$ is the reward function, where $r_t = r(s_t, a_t)$ denotes the immediate reward by taking action a_t at state s_t (e.g. $r(s, a) = -[s \neq g]$, where g is the student's learning target and when $s \neq g$, $[s \neq g] = 1$, otherwise $[s \neq g]$ is set as 0).

To maximize the long-term cumulative reward, define the cumulative reward after the current moment as Return $R_t = \sum_{i=t}^{T} \gamma^{i-t} r_i$, considering the discount factor γ which to balance the importance of the current rewards and future rewards, and T is terminal which indicates achieving the learning goal within T time steps. The Q-function or action-value function is defined as $Q^\pi(s_t, a_t) = \mathbb{E}[R_t|a_t, s_t] = \mathbb{E}_{a \sim \pi}[r_t + \sum_{k=1}^{T=t} \gamma^k r_{t+k}]$. The optimal Q^*, having the maximum expected reward achievable by the optimal policy, satisfies $Q^*(s_t, a_t) = \mathbb{E}_{s_{t+1}}[r_t + \gamma \max_{a'} Q^*(s_{t+1}, a'|s_t, at)]$.

Agent selects the recommended item a_t according to the maximum $Q^*(s_t, a_t)$. However, in a real-world recommendation scenario, with the large number of users and items, it is infeasible to estimate an action-value function $Q^*(s_t, a_t)$ for each state-action pair. Deep Q-Networks (DQN) [15] is a model-free RL algorithm for discrete action spaces. In DQN we maintain a neural network Q which approximates Q^*, i.e. $Q^*(s_t, a_t) \approx Q(s_t, a_t; \theta_q)$. The Q-Network can be trained by minimizing the mean-squared loss function, defined as Eq. 1:

$$\ell(\theta_q) = \mathbb{E}_{(s_t, a_t, r_t, s_{t+1}) \sim \mathcal{B}}[(y_t - Q(s_t, a_t; \theta_q))^2]$$
$$y_t = r_t + \gamma \max_{a_{t+1} \in \mathcal{A}} Q(s_{t+1}, a_{t+1}; \theta_q)$$

(1)

Where, $\mathcal{B} = \{(s_t, a_t, r_t, s_{t+1})\}$ is a replay buffer storing the past experiences, from which samples are taken in mini-batch training. DQN uses a target network to optimize the parameters in target y_t. Here we sketch DQN only informally, see [15] for more details. By differentiating the loss function with respect to θ_q, the gradient is as Eq. 2:

$$
\nabla_{\theta_q} \ell(\theta_q) = \mathbb{E}_{(s_t, a_t, r_t, s_{t+1}) \sim \mathcal{B}}[(r_t + \gamma \max_{a_{t+1}} Q(s_{t+1}, a_{t+1}; \theta_q)
$$
$$
- Q(s_t, a_t; \theta_q)) \nabla_{\theta_q} Q(s_t, a_t; \theta_q)]
\tag{2}
$$

Finally, the stochastic gradient descent method is used to optimize the loss function.

3   Proposed Method

Firstly, we briefly introduce the multi-goal RL for learning material recommendation problem. Then, the adaptive selection of pseudo goal for replay according to the current learning stage of the agent is introduced, which can accelerate the learning procedure of agent in the multi-goal task.

3.1   Multi-goal Agent for Adaptive Learning

HER regards failure as success, and learns from the experience of failure, thus alleviating the problem of sparse rewards in real-world situations. It is an effective method for training multi-goal agents. The idea behind HER is that after experiencing some episode $s_0, s_1, ..., s_T$, every transition $s_t \rightarrow s_{t+1}$ stored in the replay buffer is not only with the original goal used for this episode but also with a subset of other goals. HER utilize Universal Value Function Approximators (UVFA) [14] to achieve multi-goal Q-value calculation. HER can be well combined with existing off-policy RL algorithms (such as DQN, DDPG, etc.) to form an implicit curriculum, which is used to guide the agent to effectively learn multi-goal tasks in the environment with sparse rewards.

Now, we extend the goal space to the reinforcement learning scenario mentioned in Sect. 2.2.

- **Goal space** $\mathcal{G}$ is a set of goals. We set the goal to be a specific representation of student's proficiency, which is consistent with the representation of the state. Each goal $g \in \mathcal{G}$ corresponds to a reward function $r_t^g = r(s_t, a_t, g)$.

In each episode, a state-goal pair (s_0, g) is sampled as the start, and the target g remains unchanged throughout the episode. At each time step, the agent obtains the current state s_t and the target g, executes the action according to the current strategy $\pi : \mathcal{S} \times \mathcal{G} \rightarrow \mathcal{A}$, and obtains a reward $r_t^g = r(s_t, a_t, g)$. Store all transition tuples $(s_t \| g, a_t, r_t, s_{t+1} \| g)$ in the entire episode in replay buffer $\mathcal{B}$ ($\|$ indicate concatenation). In addition, select some reached states in the episode as a pseudo goal g' (the selection strategy will be explained in the section3.2).

The transition tuple $(s_t\|g', a_t, r_t^{g'}, s_{t+1}\|g')$ of the episode before reaching the pseudo goal g' is also stored in replay buffer $\mathcal{B}$.

Now, the calculation of Q-function not only depends on the state-action pair, but also on the goal, $Q^{\pi_g}(s_t, a_t, g) = \mathbb{E}[R_t^g|a_t, s_t, g] = \mathbb{E}_{a\sim\pi_g}[r_t^g + \sum_{k=1}^{T-t}\gamma^k r_{t+k}^g]$. [14] shows that in this setup it is possible to train an approximator to the Q-function using direct bootstrapping from the Bellman equation (just like in case of DQN) and that a greedy policy derived from it can generalize to previously unseen state-action pairs.

We rewrite the loss function and corresponding gradient (Eq. 1, Eq. 2) of the Q network as Eq. 3 and Eq. 4:

$$\ell(\theta_q) = \mathbb{E}_{(s_t\|g, a_t, r_t, s_{t+1}\|g)\sim\mathcal{B}_i}[(y_t - Q(s_t, a_t, g; \theta_q))^2]$$
$$y_t = r_t + \gamma \max_{a_{t+1}\in\mathcal{A}} Q(s_{t+1}, a_{t+1}, g; \theta_q) \tag{3}$$

$$\nabla_{\theta_q}\ell(\theta_q) = \mathbb{E}_{(s_t\|g, a_t, r_t, s_{t+1}\|g)\sim\mathcal{B}_i}[(r_t + \gamma \max_{a_{t+1}} Q(s_{t+1}, a_{t+1}, g; \theta_q)$$
$$- Q(s_t, a_t, g; \theta_q))\nabla_{\theta_q}Q(s_t, a_t, g; \theta_q)] \tag{4}$$

3.2 Pseudo Goal Setup and Curriculum-Oriented Replay

HER provides several ways to select pseudo goals, such as final, future, episode, and random. Among them, future is proved to be the most effective strategy for goal selection. Our method will also use this strategy to randomly select N achieved state of each episode as pseudo goals. Then mark the transition tuples in each episode with the pseudo target g' and store them in the replay buffer. Detailed process is exhibited in Algorithm 1.

Algorithm 1: Experience extension with pseudo goal

Input: An episode, replay buffer $\mathcal{B}$, N

1 **for** $t = 0, T - 1$ **do**
2    $r_t^g = r(s_t, a_t, g)$
3   Store the transition tuple $(s_t \| g, a_t, r_t^g, s_{t+1} \| g)$ in $\mathcal{B}$
4 **end**
5 Sample N states in current episode
6 **for** $n = 1, N$ **do**
7    $g' = s_\tau^n$ #s_τ^n is the final state in the sub-episode
8   Calculate the weight of g' with Equ.5
9   **for** $t = 0, \tau - 1$ **do**
10       $r_t^{g'} = r(s_t, a_t, g')$
11   Store the transition tuple $(s_t \| g', a_t, r_t^{g'}, s_{t+1} \| g')$ in $\mathcal{B}$
12   **end**
13 **end**

In order to speed up the agent learning process in hard tasks, we use the method of curriculum learning for the agent from simple to difficult learning process. Inspired from [16], we use the Euclidean distance between the pseudo goal and the real target as a measure of the simplicity of the goal g', expressed as $simp(g') = \sqrt{(g - g')^2}$. The larger the $simp(g')$, the simpler the pseudo target g' and the easier the agent can reach. Correspondingly, we use $diff(g') = c - simp(g')$ to represent the difficulty level of the pseudo target, where c is a sufficiently large constant to ensure that $diff(g') \geq 0$ for any g'. The replay priority weight of the goal g_i is set as Eq. 5:

$$w(g_i) = (1 - \frac{\alpha}{M})simp(g_i) + \frac{\alpha}{M}diff(g_i) \tag{5}$$

Where α is the current number of iterations and M is the total number of iterations. Finally, the probability of sampling target g_i is defined as Eq. 6:

$$W(g_i) = \frac{w(g_i)}{\sum_j w(g_j)} \tag{6}$$

Therefore, the curriculum-oriented multi-goal agent training process is shown in Algorithm 2.

Algorithm 2: Training of curriculum-oriented multi-goal agent

---

Input: M, T, H, ϵ
Output: An optimal policy function π^*
1 Randomly initialize parameters θ_q
2 Initialize replay buffer $\mathcal{B} \leftarrow \emptyset$
3 Pretraining the NeuralCD
4 **repeat**
5   **for** *episode = 1, M* **do**
6   Sample a learner l and learning target g
7   Initialize $X_0 = \{l\}$
8   Initialize $s_0 = \phi(X_0)$ with NeuralCD
9   a **for** $t = 0, T - 1$ **do**
10   Sample an exercise a_t w.r.t ϵ-greedy Q-value: $a_t \leftarrow \pi(s_t \parallel g)$
11   Execute a_t and receive learner's feedback f_t
12             $X_{t+1} = X_t \oplus \{a_t, f_t\}$
13   Set $s_{t+1} = \phi(X_{t+1})$
14   **end**
15   Experience extension with pseudo goal with Algorithm 1
16   Initialize a minibatch $\mathcal{B}_i \leftarrow \emptyset$
17   **for** $i=1, H$ **do**
18   sample a subset $\mathcal{G}_i$ from $\mathcal{G}$ with $g \sim W(g)$ in Equ.6
19   Sample a minibatch $\mathcal{B}_i$ of transition tuple $(s_t \parallel g, a_t, r_t^g, s_{t+1} \parallel g)$
                from $\mathcal{B}$, where $g \in \mathcal{G}_i$
20   Update θ_q via mini-batch SGD w.r.t the loss in Equ.4
21   **end**
22   **end**
23 **until** *convergence*;

---

4 Experiments

In this section, we conduct extensive experiments to evaluate the effectiveness of the proposed curriculum-oriented multi-goal agent with a real-world dataset from an Intelligent Tutoring System. We mainly focus on two factor: 1) How effective is the proposed method in learning materials recommendation with sparse rewards? 2) Does the curriculum accelerate the learning of the agent?

4.1 Dataset Description

In this paper, we use the ASSIST (ASSISTments 2009–2010 skill builder) data set, which is an open dataset collected by the ASSISTments online tutoring system. It provides student reaction logs and knowledge concepts. We will remove the invalid data, the statistics of the data set are summarized in Table 1. We split the data set according to the method of [13], in which the ratio of training set, validation set and test set is 7:1:2.

Table 1. ASSISTments 2009–2010 skill builder.

Dataset	ASSIST
Students	4,136
Exercises	17,746
Knowledge concepts	123
Response logs	324,572

4.2 Environment Setup

We set up a multi-goal learning material recommendation environment. Firstly, use the training set data to pre-train a NeuralCD model named NeuralCD_{init}, which can get the current student's knowledge proficiency $\phi(X_t^{l_i})$ where mentioned in Sect. 2.1. We take the students' proficiency obtained from NeuralCD_{init} as the initial state of each student during the interaction with the agent.

Considering that the NeuralCDM model has two functions: obtaining the student's current knowledge mastery and predicting the student's score. We make two copies of NeuralCD_{init}, named as NeuralCD_{diag} and NeuralCD_{sim}, which are trained online during the interaction with the agent. Among them, NeuralCD_{diag} is used to obtain real-time students' proficiency, and NeuralCD_{sim} is used as a student simulator to obtain students' scores on specific exercises.

Below, we set up multi-goal tasks of learning material recommendation based on reinforcement learning.

- State: Student's knowledge proficiency. Take the one-step update result of NeuralCD_{diag} trained online as a representation of the next state, i.e. $s_{t+1} = \phi(X_{t+1})$.

- Action: The currently selectable exercise id. Based on the results in the Q-network, we use ϵ-greedy strategy [4] to select actions.
- Learning targets: Expressed in terms of student knowledge proficiency. Send a batch of response logs for each student to NeuraCD$_{init}$ in turn. Get the student's knowledge proficiency in completing the last exercise, as the student's learning target g.
- Pseudo-goal: In each episode, randomly select N (the setting of N will be mentioned in Sect. 4.3) as the pseudo-goal.
- Reward: We use the binary sparse reward $r_t^g = r(s_t, a_t, g) = -[|g - s_t| > \delta]$ as the reward after reaching the goal g. That is, when $|g - s_t| \leqslant \delta, r_t^g = 0$; otherwise, $r_t^g = -1$. In addition, we set the discount factor $\gamma = 0.9$ in Eq. 3 to calculate the return.
- Experience replay strategy: Two experience replay strategies are set up for later experiment comparison: 1) Sample all transition tuples uniformly for the agent to learn (same as traditional HER). 2) Use the curriculum learning method proposed in this paper to adaptively select the replay experience according to the current iteration progress.

4.3   Experimental Setup

We set up three models in the experiment to do ablation studies, and utilize the vanilla deep-Q-network as the baseline model. The proposed method without curriculum is named as MGA (Multi-Goal Agent) and the complete model is named as CMGA (Curriculum-Oriented Multi-Goal Agent).

Firstly, in the setting of the baseline, we directly store the transition tuple generated when the student simulator interacts with the agent in the replay buffer. At each time step, randomly sample 32 transition tuples from the replay buffer and send them to the Q-network for learning. In the settings of MGA and CMGA, we store each transition tuple in the replay buffer twice: 1) Concatenate the learning targets of the students used to generate episodes with the current state and the next state respectively, and store them in the replay buffer. 2) Randomly sample N achieved states as pseudo goals in the current episode, and do the same processing as 1). During this period, the replay weight of each transition tuple is calculated according to Eq. 5. For the learning target $diff(g) = 0$ by default, and the constant $c = 3.88$.

Secondly, two types of learning targets are set according to different time steps: One is the learning target applicable to shorter time steps, where epoch is set as 100, every epoch contains 100 episodes, and each episode includes 10 time steps (e.g. target 1&2 as shown in the Fig. 2). The other is the learning target applicable to longer time steps, where epoch is set as 100, every epoch contains 100 episodes, and each episode includes 20 time steps (e.g. target 3&4 as shown in the Fig. 2). For two different time steps, we set $N = 2$ and $N = 4$ respectively, corresponding to 10-step target and 20-step target. Experiments are conducted based on two types of learning targets respectively, and the performance of the proposed method on the two types of targets will be compared in Sect. 4.4.

Finally, the input of the Q-network of the baseline is the current state representation (123-dimensional vector), and the input of the Q-network in MGA and CMGA is the concatenation of the current state and the goal (246-dimensional vector). The output dimensions of the Q-network of the three models are the size of the action space. Since the total number of exercises in this data set is as high as 17746, the huge amount of parameters makes the model training difficult. We split the exercises according to their relevance, taking 3000 exercises as a group, and conduct a lot of experiments on each group to count the success rate of the three models. All neural networks mentioned above are MLP, and all models are implemented by PyTorch using Python. All experiments are trained under a Linux server with CPU Intel Core i7-8700 @ 3.20 GHz, GPU NVIDIA GTX 1060, and 16 GB RAM.

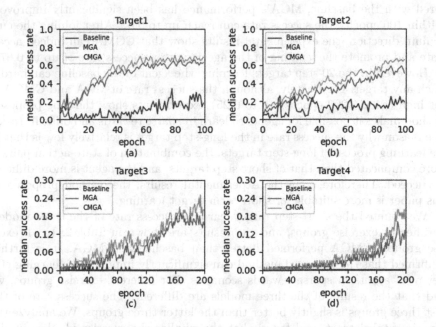

Fig. 2. Median success rates for the two types of target experiments.

Table 2. The short-step target learning success rate of the three models in different exercise groups.

Exer_id	1–3000	3001–6000	6001–9000	9001–12000	12001–15000	15001–17746
Baseline	0.1532	0.1476	0.1509	0.1353	0.1304	0.1265
MGA	0.4744	0.3345	0.4190	0.3126	0.3088	2863
CMGA	0.5232	0.4108	0.4684	0.3408	0.3260	0.3045

4.4   Experimental Results

In this section, we respectively select two experimental results for the two types of target experiments (as shown in Fig. 2). The median success rate of all episodes in each epoch is used as the evaluation criteria of three model's performance. In general, CMGA and MGA are more effective than baseline in dealing with sparse rewards.

Figure 2 shows the learning curve of four learning targets, where target 1&2 are 10-step goal and target 3&4 are 20-step goal. From the comparison of the experimental results of the two types of targets, the shorter timestamp targets get the higher success rate, and the success rate of the longer timestamp targets are lower. In the 10-step targets learning, although the baseline agent has some successful records, the overall median success rate is low (about 0.141). Compared with the baseline, MGA's performance has been significantly improved. Within 100 epochs, the success rate can reach up to 0.62. After joining the curriculum direction, the experimental results show that CGMA can indeed accelerate and promote the learning of the agent, with a success rate of up to 0.67.

However, in the 20-step targets learning, the agent of the baseline can hardly reach any target. Fortunately, although the success rate of MGA and CMGA is not high (within 200 epochs, up to 0.25), experiments show that the proposed method makes it possible for agents to learn in sparse rewards and difficult tasks. The reason why the success rate in the long-step target is relatively low is that in the learning process of long-step targets, the combination of state-action pairs is more complicated than that of short-step targets, and the agent is more difficult to succeed. Therefore, from the experimental results, the method proposed in this paper is more suitable for short-term target learning.

We counted the short-step target learning success rate of the three models in different exercise groups, and the results are shown in Table 2. In all exercise groups, CMGA performed better than baseline and MGA. It is further confirmed that the proposed method can significantly improve the learning efficiency of agents in sparse rewards scenarios. For different exercise groups, we find that the results of the three models are different. The success rate of the first three groups is slightly better than the latter three groups. We analyze the experimental dataset, and found that the smaller the exercise id, the simpler the related knowledge concepts (most 1 or 2), and the larger the exercise id, the more relevant knowledge concepts (up to 7). This may cause a large deviation in our student simulator $NeuralCD_{sim}$ in simulating student responses, and further cause the agent to learn more negative samples, which result in relative low success rate.

5   Conclusion

In this paper, we introduce a curriculum-oriented multi-goal agent to cope with multi-goal tasks with sparse rewards in learning material recommendation scenarios. We combine curriculum learning with multi-goal RL to improve the learning efficiency of the agent under multiple learning targets. Experimental results show that the method proposed can indeed make the agent learn from the sparse rewards in short-step target learning, while not applicable in long-step target learning. Future research will focus on how to improve the success rate of curriculum-oriented multi-goal agent in short-step and long-step target learning.

Acknowledgement. This research was supported by the Joint Funds of the National Natural Science Foundation of China under Grant No. U1811261, the Project of Liaoning Provincial Public Opinion and Network Security Big Data System Engineering Laboratory.

References

1. Alkhatlan, A., Kalita, J.: Intelligent tutoring systems: a comprehensive historical survey with recent developments. arXiv preprint arXiv:1812.09628 (2018)
2. Zhang, S., Chang, H.-H.: From smart testing to smart learning: how testing technology can assist the new generation of education. Int. J. Smart Technol. Learn. **1**(1), 67–92 (2016)
3. Chen, Y., et al.: Recommendation system for adaptive learning. Appl. Psychol. Measur. **42**(1), 24–41 (2018)
4. Sutton, R.S., Barto, A.G.: Reinforcement Learning: An Introduction. MIT Press, Cambridge (2018)
5. Han, R., Chen, K., Tan, C.: Curiosity-driven recommendation strategy for adaptive learning via deep reinforcement learning. Br. J. Math. Stat. Psychol. **73**(3), 522–540 (2020)
6. Zou, L., et al.: Reinforcement learning to optimize long-term user engagement in recommender systems. In: Proceedings of the 25th ACM SIGKDD International Conference on Knowledge Discovery & Data Mining (2019)
7. Portelas, R., et al.: Automatic curriculum learning for deep RL: a short survey. arXiv preprint arXiv:2003.04664 (2020)
8. Florensa, C., et al.: Automatic goal generation for reinforcement learning agents. In: International Conference on Machine Learning (2018)
9. Colas, C., et al.: CURIOUS: intrinsically motivated modular multi-goal reinforcement learning. In: International Conference on Machine Learning (2019)
10. Narvekar, S., et al.: Curriculum learning for reinforcement learning domains: a framework and survey. arXiv preprint arXiv:2003.04960 (2020)
11. von Davier, M.: The DINA model as a constrained general diagnostic model: two variants of a model equivalency. Br. J. Math. Stat. Psychol. **67**(1), 49–71 (2014)
12. Embretson, S.E., Reise, S.P.: Item Response Theory. Psychology Press (2013)
13. Wang, F., et al.: Neural cognitive diagnosis for intelligent education systems. arXiv preprint arXiv:1908.08733 (2019)
14. Schaul, T., et al.: Universal value function approximators. In: International Conference on Machine Learning (2015)
15. Mnih, V., et al.: Human-level control through deep reinforcement learning. Nature **518**(7540), 529–533 (2015)
16. Florensa, C., et al.: Reverse curriculum generation for reinforcement learning. arXiv preprint arXiv:1707.05300 (2017)

Distributed Storage and Query for Domain Knowledge Graphs

Xiaohuan Shan[1], Xiyi Shi[1], Wenyuan Ma[2], and Junlu Wang[1(✉)]

[1] School of Information, Liaoning University, Shenyang, China
wangjunlu@lnu.edu.cn
[2] School of International Education, Beijing University of Chemical Technology, Beijing, China

Abstract. The development of knowledge graph needs the support of a vast quantity of data. However, the amount of data increases rapidly is placing increasing demands on machines. Centralized data storage requires high-performance hosts to store data, which is costly and have single point of failure. Distributed data storage can reduce the cost of the machine greatly, and there is no single point of failure, but it has requirements for partition and storage of data collection. In the knowledge storage of specific domain, the way of graph data partition and storage vary from the different domain knowledge. To solve the above problems, a scheme of graph partition and distributed storage for domain-specific knowledge graphs is proposed. The proposed graph partition scheme pays attention to the correlation between the data, and divides the nodes affiliated each other into the same or similar partition. A distributed aggregation storage scheme is designed, which makes full use of cluster performance and solves the problem of data consistency during data insertion and update. The proposed distributed storage scheme based on HBase combines Neo4j to realize visual query effectively. Experimental results show the efficiency and the effectiveness of the proposed method in partition time, the number of edge-cut and update time.

Keywords: Knowledge graph · Distributed storage · Graph partition · Visualization

1 Introduction

The rapid development of information and Internet technology has led to the continuous increase in the scale of data and increasing demand for its application. As a typical application of knowledge data in a specific field, knowledge graphs can further explore the internal connections of various knowledge to infer new knowledge based on the visualization and data analysis [1]. Therefore, in addition to being used in intelligent question and answer system [2], intelligent search system [3] and personalized recommendation [4], knowledge graphs are also widely applied in different domains [5, 6]. For example, using an anti–fraud knowledge graph of credit card application, we can quickly query whether an entity has fraud risks and analyze whether a relationship is suspicious. We can also use an enterprise knowledge graph for enterprise risk assessments. Financial

© Springer Nature Singapore Pte Ltd. 2021
Q. Chen and J. Li (Eds.): APWeb-WAIM 2020 Workshops, CCIS 1373, pp. 116–128, 2021.
https://doi.org/10.1007/978-981-16-0479-9_10

knowledge graphs can be utilized to predict financial risks and investment. However, faced with the explosive growth of data scale, how to effectively store and manage the knowledge graphs will face enormous challenges.

The graph database organizes data by entity dimensions, which can better obtain the attributes of an entity and its relationship with other entities. So it is more efficient for identifying the characteristics of entities. Therefore, the mainstream method of knowledge graph storage is utilizing graph database at present. The centralized storage pattern can manage only one server. Although it is easy to implement, there are problems such as the inaccessibility of data caused by single point failure and the inability to meet the storage requirement of big data. The multi-point backup of distributed storage can effectively solve the impact of single point of failure on data query. The dynamic expansion feature enables the distributed storage pattern with great scalability, which can meet the continuously increase of the amount of data. At the same time, it can also alleviate the excessive processing pressure on a single server, so as to raise the speed of query. However, knowledge graphs in different fields have their own features. If a unified distributed storage model is adopted, the characteristics of the graph cannot be satisfied. So, it is of great significance to design a corresponding distributed storage model for the domain-specific knowledge graph.

To this end, this paper conducts in-depth research on knowledge graphs in specific fields, and proposes a distributed storage and query method for domain-specific knowledge graphs. The main contributions of this patter are as follows:

- A graph partition method based on node density and modularity is proposed, which applies the node density to initially divide the graph, and then use modularity detection to assign the remaining nodes to the more close-knit partitions. So far as possible to ensure that closely connected nodes and their relationships are stored centrally on a server to reduce network communication overhead.
- A distributed aggregation storage mode is designed. This storage schema makes full use of cluster performance, which can effectively reduce the redundancy overhead caused by repeated data storage. At the same time, it solves the problem of data consistency during data insertion and update.
- In order to realize the distributed storage and query of domain-specific knowledge graph, we design to combines HBase distributed database storage and Neo4j visual query effectively. Related entities and relationships in HBase are extracted according to the query semantics from master node. Then the information is imported into Neo4j to form sub-graphs that users concern for visual display.

The rest of this paper is organized as follows. In Sect. 2, we review related works. The details of the storage and query are discussed in Sect. 3 and 4. Experimental results and analysis are shown in Sect. 5. We finally conclude in Sect. 6.

2   Related Work

2.1   Knowledge Graph Storage

The knowledge graph is composed of nodes and relationships. Through the association of different knowledge, a network-like knowledge structure is formed to intuitively model various real-world scenarios. There are two main current mainstream ways to store the knowledge graphs.

The first kind is RDF storage [7]. An important design principle of RDF is that the data should be easy to publish and share. But RDF stores data in the form of triples and does not contain attribute information, meanwhile there are problems such as high update and maintenance costs. The other is graph database storage. Compared with the RDF storage, the graph database is more general. It generally takes attribute graphs as the basic representation form, which realizes the storage of graph data by nodes, edges, and attributes in the graph structure. So it is easier to express real world business scenarios. Typically, open source graph databases are Neo4j [8], Arangodb [9], etc. Since the database itself has provided a perfect graph query language and supports various graph mining algorithms, it has efficient graph query and search functions. However, the distributed storage of graph database is expensive. With the growth of graph scale, distributed storage has become the mainstream. How to reduce the overhead of graph database distributed storage has become one of the research hotspots of knowledge graph storage.

2.2 Graph Partition

The knowledge graph stored in the graph database is to represent the relationship structure of a certain thing in the form of a graph, which is composed of nodes and edges and attributes. Therefore, the data partition problem of knowledge graph can be transformed into graph partition problem.

The problem of graph partition has been extensively studied in many application fields. Finding the optimal partition of graphs is an NP-complete problem [10], and many solutions have been proposed. In recent years, several multi-level partition algorithms have been proposed [11–13]. The idea is to coarsen large graphs into small ones, and then apply classic algorithms on the small graph. However, the optimal partition on the roughened graph may not be suitable for realistic scale-free graphs. In addition, the coarsening algorithm is very expensive and cannot be scaled on a graph of large-scale nodes. To improve scalability, several parallel partitioning solutions have been proposed. The JA-BE-JA algorithm [14] combines simulated annealing algorithm and data migration algorithm for edge cutting and point cutting, and uses the heuristic method centered on vertex to solve the equilibrium graph partitioning problem by processing each vertex of the graph data in parallel. DFEP [15] randomly assigns a partition for each node and gives an initial funding. Each node uses its funding to find its neighbors. The principle of random selection has a certain influence on the stability of the partition quality.

2.3 Semantic Query

In this paper, the query processing techniques for knowledge graphs on existing graph databases are investigated. Neo4j is the current mainstream graph database system, which uses Cypher language to perform centralized query of graphs. The main clause in Cypher is the MATCH clause, which indicates the matching of a graph pattern on the property graph. And an empty table is added to the matching result to form a new table as a result. With the scale of graphs keeping growing, the index and maintenance efficiency of centralized processing methods is greatly reduced and replaced by distributed query processing technology. Compared with the centralized processing method, distributed query processing assigns the sub-graphs among different compute nodes, decomposes the query graph according to the data division, and realizes the parallel query on each compute node. GeaBas graph database can query the relationship information quickly and efficiently through the unique data organization method and distributed parallel computing algorithm. JanusGraph is a distributed graph database, which is an attribute graph database system that supports the TinkerPop framework. Its query mechanism is Gremlin graph traversal language.

3 Distributed Storage Based on HBase

3.1 Graph Partition Based on Node Density and Modularity

In order to ensure the high-cohesion and low-coupling of graph partition, closely related nodes and relationships are divided into a sub-graph to minimize network communication overhead. This paper proposes a graph partition method based on node density and modularity (GP-NDM). Because of data increasing rapidly and complex relationships in specific fields, GP-NDM first selects hotspot nodes (nodes with large degrees) as the initial partition according to the node density. Then it uses the modularity to detect the partition effect, and the graph partition is completed by dynamically adding nodes. The algorithm in this paper effectively avoids the poor partition due to the high degree of data aggregation.

If there are N storage servers, first the N nodes with the largest degrees and no direct relationship (i.e., the direct relationship (v_i, v_j) is not allowed, the indirect contact (v_i, v_k), (v_k, v_j) exists) are selected randomly. For all the remaining nodes, GP-NDM calculates the modularity when joining a partition and adds each node to the server that makes the modularity larger, so as to ensure the tightness of internal connections in the sub-graph. The modularity formula is given as follows:

$$Q = \frac{1}{2m} \sum_{i,j} \left[A_{ij} - \frac{k_i k_j}{2m} \right] \delta(c_i, c_j) \quad Q \in [-1, 1) \ \delta(u, v) = \begin{cases} 1 & when \ u == v \\ 0 & else \end{cases} \tag{1}$$

A_{ij} represents the edges weights between two nodes. Since in this paper the edge in the knowledge graph is a relation, rather than a edge with weight, the weight of the edge is regarded as value 1. The k_i indicates the degree of node i. c_i represents the community to which the node i belongs. The m is the sum of the weights of all edges. The formula of modularity can be simplified as:

$$Q = \frac{1}{2m} \sum_{i,j} \left[A_{ij} - \frac{k_i k_j}{2m} \right] \delta(c_i, c_j) = \frac{1}{2m} \left[\sum A_{ij} - \frac{\sum_i k_i \sum_j k_j}{2m} \right] \delta(c_i, c_j)$$

$$= \frac{1}{2m} \sum_c \left[\sum cin - \frac{\left(\sum tot \right)^2}{2m} \right] = \sum_c \left[\frac{\sum cin}{2m} - \left(\frac{\sum tot}{2m} \right)^2 \right] \tag{2}$$

$\sum cin$ represents the sum of weights in community c. $\sum tot$ represents the sum of the weights connected to the nodes within the community c. As the value of modularity, Q represents the degree of tightness of nodes within the community, the larger the modularity, the better the community partition. An example is illustrated in Fig. 1.

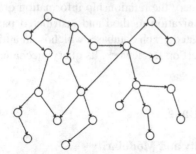 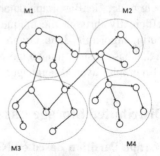

Fig. 1. The directed data graph G   **Fig. 2.** The partition result of G

Suppose that a node in graph is assigned to m_1, it can be seen from formula of modularity, the modularity degree before moving is

$$Q_1 = \left[\frac{\sum cin}{2m} - \left(\frac{\sum tot}{2m} \right)^2 \right] + \left[\frac{0}{2m} - \left(\frac{k_i}{2m} \right)^2 \right] \qquad (3)$$

The modularity after assigning the node i to m_1 is Q_2. E_i indicates that the number of new edges after node i join m_1.

$$Q_2 = \left[\frac{\sum cin + E_i}{2m} - \left(\frac{\sum tot + k_i}{2m} \right)^2 \right] \qquad (4)$$

The gain of the modularity is:

$$\Delta Q = Q_2 - Q_1 = \frac{E_i}{2m} - \frac{k_i \sum tot}{2m^2} \qquad (5)$$

After modularity detection, each node is assigned to corresponding servers according to the criterion of maximum modularity. The results are shown Fig. 2. The specific algorithm is shown in Algorithm 1.

```
Algorithm 1 GP-NDM Algorithm
Input: G(V,E), N
Output: N-way partition results
1  G'=G, Ni={0}(1≤i≤n);
2  N={N1,N2,N3,....Nn},q=−∞;
3  foreach(Ni in N(N1,N2,...Nn)) do
4    dispatchInitNode(Ni,V);
5    C the index of community of each nodes of G';
6    Initialize each nodes with its own community;
7  foreach(Vk in G(V,E)) do
8    foreach(Ni in N(N1,N2,...Nn)) do
9      while q<Q(G',C) do
10     q=Q(G',C);
11     if(LOAD(Ni<1.3*AVG(LOAD(Ni)) then
12       chooseServer(N);
13       C= MoveNodes(G');
14       G'=Aggregate(G',C);
15       C=put each node of G' In its own community;
16     else select another server;
17 return the N-way partition results;
```

3.2 The Design of Distributed Storage Mode

Faced with enormous entities and relationships, the knowledge graph storage access system needs to design a scalable storage schema to enhance the storage performance. This paper takes the knowledge graph in the financial domain as an example to illustrate. We design the storage mode based on HBase, and store enterprise entities and relationships in it.

This paper takes full advantage of the sparse, distributed, consistent, multidimensional sorting characteristics of HBase. And it is designed as a distributed storage model with a single table and multiple-column clusters. The mode not only can effectively avoid data redundancy, but also has the overall storage load distribution balance, preventing the query nodes from re-traverse all entries to meet the need for scalability of the knowledge graph storage. The storage mode is shown in Fig. 3.

As shown in Fig. 3, the distributed storage mode designed in this paper uses a table for each entity type to store relationships and attribute values between entities. Each row stores the attribute values and relationship objects of an entity. The row key stores the table name to which the entity belongs, the entity and another entity associated with it. The attributes store the entity's attribute values, and object stores the corresponding entity. The value in the cell stores the corresponding attribute value or entity, where the entity representation is consistent with the entity representation of the row key. Storing attributes and relationships with two column clusters is not only easy to manage, but also reduces the number of columns loaded in memory during query, which helps to load more entities into memory and speed up query. In order to meet the requirements

Row key	attributes		Object	
	Property 1	...	Relation 1	...
tname:object 1:object 2	Value 1	...	Object 2	...
...	...		...	
tname:object p:object x	...		...	
...				
tname:object t:object y	...		...	
...	...		...	
tname:object n:object m	Value n		Object m	

Fig. 3. The storage mode

of the knowledge graph, the row key format of this storage mode is designed as "tname: object1:object2". "tname" is the table name corresponding to the stored entity data, "object1" corresponds to the first entity, "object2" corresponds to the second entity associated with first entity, and ":" is the custom delimiter.

The distributed aggregation storage mode designed in this paper not only reduces data redundancy caused by repeated data storage, but also avoids data inconsistency caused by multiple table data insertion and update operations. It can also make full use of cluster performance, improve parallelism and ensure load balancing. The entity storage has the characteristics of overall storage load distribution and local node aggregation storage which fully meets the requirements of knowledge graph storage.

3.3 Load Balancing

In order to solve the problem of load balancing, this paper adopts an improved algorithm of consistent hashing method [16], i.e., a method of increasing the upper limit of the load to solve this problem. The algorithm adding to each server a maximum load limit, where the maximum load limit is $(1 + e)$ times the average load. The custom e value is 0.3, i.e., the average load of the storage node server is 100, if the current node and relationship to be added to the N_i server will result in the load of this server to be 30% higher than the average load, the current selected server would be excluded. And the node will select the server with the second largest modularity to further determine the load of the server at this time. If the maximum load limit is met, add the node to the server, otherwise continue to filter the server.

4 Visual Query Based on Neo4j

4.1 Problem Description

Neo4j is currently the most widely used open source graph database, which can intuitively and vividly represent real-world application scenarios. Therefore, this paper takes the knowledge graph in the financial field as an example to study the visual display and query strategy based on Neo4j. The complex, difficult and diverse knowledge in the financial field is visually presented in a graphical way. The implicit knowledge is manifested and the external knowledge is materialized. And the relevant knowledge in the financial field will be constructed, connected and integrated. In this section, we use the constructed financial knowledge graph as the back-end data source. By designing specific query statements, the query result obtained is the sub-graph that meets the limited conditions, which is inside the users' scope of concern.

Figure 4 shows the visual query architecture of the knowledge graph in this paper. Among them, the user enters a query statement through the query interface, and the query condition is sent to the background processing program. The HBase database interface is logically called by the background code, according to the query condition to find the satisfaction in the HBase database. Query the condition data and write it in Neo4j. Neo4j correlates the corresponding nodes according to the written data, draws the map, and finally returns the map to the user.

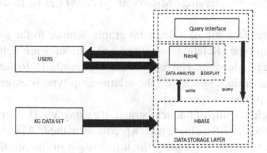

Fig. 4. Visual query architecture

4.2 Visual Query Based on Property Graph

The knowledge graph created by Neo4j is based on the property graph, and the query language on it is Cypher, which can query, modify and update data through the nodes and relationships in the pattern matching graph database without writing complex query statements. It lays a good foundation for data analysis and expansion of knowledge graphs in the financial field. The entity information and semantic relations involved in the graph are stored in the visual query architecture of this paper. The operation content and implementation method of data update and query of financial knowledge graph based on Cypher language are introduced in detail below.

(1) Create financial graph entity nodes, including enterprise entities and business personnel entities. Formally expressed as (Variable: Lable1: Label2 {Key1:Value1, Key2:Value2}). The label of the node is equivalent to the table name of the relational database (RDB), and the attribute is equivalent to the column of the relational database. Each node contains the default internal property id. When creating nodes, Neo4j graph data server will automatically assign an integer id to it. In the entire graph database, the id value of the node is incremented by default and unique. As shown in Fig. 5, creating a Cypher statement for an enterprise entity:

(2) Query the entity node of the financial graph. Cypher query language depends on matching a graph model. The keyword MATCH graph pattern is used to match the

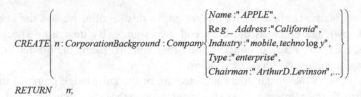

$$CREATE\left|\begin{array}{l}n: CorporationBackground : Company\left\{\begin{array}{l}Name:"APPLE",\\ \operatorname{Re}g\_Address:"California",\\ Industry:"mobile, techno\log y",\\ Type:"enterprise",\\ Chairman:"ArthurD.Levinson",...\end{array}\right.\end{array}\right.$$

$RETURN\quad n;$

Fig. 5. Creating an enterprise entity by Cypher

existing entity nodes in the database. The MATCH clause is used to specify the search model (pattern). And the WHERE clause adds a predicate to the MATCH pattern constrain the pattern. Query the node of the specified attribute. Such as the Cypher statement of querying "MicroSoft" is *"MATCH (n {Name: "MicroSoft"}) RETURN n"*.

(3) Create entity relationship of a financial graph. Similar to the syntax of the node, the relationship type (RelationshopType) and attributes are defined in the square brackets of the relationship. The relationship type is similar to the node label. When creating a relationship, specifying the relationship type is essential, but only one relationship type can be specified.

(4) Query entity relationship of financial graph. By using MATCH clause to specify the search mode, the WHERE clause adds a predicate to the MATCH mode to constrain the StartNode node, so as to query the information of the StartNode node and its related nodes with a layer of direct relationships.

4.3   The Display of Neo4j Visual Query

By inputting the corresponding query statement to the knowledge graph, the user can concentrate on querying the graph inside his scope of concern, while the other unrelated partial graphs are not displayed. In this paper, through the collection of financial data from professional financial network, we realize the construction of the financial knowledge graph by the process of data cleaning and extraction. A total of 3548 entities have been constructed in the knowledge base.

In Neo4j, the financial domain knowledge graph stores knowledge with nodes and edges. A part of the entities and relationships of financial knowledge that contains the keyword "GuangdongHongdaBlasting Co., Ltd." are displayed in Neo4j as shown in Fig. 6. Different entity classes are distinguished by different colors. Red nodes represent business entities, blue nodes represent product entities, and orange nodes represent human entities. These nodes are accompanied by their own attribute information. The relationship between entities and entities is represented by edges. The edges contain relationship attributes, start node *id* and end node *id*.

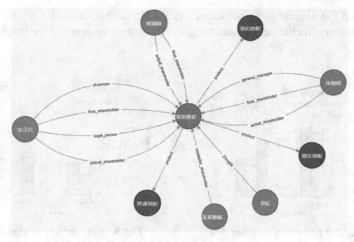

Fig. 6. Partial financial knowledge queried by user

5 Experiments

5.1 Experimental Settings and Datasets

The experimental environment of this paper is Inter Core i7–8750 CPU @ 1.8 Hz 2.00 GHz processor, and the computer with 8G memory is used as the host of Neo4j graph database. Three other servers with 64 GB memory and 512 GB hard disk and Ubuntu operating system are applied as devices for deploying HBase distributed database. The host and server communicate with each other through deployment in the same local area network.

In the selection of data sources, the financial knowledge graph studied in this paper covers the basic information of the company, shareholder information, executive information, corporate news, and corporate credit information. Use crawlers for large-scale data acquisition on selected data sources, such as Royalflush Finance News, Sohu Finance News and Tianyancha. After obtaining the data, we perform basic statistical analysis and processing for subsequent data partition and distributed storage. Build basic connections between enterprises. The original datasets is split into two sets of different sizes. The node numbers of both datasets are 13832 and 21299; the numbers of edges are 69160 and 106440.

5.2 Efficiency Analysis of Graph Partition

This paper compares the proposed GP-NDM algorithm with BS and DynamicDFEP in terms of the partition time and the number of edge cuts. Each partition algorithm is executed three times, and the result is averaged. With the increasing graph scale, the partition time of GP-NDM does not increase greatly as shown in Fig. 7, and the effect is good for large-scale dynamic graphs. DynamicDFEP is more complicated and its time complexity is relatively large. In the experiments, DynamicDFEP is used to cyclically allocate nodes on N servers. As the result the time complexity of the algorithm will further increase, and the algorithm is inefficient. As for BS architecture, the BS algorithm is fast, but if the graph changes dynamically, the BS cannot respond to the graph division in real time.

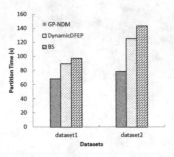

Fig. 7. Comparison of partition time

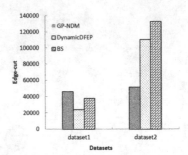

Fig. 8. Comparison of edge-cut

Figure 8 shows the comparison of edge cutting on different datasets. Edge cutting is the number of edges with endpoints in different partitions, and the quality of the partition can be verified by edge cutting. In order to ensure the partitioning principle of high cohesion and low coupling, fewer cutting edges indirectly prove that the segmentation quality is better. BS switches nodes to improve the division result, but ignores the influence of weight on closeness. DynamicDFEP utilizes the principle of random selection, which has a certain influence on the segmentation quality. GP-NDM considers the influence of modularity and node degree, so we exchange nodes to improve the node's modularity.

5.3 Performance Analysis of Incremental Dynamic Maintenance

We evaluate the update efficiency on different numbers of partitions. Since BS is an algorithm for static graphs, it can be updated only by repartitioning the graph, which is much lower than the incremental update method. Therefore, we compared GP-NDM with the DynamicDFEP. As shown in Fig. 9, DynamicDFEP algorithm is sensitive to update, and it is not applicable to the situation where the freshness of the graph exceeds 20%. In the stage of graph update and maintenance, the DynamicDFEP assigns initial "funds" to the initial graph partitioning interactions up to the final vertex. In repeating the initial graph partitioning steps, the information of the boundary nodes needs to be stored in the partition. Due to the incremental update of the graph which leads to the expansion of the graph size, the cost of space and time is close to running the DFEP algorithm starting from the beginning. GP-NDM only need execute to perform the module degree calculation to complete the update according to the newly added nodes or edges. And the algorithm does not need to be run from scratch.

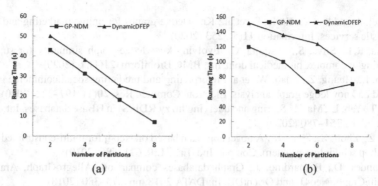

Fig. 9. Comparison of incremental dynamic maintenance

6 Conclusion

This paper conducts an in-depth study of knowledge graphs in specific fields, and proposes a distributed storage and query method for domain-specific knowledge graphs. A graph partition method based on node density and modularity is proposed to ensure as far as possible that nodes closely connected and their relationships are stored in the same partition. The network communication overhead is reduced. A distributed aggregate storage model is designed. This storage model makes full use of cluster performance and can effectively reduce the redundancy overhead caused by storing repeated data. At the same time, it solves the problem of data consistency when inserting and updating data. In order to achieve distributed storage and query of domain-specific knowledge graphs, we manage to combines HBase distributed storage with Neo4j visual query effectively. According to the query semantics of the master node, the related Entities and relationships in HBase are extracted and imported into Neo4j to form sub-graphs that users are interested in for visual display. The proposed method has a wide range of practical application value.

Acknowledgements. This work was supported by National Natural Science Foundation of China under Grant (No. 61472169, 61502215, 62072220, 61702381, U1811261); China Postdoctoral Science Foundation Funded Project (2020M672134); Science Research Fund of Liaoning Province Education Department (LJC201913); Liaoning Public Opinion and Network Security Big Data System Engineering Laboratory (No. 04-2016-0089013).

References

1. Xin, H., Jiangli, D., Jiangli, D.: Scalable aggregate keyword query over knowledge graph. Future Gener. Comput. Syst. **107**, 588–600 (2020)
2. Li, W., Song, M., Tian, Y.: An ontology-driven cyberinfrastructure for intelligent spatiotemporal question answering and open knowledge discovery. ISPRS Int. J. Geo-Inf. **8**(11), 496 (2019)
3. Barnawi, A., Alharbi, M., Chen, M.: Intelligent search and find system for robotic platform based on smart edge computing service. IEEE Access **8**, 108821–108834 (2020)

4. Fensel, A., Akbar, Z., Kärle, E., et al.: Knowledge graphs for online marketing and sales of touristic services. Information **11**(5), 253 (2020)
5. Sousa, R.T., Silva, S., Pesquita, C.: Evolving knowledge graph similarity for supervised learning in complex biomedical domains. BMC Bioinform. **21**(1), 6 (2020)
6. Yuan, L., Huang, Z., Zhao, W., et al.: Interpreting and predicting social commerce intention based on knowledge graph analysis. Electron. Commer. Res. **20**(1), 197–222 (2020)
7. Fan, T., Yan, L., Ma, Z.: Storing and querying fuzzy RDF(S) in HBase databases. Int. J. Intell. Syst. **35**(4), 751–780 (2020)
8. Zhu, Z., Zhou, X., Shao, K.: A novel approach based on Neo4j for multi-constrained flexible job shop scheduling problem. Comput. Ind. Eng. **130**, 671–686 (2019)
9. Fernandes, D., Bernardino, J.: Graph databases comparison: AllegroGraph, ArangoDB, InfiniteGraph, Neo4J, and OrientDB. In: DATA 2018, pp. 373–380 (2018)
10. Soudani, N.M., Fatemi, A., Nematbakhsh, M.: An investigation of big graph partitioning methods for distribution of graphs in vertex-centric systems. Distrib. Parallel Databases **38**(1), 1–29 (2019)
11. Filippidou, I., Kotid, Y.: Online partitioning of multi-labeled graphs. In: Proceedings of the GRADES 2015, pp. 1–6. ACM (2015)
12. Lotfifar, F., Johnson, M.: A serial multilevel hypergraph partitioning algorithm. Comput. Res. Repository (2016)
13. Preen, R.J., Smith, J.: Evolutionary n-level hypergraph partitioning with adaptive coarsening. IEEE Trans. Evol. Comput. **23**(6), 962–971 (2019)
14. Rahimian, F., Payberah, A.H., Girdzijauskas, S., et al.: JA-BE-JA: a distributed algorithm for balanced graph partitioning. In: IEEE International Conference on Self-adaptive & Self-organizing Systems, pp. 51–60. IEEE (2013)
15. Guerrieri, A., Montresor, A.: DFEP: distributed funding-based edge partitioning. In: Träff, J.L., Hunold, S., Versaci, F. (eds.) Euro-Par 2015. LNCS, vol. 9233, pp. 346–358. Springer, Heidelberg (2015). https://doi.org/10.1007/978-3-662-48096-0_27
16. Mirrokni, V., Thorup, M., Zadimoghaddam, M.: Consistent hashing with bounded loads. In: Proceedings of the Twenty-Ninth Annual ACM-SIAM Symposium on Discrete Algorithms. Society for Industrial and Applied Mathematics, pp. 587–604 (2018)

The First International Workshop on Deep Learning in Largescale Unstructured Data Analytics

Label Propagation Algorithm Based on Topological Potential

Guocheng Wang$^{(\boxtimes)}$ and Zhengyou Xia$^{(\boxtimes)}$

College of Computer Science and Technology,
Nanjing University of Aeronautics and Astronautics, Nanjing 210016, China
{wanguocheng,zhengyou_xia}@nuaa.edu.cn

Abstract. The label propagation algorithm is a label-based semi-supervised learning method, which is widely used in the division of large complex communities. This algorithm has the advantages of easy implementation and low complexity, but it also has the disadvantages of lower stability and greater randomness. Many experts and scholars have improved the dissemination of labels, especially the original labels. But most of them are not suitable for large community network discovery, because they are usually very unstable. Therefore, we propose label propagation based on the topological potential field of graphs. By using the topological potential of graph nodes as the importance measure of nodes, the stability of LPA is improved. Finally, the algorithm was tested using real network data sets and LFR benchmark network data sets. The results show that the algorithm has better accuracy and stability than some classic label propagation algorithms.

Keywords: Community detection · Label propagation · Topological potential · Real network · LFR benchmark network

1 Introduction

The advent of the information age has made the research of complex networks a hot topic. It is possible to abstract complex large-scale network problems in real life into complex network systems for research. Complex network research involves many fields such as social networks, academic networks, the World Wide Web, and protein interaction networks]. Research on community discovery can be divided into local community discovery algorithms and global community discovery algorithms. The core idea of the local community discovery algorithm is to incorporate the neighbor set into the framework. This type of algorithm is mainly based on the characteristics of the local topology of the network to reveal the local or entire network community structure. Local community discovery algorithms currently mainly include algorithms based on local expansion optimization, faction filtering and edge clustering optimization. Based on the community structure, the concept of community is put forward, which is composedof nodes with the same or similar nature and function in thenetwork, with

© Springer Nature Singapore Pte Ltd. 2021
Q. Chen and J. Li (Eds.): APWeb-WAIM 2020 Workshops, CCIS 1373, pp. 131–143, 2021.
https://doi.org/10.1007/978-981-16-0479-9_11

close internal connections and relatively sparseconnections between communities [1–3]. The classic community detection has many kinds of methods, such as algorithm-based on modular degree optimization, hierarchical clustering and tag propagation algorithm.

Raghavan proposed the label propagation algorithm (LPA) [4] in 2007. The label information of the target node is determined jointly by the label information of its neighbor nodes. The improvement work of the label propagation algorithm mainly focuses on how to improve the accuracy and stability of the algorithm. In 2009, Leung introduced the concept of labels scores in the HNPA algorithm [5]. Its core idea is to make the tag scores gradually decrease with the spread of tags to suppress the infinite spread of tags, thereby suppressing the formation of the 'monster' community. Raghhavan proposed an algorithm SLPA [6] based on the historical label of nodes in 2011. This algorithm is that each node saves the historical label record when iteratively updating the label and updates the label of the node according to the historical label list. The algorithm retains all the advantages of traditional label propagation and can detect non-overlapping communities by setting reasonable thresholds. In 2015, Xian-Kun proposed an improved label selection label propagation algorithm LPALC [7]. Its idea is that when there are multiple optimal labels when the label is updated, a local loop is used to solve the problem of label randomness. In 2014, Xing Yan proposed an NIBLPA algorithm that introduced k-shell into label propagation [8]. The algorithm uses k-shell to calculate the importance of the node. The node is closer to the edge of the community, thus distinguishing Core nodes and marginal nodes in the network. In 2016, based on the theory of random walk, Chang proposed the label propagation algorithm RWLPA using random walk matrix to calculate the importance of nodes [9].

Although the above algorithm is greatly optimized on the basis of the label propagation algorithm, it fails to take into account both accuracy and stability. For example, the HNPA algorithm does not consider the problem of node oscillation and node update randomness, so there is an unstable situation. In the LPALC algorithm, if there is no local loop in the node, the label must still be selected randomly, which makes the LPALC algorithm still have the problem of node label oscillation. In this paper, the importance of nodes is calculated and ranked. This sequence is used to optimize the node update sequence, and at the same time, the node importance restriction is added to the label propagation process, so that the improved label propagation algorithm takes into account both accuracy and stability.

The rest of this paper is organized as follows. Section 2 discusses the motivation and algorithm of this article in detail, and finally analyzes the time complexity of the algorithm. Section 3 takes the real network data set and the LFR benchmark network data set as examples to verify the label propagation algorithm based on topological potential (TPLPA). Section 4 summarizes our work.

2 Label Propagation Algorithm Based on Topological Potential

2.1 Motivation

Many scholars are committed to using node importance to optimize the process of label propagation, such as NIBLPA and RWLPA mentioned above. The importance of nodes is mainly used to optimize the sequence of label updates and the process of label selection, thereby optimizing the stability and accuracy of label propagation. Therefore, the measurement of the importance of selecting nodes is particularly important.

There are many algorithms applied to the measurement of node importance, so many different metrics for node importance are produced. Among them, the more commonly used are k-shell [10], degree centrality [11], edge betweenness [12] and clustering coefficient centrality [13]. However, the measurement of the influence of these nodes has great limitations. For example, NIBLPA mentioned above uses k-shell as the measurement of node importance. K-shell's calculation of the importance of nodes is coarse-grained, which leads to the existence of many nodes of the same importance in the network. This leads to the problem of node label oscillation after using k-shell to improve the label propagation process. In addition, some measures are very inaccurate in measuring the importance of nodes. For example, the degree centrality is a measure based on local information, and only considers the situation of the neighbor nodes of the node. If the degree index is used to optimize the label propagation, the accuracy of the final partition is likely to be low. This paper introduces the topological potential to calculate the importance of nodes. Topological potential is a measure based on the global information of nodes. It can accurately quantify the importance of nodes in the network. It is rare that multiple nodes have the same importance. When evaluating the importance of nodes in complex networks, the topological potential index is superior to the above parameters. The nodes are updated according to the ranking of node importance, which optimizes the randomness problem in the order of node updates. At the same time, the rule of node importance comparison is added to the label selection of nodes, which optimizes the label oscillation of nodes. At the same time, because the nodes with higher node importance in the network are generally the core nodes of the network, the core nodes are often the core of different communities. So our algorithm also takes into account the accuracy of label propagation.

2.2 Topological Potential Label Propagation Algorithm

In 2009, Gan Wenyan proposed a network community discovery algorithm NHP [14] based on topological potential. This algorithm introduced the nuclear field theory in physics. Its core idea is to treat the network as a physical system that there is interaction force between nodes. The short-range field is used to represent the force between nodes, and the influence factor is used to control the scope of the node force.

We use G(V, E) tuple to represent complex network, where V represents the set of nodes, and E means the set of edges. The topological potential can be calculated with the following Gaussian potential function:

$$\varphi(v_j) = \sum_{j=1}^{n} [m_j \times e^{-(\frac{d_{ij}}{\sigma})^2}] \tag{1}$$

where d_{ij} is the distance between nodes i and j, and can be calculated using the shortest path distance in the network; the influence factor σ is the influence range of the node force, which is used to measure the inherent properties of the node; m_j usually the quality of node $v_j (j = 1, 2....n)$ while n is the number of nodes. Different influence factors can be obtained by simulated annealing to obtain the minimum value of the potential entropy function. The NHP algorithm defines the potential entropy function as:

$$H(\sigma) = - \sum_{i=1}^{n} \frac{\varphi(v_i)}{Z} log \frac{\varphi(v_i)}{Z} \tag{2}$$

Where $Z = \sum_{i=1}^{n} \varphi(v_i)$ is the normalization factor, and in the paper, Gan Wenyan simplified (1) into:

$$\varphi(v_j) = \frac{1}{n} \sum_{i=1}^{n} n_j(v_i) \times e^{-(\frac{d_{ij}}{\sigma})^2} \tag{3}$$

In NHP, the influence range of node v_i is controlled by $\iota = \lfloor \sigma/\sqrt{2} \rfloor$. By Gan's calculation, when σ is 1.0203, the optimal result is obtained. At this time, $\varphi(v_i)$ can represent the node importance where $n_j(v_i)$ is the j-th neighbor node of node i.

We sort the node sets in ascending order according to the importance of the nodes, so as to avoid the risk of community monsters as much as possible. The update order of the nodes is adjusted according to the importance of the nodes, which improves the stability of the algorithm. At the same time, we need to improve the label selection to further reduce the probability of random selection during the label update process. The label update rule is defined as follows: select the most labels among the current neighbor nodes as the optimal labels, if there are multiple optimal labels, select the label with the largest topological potential, if there are still multiple optimal labels with the same topological potential, select the label randomly.

Aiming at the defects of the label propagation algorithm, a label propagation algorithm TPLPA based on topological potential is proposed. The detailed description of the algorithm is as follows:

1. Initialize the labels of all nodes, using each node's own number as a label.
2. Calculate the topological potential of each node according to Eq. (3) above, and use it as the node importance.
3. Nodes are sorted in ascending order of importance to obtain node update sequence V.

4. Updating each node for sequence V, we choose label that appears most frequently in its neighbor nodes. If multiple labels exist, we choose the label with maximum label influence according to Eq. (3); if at this time, the result calculated by our method also has more than one label, then randomly choose one label from the set of labels with the same influential value.
5. If the label of all nodes is no longer changed or the number of iterations reaches a certain threshold, the label propagation process is terminated and directly goes into 6, otherwise the next iteration is continued and turns to 4.
6. Nodes belonging to the same label are assigned to the same community to complete the label propagation process.

The pseudo code is shown in Algorithm TPLPA:

Algorithm 1: TPLPA

    Input: G=(V,E)
    Output: C=C1,C2,......,Cn
1 initLabel();
2 calculateNodeImportance();
3 sortNodeByNodeImportanceInAscending(V);
4 for $iter < maxNumber$ do
5   for v in V do
6   maxLabels=getMaxLabel(v);
7   currentLabel=v.label;
8   if $len(maxLabels) > 1$ then
9   newLabels=getMaxLabelbyNodeImportance(v);
10   if $len(newLabels) > 1$ then
11   currentLabel=random(newLabels);
12   else
13   currentLabel=newLabels[0];
14   end
15   else
16   currentLabel=maxLabels[0];
17   end
18   end
19   if the $label$ of all $nodes$ are in $stable$ $state$ then
20   break();
21   end
22   iter+=1;
23 end

2.3   Time Complexity Analysis

We know that the LPA algorithm can complete the community discovery in the near linear time. The time complexity of the algorithm is $O(m+n)$, where n is the number of nodes in the network and m is the total number of edges in network. Although the TPLPA algorithm proposed by us is not better than the LPA in time complexity, the stability of the algorithm is better than LPA. AHLPA is estimated as follows:

1. The time complexity of initializing the label of all node is O(m).
2. The process of calculating the topological potential takes O(n).
3. The time complexity of sorting the nodes by ascending order of importance is O(nlogn).
4. The key step of the label propagation process costs time of O(km), where k is the iteration times. So the time complexity of the whole algorithm is O((k + 1)m + (logn + 1)n).

3   Experimental Result and Analysis

3.1   Experimental Evaluation Standard

Modularity(Q) [15] is a new quantitative index used by Newman to measure the quality of community division. The closer the value is to 1, the higher the quality of the community division result. Q can be defined as:

$$Q = \frac{1}{2m} \sum_{ij} [A_{ij} - \frac{k_i k_j}{2m}] \delta(C_i, C_j) \tag{4}$$

Where A_{ij} is an element of the adjacency matrix of the network, and its value is defined as: if node i and node j are connected, the value of A_{ij} is 1, otherwise it is 0. The value of function $\delta(C_i, C_j)$ is defined as: if node i and node j are in a community, ie $C_i = Cj$, the value is 1, otherwise it is 0. m is the total number of edges in the network. k_i and k_j represent the degrees of nodes i and j. NMI [16] (Normalized Mutual Information) is an important indicator to measure the difference between community division and real community structure. Its definition is as follows:

$$NMI(a, b) = \frac{-2 \sum_{i=1}^{C_a} \sum_{j=1}^{C_b} N_{ij} log(\frac{N_{ij}N}{N_i N_j})}{\sum_{j=1}^{C_b} N_j log\frac{N_j}{N} + \sum_{i=1}^{C_b} N_i log(\frac{N_i}{N})} \tag{5}$$

Among them, N is the total number of LFR benchmark network nodes, N_i represents the sum of the i-th row in the matrix N, and N_{ij} represents the number of nodes shared by community i and community j. C_a and C_b indicate the number of communities after the community division algorithm runs and the number of actual communities. The value of NMI is [0, 1]. The larger the value of NMI, the more similar the community division result is to the real community structure, and the smaller the opposite.

3.2 Experimental Result and Analysis

In order to verify the quality and stability of the algorithm, we will conduct a quantitative comparison of the modularity (Q) and normalized mutual information (NMI) in the real network dataset and the benchmark network dataset. The main comparison algorithms are LPA and NIBLPA, which separately use the measure of degree and improved k-shell respectively as a measure of node importance. Our program is implemented in python (Python 3.6) language, and the program runs as window 7 operating system, 4.1 GHz, 32 GB memory.

Real Network Experiment. We choose to take karate, dolphin and football as the open standard test dataset. Dataset information is followed in Table 1.

Table 1. Dataset for real networks

Name	Number of nodes	Number of edges	Average degree
Karate	34	78	4.6
Dolphins	62	159	5.1
Fotball	105	441	8.4

Results of TPLPA. Figures 1, 2 and 3 are the results of TPLPA's community division in three real networks.

Table 2. Comparsion of modularity Q values of different algorithm

Network	LPA	KBLPA	TPLPA
Karate	0.21 ± 0.21	0.20 ± 0.20	0.36
Dolphins	0.39 ± 0.12	0.43 ± 0.09	0.42
Fotball	0.56 ± 0.04	0.54 ± 0.06	0.48

Analysis of Results. It can be seen from Table 2 that the TPLPA algorithm is more stable than LPA and KBLPA. LPA and KBLPA have great instability, and even some of the divisions will have the worst result, that is, the degree of modularity is 0. It can be seen from Table 3 that the partition accuracy of TPLPA is superior to the other two methods in most cases. Although the standard mutual information of some partition results of LPA and KBLPA of some data sets is better than TPLPA, LPA and KBLPA itself have great instability, and even some partitions will have completely wrong partition results. By comparing on three real networks, we prove that TPLPA is more accurate and stable than the other two algorithms.

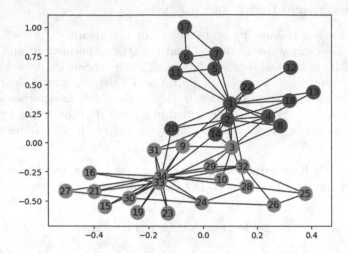

Fig. 1. Result of karate.

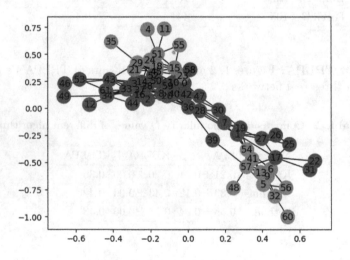

Fig. 2. Result of dolphins.

Table 3. Comparsion of NMI values of different algorithm

Network	LPA	KBLPA	TPLPA
Karate	0.58 ± 0.58	0.13 ± 0.13	0.83
Dolphins	0.51 ± 0.18	0.47 ± 0.22	0.48
Fotball	0.86 ± 0.24	0.85 ± 0.13	0.67

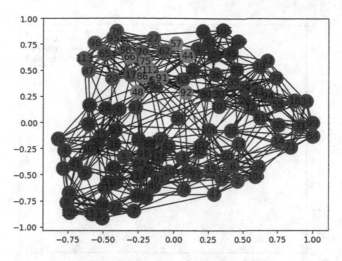

Fig. 3. Result of football.

Table 4. LFR benchmark network parameters

Parameters	Meaning
N	The number of nodes
K	The average degree
maxK	The maximum degree
γ	The exponent for the degree distribution
β	The exponent for community size distribution
mu	The mixing parameter of topology
minc	The minimum for the community sizec
maxc	The maximum for the community size

LFR Benchmark Network Experiment. Using the LFR benchmark for network community division performance testing, you can generate a specified real-world distribution network, which includes not only the distribution of node degrees here, but also the distribution of the number of nodes in the community (Table 4).

We set up two sets of experiments, the network size is 500 nodes and 1000 nodes. The network parameters are set to K = 15, maxK = 50, minc = 20, maxc = 50, and each algorithm is executed 100 times.

Figure 4 shows that when the number of artificial reference network nodes is 500, for different u, the NMI results of different methods. As u gradually becomes larger, the community structure becomes more and more difficult to determine, which indicates that the detection of the community becomes more and more difficult. When u is in the range of [0.1, 0.4], TPLPA performs better than the

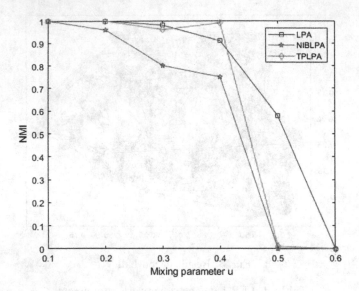

Fig. 4. Result of NMI at network scale N = 500.

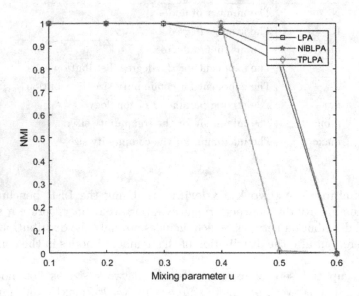

Fig. 5. Result of NMI at network scale N = 1000.

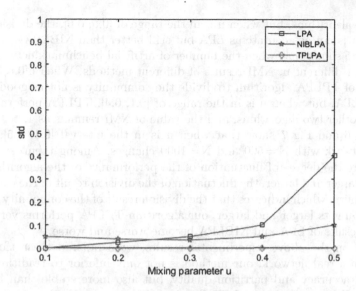

Fig. 6. Experimental result of std at network scale N = 500.

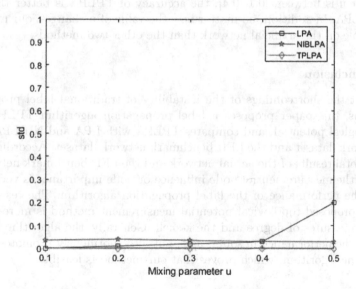

Fig. 7. Experimental result of std at network scale N = 1000.

other two algorithms, but when u is in the range of [0.5, 0.6], the division result of TPLPA is not as accurate as LPA but still better than NIBLPA.

Figure 5 shows that when the number of artificial benchmark network nodes is 1000, for different u, NMI results of different methods. When u[0.5, 0.6], the accuracy of TPLPA algorithm to divide the community is not as good as LPA and NIBLPA, but when u is in the range of [0.1, 0.4], TPLPA performs better than the other two algorithms, and the value of NMI remains as 1.

Figure 6 and Fig. 7 show that when u is in the interval [0.1, 0.5], the std of the network with N = 500 and N = 1000 changes. Among them, std is used to measure the degree of fluctuation of the performance of the algorithm. As u becomes larger and larger, the fluctuation of the division result of the community becomes huge, which indicates that the division result of the community becomes fuzzy. As u gets larger and larger, our algorithm TPLPA performs very stable, and the results of LPA and NIBLPA become worse and worse.

Based on the above experimental results, we compared these three algorithms. In a real network, our method is not only inferior to traditional algorithms in accuracy and partition quality, but also more stable than LPA and NIBLPA. When it comes to LFR benchmark network, whether on a smaller-scale network (N = 500) or a larger-scale network (N = 1000), when the mixing parameter u is between [0.1, 0.4], the accuracy of TPLPA is better than LPA and NIBLPA. In addition, no matter how the value of u changes, our method is more stable on the artificial network than the other two methods.

3.3 Conclusion

Aiming at the shortcomings of the instability of traditional label propagation algorithms, this paper proposes a label propagation algorithm TPLPA based on topological potential, and compares TPLPA with LPA and NIBLPA on the real network dataset and the LFR benchmark network dataset. According to the experimental results of the actual network and the LFR benchmark network, we find that the measurement of node influence or node importance is very important to the performance of the label propagation algorithm. The results show that our proposed topological potential measurement method is more effective than the measures of degree and the k-shell. Generally, the algorithm not only improves the performance in some cases, but also enormously promotes the stability of the algorithm, which proves that our method is feasible.

References

1. Fortunato, S.: Community detection in graphs. Phys. Rep. **486**(3–5), 75–174 (2009)
2. Chen, W., Wang, S., Zhang, X., et al.: EEG-based motion intention recognition via multitask RNNs, pp. 279–287. Society for Industrial and Applied Mathematics (2018)
3. Yue, L., Chen, W., Li, X., Zuo, W., Yin, M.: A survey of sentiment analysis in social media. Knowl. Inf. Syst. **60**(2), 617–663 (2019). https://doi.org/10.1007/s10115-018-1236-4

4. Raghavan, U.N., Albert, R., Kumara, S.: Near linear time algorithm to detect community structures in large-scale networks. Phys. Rev. E **76**(3), 036106 (2007)
5. Leung, I.X., Hui, P., Liò, P., Crowcroft, J.: Towards real-time community detection in large networks. Phys. Rev. E **79**(6), 066107 (2009)
6. Xie, J.R., Szymanski, B.K., Liu, X.M.: SLPA: uncovering overlapping communities in social networks via a speaker listener interaction dynamic process. In: Proceedings of the 11th IEEE International Conference on Data Mining Workshops, pp. 344–349, December 2011
7. Zhang, X.-K., Fei, S., Song, C., Tian, X., Ao, Y.-Y.: Label propagation algorithm based on local cycles for community detection. Int. J. Modern Phys. B **29**, 1550029 (2015)
8. Xing, Y., et al.: A node influence based label propagation algorithm for community detection in networks. Sci. World J. **2014** (2014). Article ID: 627581
9. Su, C., Jia, X., Xie, X., Yu, Y.: A new random-walk based label propagation community detection algorithm, pp. 137–140. IEEE (2016)
10. Kitsak, M., et al.: Identification of influential spreaders in complex networks. Nat. Phys. **6**, 888–893 (2010)
11. Sohn, J., Kang, D., Park, H., Joo, B.-G., Chung, I.-J.: An improved social network analysis method for social networks. In: Huang, Y.-M., Chao, H.-C., Deng, D.-J., Park, J.J.J.H. (eds.) Advanced Technologies, Embedded and Multimedia for Human-centric Computing. LNEE, vol. 260, pp. 115–123. Springer, Dordrecht (2014). https://doi.org/10.1007/978-94-007-7262-5_13
12. Green, O., Bader, D.A.: Faster betweenness centrality based on data structure experimentation. Procedia Comput. Sci. **18**, 399–408 (2013)
13. Subelj, L., Bajec, M.: Group detection in complex networks: an algorithm and comparison of the state of the art. Phys. A **397**, 144–156 (2014)
14. WenYan, G.A.N., Nan, H.E., DeYi, L.I.: Community discovery method in networks based on topological potential. J. Softw. **20**(8), 2241–2254 (2009)
15. Newman, M.E.J., Girvan, M.: Finding and evaluating community structure in networks. Phys. Rev. E **69**(2), 026113 (2004)
16. Danon, L., Díaz-Guilera, A., Duch, J., et al.: Comparing community structure identification. J. Stat. Mech. Theory Exp. (9), P09008 (2005)

LBNet: A Model for Judicial Reading Comprehension

Hao Liu and Jungang Xu[✉]

Chinese Academy of Sciences University, Beijing, China
liuhao172@mails.ucas.edu.cn, xujg@ucas.ac.cn

Abstract. In this paper, a new model for judicial reading comprehension called LBNet that combines an end-to-end network with a BERT structure is proposed, which aims to answer questions from a given passage in judicial files. Firstly, BERT is used to extract the representation of the passage and the question, and. self-matching attention mechanism is introduced to refine the representation by matching the passage against itself, which can effectively encode information from the whole passage. In the question and answer model, the pointer networks is used to locate the positions of answers from the passages. Experimental results on the CAIL2019 datasets (Chinese Judicial Reading Comprehension), show that our model can achieve good results.

Keywords: Question answering task · BERT · Judicial reading comprehension

1 Introduction

Machine reading comprehension (MRC) is a frontier field in natural language processing (NLP), which requires that machine can read, understand, and answer questions about a text. Benefiting from the rapid development of deep learning techniques (Hermann et al. 2015; Rajpurkar et al. 2016), the end-to-end neural methods have achieved promising results on MRC task (Seo et al. 2016; Huang et al. 2017; Chen et al. 2016; Clark and Gardner 2017; Hu et al. 2017; Devlin et al. 2018; Rajpurkar et al. 2018). LSTM, CNN, and attention mechanism is the common structures used in MRC. With the introduction of a series of larger and more systematic text representation models, such Bidirectional Encoder Representation from Transformers (BERT), the status of sequence representation models has been challenged. compared with the sequence representation model, a better understanding of semantics and adequate training of the article are the advantages of the pre-training model. After pre-training, simple fine-tuning can handle the problem that the sequence representation model takes a lot of time to solve. In this paper, we combine the BERT and end-to-end network models and apply them to the question and answer task.

SQuAD (Rajpurkar et al. 2018), Dureader (He et al. 2017), CoQA (Reddy et al. 2019), are the large-scale and different datasets for reading comprehension, which requires to answer questions given a passage. And in addition to the general types, the prospects for specific industry applications are now very well. In this paper, we focus on the CAIL

© Springer Nature Singapore Pte Ltd. 2021
Q. Chen and J. Li (Eds.): APWeb-WAIM 2020 Workshops, CCIS 1373, pp. 144–155, 2021.
https://doi.org/10.1007/978-981-16-0479-9_12

(Xiao et al. 2018) datasets (Chinese Judicial Reading Comprehension dataset), The law is closely related to people's daily lives. Almost every country in the world has laws. Everyone must abide by the laws to enjoy their rights and perform their duties. Every day, tens of thousands of traffic accidents, private loans, and divorce disputes occur. At the same time, in the process of handling these cases, many judgments will be made. The verdict is usually a summary of the entire case, involving the description of the event, the opinion of the court, the result of the verdict, etc. However, there are relatively few legal staff and factors such as uneven judges can often lead to wrong decisions. Moreover, even in similar cases, the judgment results can sometimes be very different. In addition, a large number of documents makes extracting information from them extremely challenging. Therefore, introducing artificial intelligence into the legal field will help judges make better decisions and work more effectively. CAIL requires to answer questions given a civil and criminal judgment documents. The referee documents contain a wealth of case information, such as time, place, relationship, etc., through the intelligent reading and understanding of the judgment documents, the results can help judges, lawyers and the general public to obtain the required information more quickly and conveniently. This dataset is the first reading comprehension dataset based on Chinese judgment documents, which belongs to the Span-Extraction Machine Reading Comprehension. In order to increase the diversity of questions, refer to the SQuAD and CoQA. This dataset adds unanswerable and YES/NO problem. In view of the fact that the civil and criminal judgment documents differ greatly in the factual description, the corresponding types of questions are not the same. In order to take into account the two types of judgment documents at the same time, CAIL dataset will set up civil and criminal test set. An example of CAIL dataset is shown in Fig. 1.

经审查表明，原、被告于2010年11月5日登记结婚，婚生子王凯翔（现改名为那8）于2012年2月10日出生。2013年1月14日，经本院主持调节，双方当事人就抚养权自愿达成如下协议：婚生子王凯翔由葛某抚养，王某从2013年1月起每月承担抚养费10000元至王翔凯独立生活之日止。2012年9月22日，原告王某与他人孕育一男孩，离婚后原、被告均已重组家庭，现原、被告双方都有稳定的工资收入，原告王某之妻没有固定收入来源，孕育两个男孩，居住于原告王某父母房屋，被告葛某之夫有收入来源，带有一女，一家住XXXX，现就读于准格尔旗民族幼儿园。以上事实由原、被告陈述及原告出示的工资收入及存款证明、葛某、那8常驻人口登记卡、出生医学证明在案予以证实。

According to the review, the plaintiff and the defendant were registered to marry on November 5, 2010. The married son Wang Kaixiang (now renamed Na ba) was born on February 10, 2012. On January 14, 2013, after the host presided over the adjustment, the two parties voluntarily reached the following agreement on custody: Wang Kaixiang, a legitimate child, was raised by Ge, and Wang took 10,000 yuan a month from January 2013 until Wang Xiangkai Living independently. On September 22, 2012, the plaintiff Wang and other women gave birth to a boy. After the divorce, both the plaintiff and the defendant had reorganized the family. Both the plaintiff and the defendant have stable wage income. The wife of the plaintiff, Wang, has no fixed source of income and raises two boys. They live in the plaintiff's parents' house. The defendant Ge's husband has a source of income and a daughter. Now living in XXXX, her daughter is currently enrolled in the Zhungeer Banner National Kindergarten. The above facts are stated by the plaintiff and the defendant. The wage income and deposit certificate presented by the plaintiff, the resident resident registration card of Ge and Na ba and the birth medical certificate were confirmed on the case.

Q1:The two sides agree on how much money Wang pays each month.   A1:February 10, 2012
Q2:Where is the stepdaughter of the defendant Ge Mou currently studying?   A2:10,000 yuan
Q3:When is the date of birth of Wang Kaixuan?   A3:Zhungeer Banner National Kindergarten
Q4:Whether the plaintiff and the defendant respectively formed a new family   A4:Yes
Q5:Does Wang Kaixuan have the will to live with the plaintiff Wang?   A5:Unk

Fig. 1. An example item from dataset CAIL.

To understand the properties of CAIL, we analyze the questions and answers in the development set. Specifically, we explore the numbers of two types of judgment documents, and the proportion of different answer types, and distribution of documents length (Figs. 2 and 3).

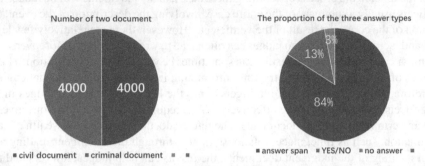

Number of two document   The proportion of the three answer types

■ civil document   ■ criminal document ■ ■   ■ answer span ■ YES/NO ■ no answer ■

Fig. 2. Analysis of the data set

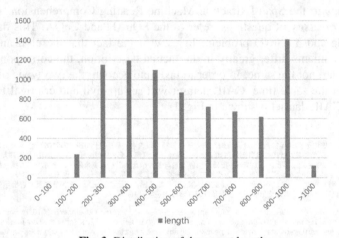

■ length

Fig. 3 Distribution of document length

The composition of the CAIL training set is mainly segment extraction, which also contains 13% of YES/NO questions and 3% of questions that cannot be answered. A reasonable solution is needed to deal with different types of questions. The length of CAIL documents is generally longer, more than 50% of the documents are longer than 500, and the long-text related issues should be considered in the model design.

To do well on MRC with unanswerable questions, the model needs to comprehend the question, reason among the passage, judge the unanswerability and then identify the answer span. When the question is answerable, the main challenge of this task lies in how to reliably determine whether a question is not answerable from the passage.

There are two kinds of approaches to model the answerability of a question. One approach is to directly extend previous MRC models by introducing a no-answer score to the score vector of the answer span (Levy et al. 2017; Clark and Gardner 2017). But this kind of approaches is relatively simple and cannot effectively model the answerability of a question. Another approach introduces an answer verifier to determine whether the question is unanswerable (Hu et al. 2018; Tan et al. 2018). However, this kind of approaches usually has a pipeline structure. The answer pointer and answer verifier have their respective models, which are trained separately. Intuitively, it is unnecessary since the underlying comprehension and reasoning of language for these components is the same.

In this paper, we divide the questions into three categories, the answerable question, and the unanswerable question, the YES/NO question. If the question is judged to be YES/NO, it is turned into a classification question. Otherwise, first judge whether it can answer, if possible, give the start point and end point.

We propose a model called LBNet (Long-term recurrent attention network from Bert) to incorporate these three sub-tasks into a unified model: (1) an answer pointer to predict a candidate answer span for a question; (2) a no-answer pointer to avoid selecting any text span when a question has no answer; and (3) an answer verifier to determine the probability of the "YES/NO" of a question with candidate answer information Our experimental results on the CAIL dataset show that LBNet effectively predicts the unanswerability of questions and achieves an F1 score of 83.5.

2 LBNet Model

For reading comprehension style question answering, a passage P and question Q are given, our task is to predict an answer A to question Q based on information found in P. The CAIL dataset further constrains answer A either to be a continuous sub-span of passage P or is YES/NO. Answer A often includes non-entities and can be much longer phrases. This setup challenges us to understand and reason about both the question and passage in order to infer the answer.

The BERT model is based on the powerful model of Transformer, which itself has broken the record of many natural language processing directions created by the deep neural network model. In general, it has been able to deal with many problems and achieve good results, However, the traditional long short-term memory network also has its advantages because that it can handle the contextual relationship well and retain the key information. So, people wish to achieve better results by combining these two models. Therefore, we made some changes based on the original BERT model and explored a new model, called LBNet (Long-term Recurrent Integrate BERT Network), which can handle machine reading task better.

LBNet is a contextual attention-based deep neural network for the task of conversational question answering, in which, the bottom layer is the input vector, and it is constructed in the same way as BERT, which is a combination of Position Embeddings, Token Embeddings and Segment Embeddings. LBNet has similar stems with existing machine reading comprehension models, but it also has several unique characteristics to tackle contextual understanding during conversation. Firstly, LBNet applies self-attention on passage and question to obtain a more effective understanding of the passage and dialogue history. Secondly, LBNet leverages the latest breakthrough in

BERT contextual embedding (Devlin et al. 2018). Different from the canonical way of appending a thin layer after BERT structure according to (Devlin et al. 2018), we innovatively employed the BiLSTM layer outputs, with locked BERT parameters. Empirical results show that each of these components has substantial gains in prediction accuracy. An illustration of LBNet model is shown in Fig. 4.

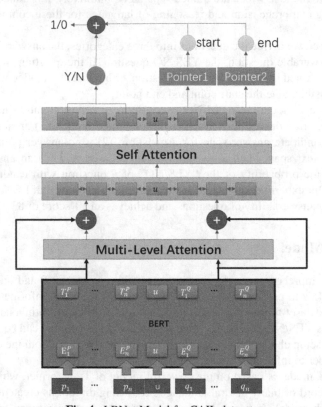

Fig. 4. LBNet Model for CAIL datasets

Formally, we can represent the MRC problem as: given a set of tuples (Q, P, A), where $Q = (q_1, q_2, \ldots, q_m)$ is the question with m words, $P = (p_1, p_2, \ldots, p_n)$ is the context passage with n words, and $A = p_{(r_s):(r_e)}$ is the answer with r_s and r_e indicating the start and end points, the task is to estimate the conditional probability $P(A|Q, P)$, LBNet consists of four major blocks: Bert & BiLSTM Encoding, Multi-Level Attention, Final Fusion, and Prediction.

We first combine the embedded representation of the question and passage with a universal node u and pass them through a Bert and BiLSTM to encode the whole text. We then use the encoded representation to deal the information interaction. Then we use the encoded and interacted Representation to fuse the full representation and feed them into the final prediction layers to do conduct the prediction. We will describe our model in details in the following.

2.1 BERT and BiLSTM Encoding

Embedding

We first segment Chinese sentences into words. Then embed both the question and the passage with the following features. Glove embedding (Pennington et al. 2014) and Elmo embedding (Peters et al. 2018) are used as basic embeddings. Besides, we use POS embedding and NER embedding (Luo et al. 2019), we use 12 dimensions to embed POS tags, 8 for NER tags, and a feature embedding that includes the exact match, lower-case match, lemma match, and a TF-IDF feature. Now we split the question Q into $Q = \left\{w_t^Q\right\}_{t=1}^m$, and the passage P into $P = \{w_t^P\}_{t=1}^n$.

Consider the question $Q = \left\{w_t^Q\right\}_{t=1}^m$ and the passage $P = \{w_t^P\}_{t=1}^n$. We first convert the words to their respective word-level embeddings ($\left\{e_t^Q\right\}_{t=1}^m$ and $\{e_t^P\}_{t=1}^n$) and character-level embeddings ($\left\{c_t^Q\right\}_{t=1}^m$ and $\{c_t^P\}_{t=1}^n$). The character-level embeddings are generated by taking the final hidden states of a bi-directional recurrent neural network (RNN) applied to embeddings of characters in the token. And E_Q denotes Q's segment embeddings. E_P denotes P's segment embeddings. E_i^{m+n+1} denotes position embeddings. The input embeddings is the sum of the token embeddings (word-level and character-level), the segment embeddings and the position embeddings. Now we get the question representation $Q = q_{i=1}^m$ and the passage representation $P = p_{i=1}^n$, where each word is represented as a d-dim embedding by combining the features/embedding described above.

The universal node u is first represented by a d-dim randomly-initialized vector. The universal node u can connect passage and questions. We concatenated question representation Q, universal node representation u, passage representation P together as:

$$V = [Q, u, P] = \left[q_1, q_2 \ldots q_m, u, p_1, p_2, \ldots, p_n\right] \tag{1}$$

$V \in \mathbb{R}^{d \times (m+n+1)}$ is a joint representation of question universal node, and passage.

Word-Level Fusion

Then we first use Bert model (Devlin et al. 2018) and bidirectional LSTM (BiLSTM) to fuse the joint representation of question, universal node, and passage.

$$H^1 = Bert(V) \tag{2}$$

And we pass it through the third BiLSTM and obtain a full representation H^f

$$H^f = BiLSTM\left(H^1\right) \tag{3}$$

We concatenate H^1 and H^f together, Thus, $H = \left[H^1; H^f\right]$ represents the deep fusion information of the question and passage on word-level. When a BiLSTM is applied to encode representations, it can learns the semantic information bi-directionally.

2.2 Multi-level Attention

To fully fuse the semantic representation of the question and passage, we use the attention mechanism (Bahdanau et al. 2014) to capture their interactions on different levels.

We first divide H into two representations: attached passage H_q and attached question H_p, and let the universal node representation h_{m+1} attached to both the passage and question, i.e.

$$H_q = \left[h_1, h_2, \ldots, h_{m+1}\right] \tag{4}$$

$$H_p = \left[h_{m+1}, h_{m+2}, \ldots, h_{m+n+1}\right] \tag{5}$$

Since both $H_q = \left[H_q^l, H_q^f\right]$ and $H_p = \left[H_p^l, H_p^f\right]$ are concatenated by three-level representations, we followed previous work FusionNet (Huang et al. 2017) to construct their iterations on three levels. Take the first level as an example. We first compute the affine matrix of H_l^q and H_p^l by

$$S = \left(\mathrm{ReLU}\left(W_1 H_q^l\right)\right)^T ReLU\left(W_2 H_p^f\right) \tag{6}$$

where $S \in \mathbb{R}^{(m+1) \times (n+1)}$; W_1 and W_2 are learnable parameters. Next, a bi-directional attention is used to compute the interacted representation $\widetilde{H_q^l}$ and $\widetilde{H_p^l}$.

$$\widetilde{H_q^l} = H_q^l \times \mathrm{softmax}\left(S^T\right) \tag{7}$$

$$\widetilde{H_p^f} = H_q^l \times \mathrm{softmax}(S) \tag{8}$$

where softmax($\cdot$) is column-wise normalized function. We use the same attention layer to model the interactions for all the three levels, and get the final fused representation $\widetilde{H_q^l}, \widetilde{H_p^f}$ for the question and passage respectively.

2.3 Final Fusion

After the three-level attentive interaction, we generate the final fused information for the question and passage. Following the work of Sun (2018), we concatenate all the history information: we first concatenate the encoded representation H and the representation after attention $\tilde{H}$ (again, we use H^l, H^f, and $\widetilde{H}^l$, $\widetilde{H}^f$ to represent two different levels of representation for the two previous steps respectively).

First, we pass the concatenated representation H through a BiLSTM to get H^A.

$$H^A = \mathrm{BiLSTM}\left(\left[H^l; H^f; \widetilde{H}^l; \widetilde{H}^f\right]\right) \tag{9}$$

where the representation H^A is a fusion of information from different levels.

Then we concatenate the original embedded representation V and H^A for better representation of the fused information of passage, universal node, and question

$$A = \left[V; H^A\right] \tag{10}$$

Finally, we use a self-attention layer to get the attention information within the fused information.

$$\tilde{A} = A \times \text{softmax}(A^T A) \tag{11}$$

Next we concatenate H^A and $\tilde{A}$ and pass them through another BiLSTM layer.

$$O = \text{BiLSTM}[H^A; \tilde{A}] \tag{12}$$

We divide O into two parts: O^P, O^Q, which denote the fused information of the question and passage respectively

$$O^P = [o_1; o_2; \ldots; o_m] \tag{13}$$

$$O^Q = [o_{m+1}; o_{m+2}; \ldots; o_{m+n+1}] \tag{14}$$

2.4 Prediction

We follow the work of Wang and Jiang (2015) and use pointer networks (Vinyals et al. 2015) to predict the start and end position of the answer.

First, we use a function shown below to summarize the question information O^Q into a fixed-dim representation c_q.

$$c_q = \frac{\exp(W^T o_i^Q)}{\sum_j \exp(W^T o_j^Q)} o_i^Q \tag{15}$$

We use two trainable matrices W_s and W_e to estimate the probability of the answer start and end boundaries of the i_{th} word in the passage, α_i and β_i.

$$\alpha_i \propto \exp(c_q W_s o_i^P) \tag{16}$$

$$\beta_i \propto \exp(c_q W_e o_i^P) \tag{17}$$

And we use the weight matrix obtained from the answer pointer to get two representations of the passage.

$$c_s = \sum_i \alpha_i \cdot o_i^P \tag{18}$$

$$c_e = \sum_i \beta_i \cdot o_i^P \tag{19}$$

To train the network, we minimize the sum of the negative log probabilities of the ground truth start and end position by the predicted distributions.

3 Experiment

3.1 Dataset

The dataset used in the technical evaluation of this task is provided by HKUST Xunfei. The dataset mainly comes from the referee documents of China Referee Documents Network, which includes criminal and civil first instance referee documents.

The training set contains about 40,000 questions, and the development set and test set each have about 5000 questions respectively. For the development set and the test set, each question contains 3 manually labeled reference answers.

In view of the large differences in the factual description of the civil and criminal adjudication documents, and the corresponding types of questions are not the same, in order to take into account both types of adjudication documents at the same time, thereby covering most of the adjudication documents, they are divided into civil and criminal test sets.

3.2 Metrics

This task is evaluated using a macro-average F1 that is consistent with the CoQA competition. For each question, need to be calculated with N standard answers to get N F1 scores, and the maximum value is taken as its F1 value. However, in assessing Human Performance, each standard answer requires an F1 value to be calculated with N-1 other criteria. In order to compare indicators more fairly, N standard responses need to be divided into N groups according to the N-1 group. Finally, the F1 value of each problem is the average of the N groups F1. The F1 value of the entire data set is the average of all data F1. The F1 value of the entire data set is the average of all data F1.

$$Lg = len(gold) \tag{20}$$

$$Lp = len(pred) \tag{21}$$

$$Lc = InterSec(gold, pred) \tag{22}$$

$$precision = \frac{Lc}{Lp} \tag{23}$$

$$recall = \frac{Lc}{Lg} \tag{24}$$

$$f1(gold, pred) = \frac{2 \times precision \times recall}{precision + recall} \tag{25}$$

$$Avef1 = \frac{\sum_{i=1}^{count_{ref}} \max(f1(gold_i, pred))}{Count_{ref}} \tag{26}$$

$$F1_{macro} = \frac{\sum_{i=1}^{N} Avef1_i}{N} \tag{27}$$

InterSec calculates the intersection of the predicted answer and the standard answer (in words), Countref represents the number of standard answers (three), max part takes the predicted answer and each standard answer, the maximum value of the F1 value. The final score is the average of the average F1 values for the criminal and civil test sets.

3.3 Implementation Details

We use Spacy to process each question and passage to obtain tokens, POS tags and NER tags of each text. We use 10 dimensions to embed POS tags, 10 for NER tags (Luo et al. 2019). We use 100-dim Glove pretrained word embeddings and 1024-dim Elmo embeddings. All the LSTM blocks are bi-directional with one single layer. We set the hidden layer dimension as 125, attention layer dimension as 250. We added a dropout layer over all the modeling layers, including the embedding layer, at a dropout rate of 0.3. We use Adam optimizer with a learning rate of 0.002.

3.4 Experimental Results and Analysis

Baseline Moels and Metrics

We compare LBNet with the following baseline models: LibSVM (Chang et al. 2011), BiDAF (Seo et al. 2016), (Devlin et al. 2018), ERNIE (Zhang et al. 2019). The dataset is randomly partitioned into a training set (80%), a development set (20%). We use F1 as the evaluation metric, which is the harmonic mean of precision and recall at word level between the predicted answer and ground truth.

4 Results

Table 1 shows the experimental results of LBNet and baseline models on CAIL datasets. As shown in Table 1, LBNet achieves better results than all baseline models. In detail, LBNet model improves F1 by 19.8, 16.4, 7.8, 6.7 on civil dataset and 17.3, 14.8, 7, 4.2 on criminal dataset compared with LibSVM, BiDAF, ERNIE and BERT, respectively. To be noted that we use the pretrain model of BERT and ENGIE. BERT uses MLM (Masked Language Model) to obtain context-relevant bidirectional feature representations. ENRIE introduces knowledge, combining entity vectors with textual representation. Different from the previous models, we use a unified representation to encode the question and passage simultaneously, and introduce a universal node which plays an important role to predict the unanswerability of a question, and we use the BiLSTM for encoding the embedded representation, which is very effective to fuse information of the question and passage.

Table 1. Experimental results (F1) on the CAIL dataset

Model	Civil data set	Criminal data set
LibSVM	63.5	63.8
BiDAF	66.8	66.5
ERNIE	75.2	74.3
BERT	78.2	77.3
LBNet	82.9	80.9

5 Conclusions

In this paper, we propose a novel contextual attention-based model, LBNet, to tackle Judicial Reading Comprehension tasks. For the joint learning of different types of questions to design an "answer fragment extraction" and "YES/NO classification and unanswerable question" three tasks of the end-to-end model, the different types of problems unified learning. For the long text problem, draw on the idea of pre-processing in the fine-tune solution for the SQuAD dataset, which is to use the sliding window method to cut the long text into multiple doc_span when data is preprocessed, for words that appear in multiple spans, the doc_span of the word with "maximum context" prevails when the score is subsequently calculated. Following an in-depth analysis of the data set, we found that some of the problems have some laws or the answers to the model prediction can be further corrected, so the post-processing module was added to the overall model structure to further improve performance. By leveraging inter-attention and self-attention and using BiLSTM on passage and conversation history, the model is able to comprehend dialogue flow and fuse It with the digestion of passage content. Furthermore, we incorporate the latest breakthrough in NLP, BERT, and leverage it in an innovative way. LBNet achieves good results over previous approaches. On the dataset CAIL, LBNet achieves F1 score 83.5 and 81.3 accuracy. In the future, we will further optimize the network structure and parameters to get more accurate results.

References

Rajpurkar, P., Zhang, J., Lopyrev, K., Liang, P.: Squad: 100,000+ questions for machine comprehension of text. arXiv preprint arXiv:1606.05250 (2016)

Hermann, K.M., et al.: Teaching machines to read and comprehend. In: Advances in Neural Information Processing Systems (2015)

Reddy, S., Chen, D., Manning, C.D.: CoQA: A conversational question answering challenge. Trans. Assoc. Comput. Linguist. **7**, 249–266 (2019)

Huang, H.Y., Zhu, C., Shen, Y., Chen, W.: Fusionnet: Fusing via fully-aware attention with application to machine comprehension. arXiv preprint arXiv:1711.07341 (2017)

Clark, C., Gardner, M.: Simple and effective multi-paragraph reading comprehension. arXiv preprint arXiv:1710.10723 (2017)

He, W., et al.: Dureader: a chinese machine reading comprehension dataset from real-world applications. arXiv preprint arXiv:1711.05073 (2017)

Hu, M., Peng, Y., Huang, Z., Qiu, X., Wei, F., Zhou, M.: Reinforced mnemonic reader for machine reading comprehension. arXiv preprint arXiv:1705.02798 (2017)

Xiao, C., Zhong, H., Guo, Z., et al.: CAIL2018: a large-scale legal dataset for judgment prediction. arXiv preprint arXiv:1807.02478 (2018)

Devlin, J., Chang, M. W., Lee, K., Toutanova, K.: BERT: pre-training of deep bidirectional transformers for language understanding. arXiv preprint arXiv:1810.04805 (2018)

Rajpurkar, P., Jia, R., Liang, P.: Know what you don't know: Unanswerable questions for SQuAD. arXiv preprint arXiv:1806.03822 (2018)

Luo, R., Xu, J., Zhang, Y., et al.: PKUSEG: a toolkit for multi-domain Chinese word segmentation. arXiv preprint arXiv:1906.11455 (2019)

Bahdanau, D., Cho, K., Bengio, Y.: Neural machine translation by jointly learning to align and translate. arXiv preprint arXiv:1409.0473 (2014)

Wang, S., Jiang, J.: Learning natural language inference with LSTM. arXiv preprint arXiv:1512.08849 (2015)

Vinyals, O., Fortunato, M., Jaitly, N.: Pointer networks. In: Advances in Neural Information Processing Systems, pp. 2692–2700 (2015)

Sun, F., Li, L., Qiu, X., Liu, Y.: U-Net: machine reading comprehension with unanswerable questions. arXiv preprint arXiv:1810.06638 (2018)

Dhingra, B., Yang, Z., Cohen, W.W., Salakhutdinov, R.: Linguistic knowledge as memory for recurrent neural networks. arXiv preprint arXiv:1703.02620 (2017)

Dhingra, B., Liu, H., Yang, Z., Cohen, W.W., Salakhutdinov, R.: Gated-attention readers for text comprehension. arXiv preprint arXiv:1606.01549 (2016)

Chen, D., Bolton, J., Manning, C. D.: A thorough examination of the CNN/daily mail reading comprehension task. arXiv preprint arXiv:1606.02858 (2016)

Seo, M., Kembhavi, A., Farhadi, A., Hajishirzi, H.: Bidirectional attention flow for machine comprehension. arXiv preprint arXiv:1611.01603 (2016)

Sun, F., Li, L., Qiu, X.: U-Net: machine reading comprehension with unanswerable questions. arXiv preprint arXiv:1810.06638 (2018)

Zhang, Z., Han, X., Liu, Z., Jiang, X., Sun, M., Liu, Q.: ERNIE: enhanced language representation with informative entities. arXiv preprint arXiv:1905.07129 (2019)

Deep Semantic Hashing for Large-Scale Image Retrieval

Yulin Yang[1], Rize Jin[1,2(✉)], and Caie Xu[3]

[1] School of Computer Science and Technology, Tiangong University, Tianjin, China
jinrize@tiangong.edu.cn
[2] Tianjin International Joint Research and Development Center of Autonomous Intelligence Technology and Systems, Tianjin, China
[3] University of Yamanashi, Yamanashi-ken, Japan

Abstract. With the rapid growth of volumes of unstructured data in the Internet, it is increasingly important to develop image-based search methods in the field of information retrieval. Hashing methods have been widely studied in favor of the low storage cost and fast retrieval speed. However, traditional hashing methods generate binary codes from handcrafted features, which limited its accuracy since the handcrafted features is hard to represent the semantic feature of the image. Recent studies have indicated that deep leaning models are superior in terms of feature extraction. Hence, in this paper, we employ the transfer learning strategy with attention mechanism on the extraction of semantic features and using difference hash algorithm to generate binary codes for image retrieval. In addition, the pre-trained CNN models also show good performance in semantic feature extraction. Instead of using the last layer of the pre-trained CNN model directly, we can provide a guidance on how to select semantic features in the task of image retrieval, by observing some changes between mean average precision and semantic features extracted from the pre-trained CNN model. Experimental results demonstrate that the mean average precision of proposed model achieves 0.944, 0.568 and 0.310 on the MNIST, Cifar-10 and Cifar-100 dataset respectively, which indicates that the transfer learning strategy with attention mechanism is effective in image retrieval.

Keywords: Image retrieval · Difference Hash Algorithm · Deep learning · Hamming distance

1 Introduction

As the information technology spreads fast, we have entered the age of big data - an extremely large volume of visual data is created every day, which brought about the issue that how to efficiently and effectively retrieve the target data from large amounts of unstructured data. There are many studies [1–5] dedicated to this topic. And the methods employed can be divided into three categories which are text-based image retrieval (TBIR), content-based image retrieval (CBIR), and semantic-based image retrieval (SBIR). The TBIR [6] is the first image retrieval framework that utilizes the description of image for searching. The descriptor is extracted from image tags such

© Springer Nature Singapore Pte Ltd. 2021
Q. Chen and J. Li (Eds.): APWeb-WAIM 2020 Workshops, CCIS 1373, pp. 156–168, 2021.
https://doi.org/10.1007/978-981-16-0479-9_13

as author, name, etc. The drawback of this approach is obvious: tags must be manually annotated, and there will be disagrees among annotators [7]. CBIR is proposed as an alternative approach, and has widely been used in the image retrieving process [7]. However, building the correlation between the pixel-level representation and the semantics from human perception is the most challenging task [8, 9]. To reduce the sematic gap, the work [10] describes an approach to image retrieval based on the underlying semantics of the image. Without designing handcrafted features, deep learning models, such as convolutional neural networks (CNNs), feature-based transfer learning, or feature-based pre-training CNN model outperform the traditional algorithms in extracting the semantic feature of images. Therefore, there is a growing re-search interest in SBIR.

Hashing methods can map similar data to similar hash codes that have smaller hamming distance, due to the low storage cost and fast retrieval speed, hashing methods have been receiving broad attention in many applications, such as image retrieval [2, 10] and video retrieval [6, 7, 11]. Among conventional wisdom and early research of hash code, including Average Hash or Mean Hash (aHash), Perceptive Hash (pHash) and Difference hash (dHash), dHash has better explanatory and faster speed in large-scale image retrieval. However, it requires different handcrafted features for generating hash code in different datasets. Recently, some image retrieval models based on deep learning was proposed. For instance, the semi-supervised deep hashing (SSDH) was proposed in [1], which performs hash code learning and feature learning simultaneously. There are still some remaining issues in SSDH, such as the training process isn't an end-to-end model and the update of binary hash coding is internally inconsistent with its label [23]. A number of researches are therefore focusing on developing effective deep learning-based methods to generate the hash code, such as network in network hashing (NINH) [23], convolutional neural network hashing (CNNH) [24]. Even though these deep hashing models have achieved convincing results in image retrieval, they all need to train a specific model on a specific dataset to a certain extent. It is also impossible to apply it in practical, like image search on Google or Baidu browser, as the category of the query image is difficult to confirm.

Motivated by human attention mechanism theories, attention mechanism has been successfully introduced in the tasks of deep learning, for example, image generation [20], image Segmentation [21], image-to-image [22]. Rather than compressing an entire image or a sequence into a static representation, attention allows the model to focus on the most relevant part of images, which is conducive to exhibits a better balance between the ability to model long-range dependencies to a certain degree. [20] propose the Self-Attention Generative Adversarial Network (SAGAN) which introduce a self-attention mechanism into convolutional GANs. Armed with the self-attention, the generator can draw images in which fine details at every location are carefully coordinated with fine details in distant portions of the image. [21] propose a Dual Attention Network (DANet) for Scene Segmentation, which can adaptively integrate local features with their global dependencies. Squeeze-and-Excitation Networks (SENet) [22] propose a novel architectural unit (SENet), that adaptively recalibrates channel-wise feature responses by explicitly modelling interdependencies between channels.

Based on the above observation, we propose to combine both the transfer learning strategy with position attention mechanism and difference hash methods for large scale image retrieval. Specifically, Image classification model based on transfer learning and position attention mechanism is designed for extracting semantic features, and then difference hash algorithm was used for generating hash codes, finally, the Hamming distance is used for image matching.

In the remainder of this paper, we first briefly describe the related work in Sect. 2, and then present the proposed method in details in Sect. 3. Section 4 provides experimental results. Finally, we conclude the paper by discussing limitations of the study and presenting future research directions in Sect. 5.

2   Related Work

2.1   Feature Extraction Based on CNN

Generally speaking, feature extraction based on CNN models mainly includes two methods: pre-trained CNN model, CNN model based on Transfer learning. The former refers to use a layer of CNN models trained on in large-scale dataset as a feature extractor directly. Specifically, for the hidden layer before the full connection layer of the pre-trained model, the same parameters are directly used. The benefit of this approach are as follows: the first is that we can use the increasingly abstract characteristics of from low to high directly, as pre-trained CNN model can learn feature hierarchies with features from higher levels of the hierarchy formed by the composition of lower level features [17]; the second is that we can get excellent semantic features of images without training a CNN model. However, when the dataset is quite different from the dataset used in pre-training CNN model, the effect of semantic feature extraction of image will be affected. Hence, semantic feature extraction based on Transfer learning was proposed.

Transfer learning is actually a research hotspot in machine learning (ML) that focuses on storing knowledge while solving one problem and applying it to a different but related task [12]. With the rapid development of CNNs, Transfer Learning has been widely applied in deep learning when the target dataset is significantly smaller than the original dataset [13]. If the pre-trained CNN model (for example, VGG-16 [12]) is used directly for extracting image features, the effect will be reduced. Therefore, it is necessary to fine-tune the parameters of the pre-trained model. In the work, we follow the basic process of fine-tuning: start with the learned weight on the ImageNet dataset and modify the last fully connected layer to suit the class of new dataset.

2.2   Difference Hash Algorithm

Difference hash algorithm converts the input image to grayscale and then scales it down. In detail, the average of all gray values of the image is calculated and then the pixels are examined one by one from left to right. If the gray value is larger than the average, a 1 is added to the hash, otherwise a 0. Since the Difference Hash calculate the difference between adjacent pixels, the hash value won't change even if the image is scaled or the length-width ratio, brightness, or contrast is altered.

After getting hash codes of input images, the remaining issue is how to measure with the similarity among them. Usually, the hamming distance is adopted for comparing hashes. It measures the number of mismatches in bits. The two hashes are identical when their hamming distance is zero because there are no mismatched bits. The larger the hamming distance, the less similar two images are in contents images.

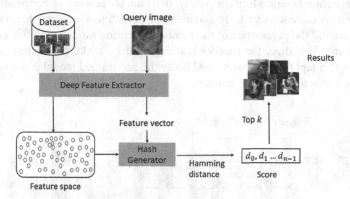

Fig. 1. The architecture of proposed method

2.3 Principal Component Analysis

Principal component analysis is a statistical procedure and it usually is used for reducing the dimensionality of large datasets. It transforms a large set of variables into a smaller one which still preserve most of the information of the original set. The trans-formation process typically follows: 1) standardize initial variables to ensure all the variables in the same scale. 2) compute covariance matrix to obtain the correlations between the variables. 3) compute the eigenvectors and eigenvalues of the covariance matrix to identity the principal components. The principal components are new variables which are uncorrelated and remain most of the information of the initial variables. 4) map the initial variables to the ones represented by the principal components. This procedure is sensitive to the size of dataset.

3 Proposed Method

As shown in Fig. 1, the architecture of our work consists of three components: feature extraction, hash code calculation, and similarity measurement. First, feature-based transfer learning is applied for extracting features from the datasets and construct the feature space. We then obtain the binary sequences of a certain length by adopting difference hash algorithm to transform and compress it into hexadecimal values. Given hexadecimal values of query image, the hamming distance function acts on it to measure the similarity degree between query image and queried images. We denote n, a parameter, as threshold value to restrict the number of the candidates.

3.1 Deep Feature Extractor

The deep feature extractor is shown in Fig. 2, which can be divided into three parts: a few stacked convolution neural network layers, a position attention module and a few full connection layers. More concretely, first, the framework of convolution neural network layers is same with VGG-16 and the same parameters are fixed that is trained on ImageNet; second the parameters of the position attention module and full connection layers randomly initialize, the transfer learning is used make parameters of random initialization to adapt to our datasets, and lastly the pre-trained model is used as feature extractor for extracting semantic features.

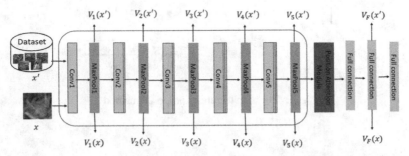

Fig. 2. The proposed deep feature extractor. From MaxPool1 to MaxPool5 is the convolution layer of VGG-16 model which is pre-trained by ImageNet dataset. The full connection is fine-tuned the parameters using the target dataset. The parameters of Full connection are 4096, 4096, C (categories of datasets).

3.2 Position Attention Module

Most image classification models based on deep learning are built using the stacking of convolutional layers or residual network. Convolution processes the information in a local receptive field, thus using convolutional layers alone is computationally inefficient for modelling long-range dependencies, which will have a certain impact on extracting image features [20]. In order to resolve this problem, Position Attention Module (PAM) is introduced into the GANs framework. The PAM model explicitly captures global dependencies regardless of locations, which adaptively aggregate long-range contextual information to make the framework context-aware. Hence, The PAM will be conducive for the proposed model to extract features better. PAM is shown in Fig. 3.

Let $x \in R^{C \times H \times W}$ denote the input feature that is fed to the algorithm. Firstly, x is fed it into three parallel convolution layers to generate three new feature maps Q(x), K(x) and V(x) respectively, here $(Q(x), K(x), V(x)) \in R^{C \times H \times W}$. Then we reshape them to $R^{C \times N}$, where $N = H \times W$ and perform a matrix multiplication between the transpose of Q(x) andK(x), and apply a softmax layer to generate the spatial attention map $S(x) \in R^{N \times N}$. After that we perform a matrix multiplication between V(x) and the transpose of $S(x)$ and reshape the result to $R^{C \times H \times W}$. Finally, we multiply the result by a scale parameter

α and perform an element-wise sum operation with the input features x to obtain the final output $A(x) \in R^{C \times H \times W}$ as follows:

$$A(x) = \alpha \times \left(S(x)^T \times V(x)\right) + x \tag{1}$$

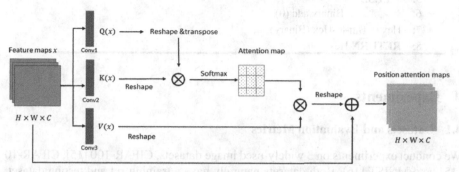

Fig. 3. The broad graphical of position attention module.

where α is initialized as 0 and gradually learns to assign more weight.

3.3 Hash Code Calculation and Similarity Measurement

Compared with image retrieval based on numerical features, binary codes can be used to greatly improve the speed of image retrieval. Because the comparison of Hamming distance can be based on bit operation. In addition, converting binary to hexadecimal also saves storage. The process of difference hashing algorithm generating binary hash codes is shown in Algorithm 1: Fea_i represents that the value of the i_{th} bit of the input feature, which is a number. Binary is binary codes, Hex represents hexadecimal value, which is obtained by converting binary. Compared to using binary hash code, hexadecimal value can save more storage space.

The smaller the Hamming distance is, the more consistent the two sequences are. Hence, we choose the Hamming distance as metrics to measuring the degree of similarity between the hash code of retrieve image and retrieved image in this paper. In detail, we first calculate the Hamming distance between the hash code of the retrieve image and all the hash code in the dataset one by one, then use Quick Sort algorithm to sort the Hamming distance according to ascending order, and top 6,000 reserved. Finally, if the queried image and retrieval images belong to the same category, it means that the retrieval is correct, otherwise failed.

Algorithm 1. Difference Hash Algorithm for Generating Hash Code

Input: Fea $_i = [f_1, f_2, ..., f_n]$
Output: Hex
1:   **WHILE** i < n **DO**
2:       **IF** Fea[i] > Fea[i+1] **THEN**
4:                Binary.add (1)
5:       **ELSE**
6:                Binary.add (0)
7:   Hex = Bin-to-Hex (Binary)
8:   **RETURN** Hex

4 Experiments

4.1 Datasets and Evaluation Metrics

We conduct experiments on 3 widely-used image datasets, CIFAR-100 [15], CIFAR-10 [15], and MNIST [16]. Both datasets naturally have a training set and testing dataset. The more detailed settings of each dataset are as follow.

The CIFAR-10 dataset consists of 60,000 color images in the training set and 10,000 color images in the test set, and the image resolution is 32 × 32. For fair comparison, 100 images are randomly selected from the test dataset as the query set, all images in the training set data are used as the retrieval database. The CIFAR-100 dataset is very similar to CIFAR-10, except that the CIFAR-100 has 100 classes containing 600 images (500 training images and 100 testing images) each. Each image has two labels: a *fine* label (the class to which it belongs) and a *coarse* label (the superclass to which it belongs) in the CIFAR-100.

The MNIST dataset contains 70,000 gray scale handwritten images from 0 to 9 with the resolution of 28 × 28 in the training set and 10,000 images in the test set. 1,000 images are randomly selected from the test set as the query set, the rest images are used as the retrieval database.

To objectively and comprehensively evaluate the retrieval accuracy of the proposed approach and all compared methods, we use *mean average precision* (MAP) for evaluating models. MAP presents an overall measurement of the retrieval performance, which is the mean of the *average precision* (AP) for each query, where AP is defined as following:

$$AP = \frac{1}{R} \sum_{i=1}^{n} \frac{i}{R_i} \times rel_i \tag{2}$$

where n is the size of training dataset, R is the number of relevant images in dataset, R_k is the number of relevant images in the top k returns, and $rel_i = 1$ if the image ranked at k_{th} position is relevant and 0 otherwise.

4.2 Experiments with Deep Representations

There are two kinds of network layers fixed-weight in pre-trained model, which are convolution and pooling layers. The convolution layer convolves the input information

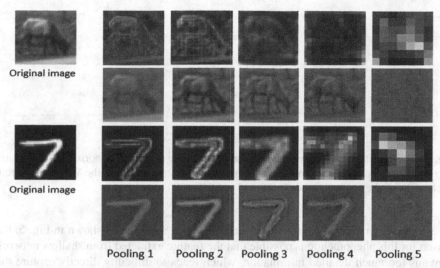

Pooling 1   Pooling 2   Pooling 3   Pooling 4   Pooling 5

Fig. 4. Evolution of samples during the layer of pre-trained model, the first column shows four samples randomly selected from cifar-10 and MNIST. From left to right in the rest columns are corresponding feature samples obtained from pooling layers. The first line is showing visualized features and the second line feature inversions.

through multiple kernels/filters to extract diverse image features. And the features are down-sampled by the pooling layer. By analyzing the changes of input image after getting through the convolution-pooling layer, which will provide a guidance for selecting the layer in feature extraction. In this paper, we use two technologies to analysis the changes of input image: a technique proposed by Matthew [19] that can visualize the features; feature inversion proposed by Mahendran [18] that can use perceptual loss functions and features extracted from pre-training model to generate images. The result is shown in Fig. 4. we observe the following: for both MNIST, CIFAR-10 and CIFAR-100 datasets, the features of the original image can be well preserved in shallow layers, and they become more abstract as we increase the depth of the network.

4.3 The Influence of Different Semantic Features on Image Retrieval

We conducted experiments for exploring the effect of the feature extracted from each pooling layer of the VGG-16 model on image retrieval. The VGG-16 model is pre-trained with the ImageNet dataset. Extracted features are input into the image retrieval system instead of the original image for searching. However, in this way, a big problem is that the number of features extracted from different layers is different, which is not fair in image retrieval. Hence, when extracting image features from pooling layer of VGG-16 model, we further use PCA technology to reduce the dimensionality of the extracted features to 100-dimensions. The result is shown in Fig. 5, from which we can draw the following conclusions: the first is that the performance of image retrieval will gradually increase as the depth of the network deepens, from the first layer of pooling to the fourth one; the second is that compared with the fourth layer, the performance of the fifth

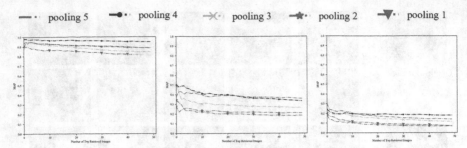

Fig. 5. The influence of different semantic features on image retrieval. The horizontal coordinate-axis is the number of retrieval images, the longitudinal coordinate-axis is the MAP score. From left to right are the result on MNIST, Cifar-10 and Cifar-100 respectively.

layer is slightly reduced. Combining the results from Sect. 4.2, as shown in Fig. 5, the reason for this phenomenon is possible that the feature extracted from shallow network contains too much detailed information, which leads to difficulty directly capture the semantic features, which causing the poor results. As the depth of the network increase, the details of the image are gradually ignored, and the semantic features of the image are gradually emphasized. Therefore, the results of image retrieval are getting better with the increases of depth of the network; and finally there is a slight drop in the result when using the feature extracted from fifth pooling layer, we can learn from Fig. 5, the output of fifth pooling layer of the model can hardly be used to reconstructed image because the features of this layer contain too little information of the image. That will arouse the retrieval results is not so good. Base on this situation, it is recommended to use features from the fourth pooling layer when using pre-trained models for extracting image features.

4.4 The Effect of Fine-Tuning CNN Model on Image Retrieval

Undoubtedly, there are many benefits to use a pre-trained model for image feature extraction. For instance, we can get the semantic features of images without training model and it can be used on any datasets. However, in many cases, the dataset used for training the pre-trained model is different from the dataset we actually use for image retrieval. Practically, the sample distribution between the datasets is quite different, which greatly affects the retrieval result and retrieval efficiency of image retrieval. Aim to address such a problem, we train an image classification model using transfer learning with attention mechanism, then apply the trained model for feature extraction. In this paper, we first extracted the feature of input images from the second-to-last full connection layer both pre-trained vgg-16 model and fine-tuning model, and then PCA is used to reduce the dimension of input features for faster retrieval speed. We can see the following phenomena from Fig. 6: first, compared with using the pre-trained vgg-16 model, the fine-tuned model that use position attention module or not show better the scores of MAP; second, the scores of MAP of the fine-tuned model with position attention module is more stable than pure fine-tuned model on Cifar-10 dataset, which indicates that position attention module be conducive to extract image semantic features better.

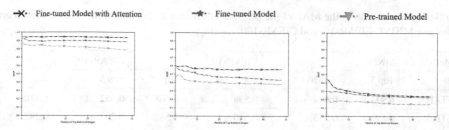

Fig. 6. The effect of fine-tuning CNN model on image retrieval, the blue, red and black line represents the result of pre-trained model, fine-tuned model and fine-tuned model with position attention model. From left to right are the result on MNIST, Cifar-10 and Cifar-100 respectively.

4.5 Results and Analysis

Quantitative and qualitative analysis are used to illustrate that the difference of different models on image retrieval in this section. We referred to Difference Hash Algorithm as DHA, image features extractor based on pre-trained CNN model as PHA, image features extractor based on fine-tuned CNN model as FTHA and image features extractor based on fine-tuned CNN model with attention mechanism as FTAHA. The results are shown in Fig. 7 and Table 4. From which we can see that: 1) compared to the traditional hash algorithm based on the hand-crafted features like DHA, image features extractor based on CNN models has shown better performance in image retrieval, which indicates that image feature extraction based on pre-trained CNN have stronger capabilities of semantic feature extraction than hand-crafted features. 2) compared to the FTHA hash algorithm, FTAHA that image features extractor based on CNN models with Position Attention Module has shown better performance in image retrieval. For example, the FTAHA improves the average MAP from (89.6%, 89.3%) to (94.4%, 94.4%) on MNIST dataset, from (29.2%, 28.2%) to (35.2%, 31.0%) on CIFAR10 dataset and from (58.0%, 54.2%) to (59.6%, 56.8%) on CIFAR100 dataset, when the number of retrieved images is top 5 and top 10. The Improvement of MAP score indicates that PAM is conducive to improve the quality of image retrieval; 3) From the Fig. 7, we can find out that retrieved images with same shape of retrieve images have more favored by the DHA model especially in CIFAR-100 dataset, which is a clear demonstration of the failure of DHA to extract image features. However, the CNN models particularly fine-tuned model like FTHA and FTAHA do not have this phenomenon, which can retrieve the images of corresponding categories very well. A reasonable conjecture is that the semantic features obtained from CNN model is more effective (Table 1).

Table 1. Comparison of the MAP of the proposed method and the other hash methods based on database MNIST, CIFAR-10, and CIFAR-100.

Method	MNIST		CIFAR-10		CIFAR-100	
	Top 5	Top 10	Top 5	Top 10	Top 5	Top 10
FTAHA	**0.944**	**0.944**	**0.596**	**0.568**	**0.352**	**0.310**
FTHA	0.896	0.893	0.580	0.542	0.292	0.282
PHA	0.844	0.846	0.551	0.425	0.172	0.184
DHA	0.880	0.867	0.108	0.122	0.084	0.074

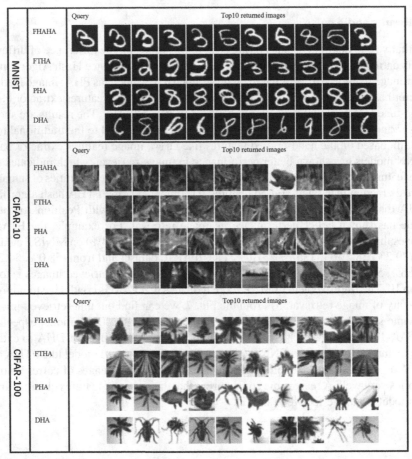

Fig. 7. Some retrieval results of MNIST, CIFAR-10 and CIFAR-100 about failure is shown above. The first column of image is used for retrieval, from left to right in rest columns are result that Hamming distance increase progressively.

5 Conclusion

This paper presents an end-to-end approach, combining image features extractor based on fine-tuned CNN model with attention mechanism and difference hash algorithm, to search out the desired images from large-scale datasets. It utilizes transfer learning technique for extracting image features, and then uses difference hash algorithm to generate hash code, finally, applying the Hamming distance to compute the similarity degree between the samples of the dataset to queried image. Meanwhile, we also focused on exploring the influence of image representation extracting from different layers of pre-trained model on the quality of image retrieval. Finally, we compare the performance of pre-trained model and fine-tuned model on the task of image retrieval. The experimental results show that fine-tuned model significantly outperforms the pre-trained model.

Acknowledgments. This work was supported in part by the National Natural Science Foundation of China (NSFC) under Grant 61806142, in part by the Natural Science Foundation of Tianjin under Grant 18JCYBJC44000, and in part by the Tianjin Science and Technology Program under Grant 19PTZWHZ00020.

References

1. Liu, H.M., Wang, R., Shan, S.G., Chen, X.L.: Deep supervised hashing for fast image retrieval. In: IEEE Conference on Computer Vision and Pattern Recognition, pp. 2064–2072 (2016)
2. Gionis, A., Indyk, P., Motwani, R.: Similarity search in high dimensions via hashing. VLDB **99**, 518–529 (1999)
3. Jiang, H., Learned-Miller., E.: Face detection with the faster R-CNN. In: 12th IEEE International Conference on Automatic Face and Gesture Recognition, pp. 650–657 (2017)
4. Ren, S.Q., He, K., Girshick, R., Sun, J.: Faster R-CNN: Towards real-time object detection with region proposal networks. In: Advances in Neural Information Processing Systems, pp. 91–99 (2015)
5. Karen, S., Andrew, Z.: Very deep convolutional networks for large-scale image recognition, arXiv preprint arXiv, pp. 1409–1556 (2014)
6. Rui, Y., Huang, T.S., Chang, S.-F.: Image retrieval: current techniques, promising directions, and open issues. J. Vis. Commun. Image Represent. **10**, 39–62 (1999)
7. Alkhawlani, M., Elmogy, M., El-Bakry, H.M.: Text-based, content-based, and semantic-based image retrievals: a survey. Int. J. Comput. Inf. Technol. **4**, 58–66 (2015)
8. Smeulders, A.W., Worring, M., Santini, S., Gupta, A., Jain, R.: Content-based image retrieval at the end of the early years. IEEE Trans. PAMI **22**(12), 1349–1380 (2000)
9. Wan, J., Wang, D.Y., HOI., S.C.H., Wu, P., Zhu. J., Zhang. Y., Li. J.: Deep learning for content-based image retrieval. a comprehensive study. In: Proceedings of the ACM MM, pp. 157–166 (2014)
10. Ben, B.: Semantic based image retrieval: a probabilistic approach. In: Proceedings of the Eighth ACM International Conference on Multimedia, pp. 167–176 (2000)
11. Chauhan, N.K., Goyani, M.M.: Enhanced multistage content based image retrieval. IJCSMC **2**(5), 175–179 (2013)
12. Guan, Q., et al.: Deep convolutional neural network VGG-16 model for differential diagnosing of papillary thyroid carcinomas in cytological images: a pilot study. J. Cancer **10**, 4876 (2019)
13. Calder, A.J., Burton, A.M., Miller, P., Young, A.W., Akamatsu, S.: A principal component analysis of facial expressions. Vis. Res. **41**(9), 1179–1208 (2001)

14. Liu, T.: Learning to Rank for Information Retrieval. Springer, Heidelberg (2011). https://doi.org/10.1007/978-3-642-14267-3
15. Krizhevsky, A., Hinton, G.: Learning multiple layers of features from tiny images, Technical report, University of Toronto (2009)
16. LeCun, Y., Bottou, L., Bengio, Y., Haffner, P.: Gradient-based learning applied to document recognition. In: Proceedings of the IEEE, vol. 86, no. 11, pp. 2278–2324 (1998)
17. Erhan, D., et al.: Why does unsupervised pre-training help deep learning? J. Mach. Learn. Res. **11**(19), 625–660 (2010)
18. Mahendran, A., Vedaldi, A.: Understanding deep image representations by inverting them. In: 2015 IEEE Conference on Computer Vision and Pattern Recognition (CVPR), pp. 5188–5196 (2015)
19. Zeiler, M.D., Fergus, R.: Visualizing and understanding convolutional networks. In: Fleet, D., Pajdla, T., Schiele, B., Tuytelaars, T. (eds.) ECCV 2014. LNCS, vol. 8689, pp. 818–833. Springer, Cham (2014). https://doi.org/10.1007/978-3-319-10590-1_53
20. Zhang, H., et al.: Self-attention generative adversarial networks. In: ICML 2019: Thirty-Sixth International Conference on Machine Learning, pp. 7354–7363 (2019)
21. Fu, J., et al.: Dual attention network for scene segmentation. In: 2019 IEEE/CVF Conference on Computer Vision and Pattern Recognition (CVPR), pp. 3146–3154 (2019)
22. Hu, J., et al.: Squeeze-and-Excitation Networks. In: 2018 IEEE/CVF Conference on Computer Vision and Pattern Recognition, pp. 7132–7141 (2018)
23. Zhu, H., et al.: Deep hashing network for efficient similarity retrieval. In: 2016 the Thirtieth AAAI Conference on Artificial Intelligence, pp. 2415–2421 (2016)
24. Wu, D., et al.: Deep incremental hashing network for efficient image retrieval. In: 2019 IEEE/CVF Conference on Computer Vision and Pattern Recognition (CVPR), pp. 9069–9077 (2019)

Author Index

Printed in the United States
by Baker & Taylor Publisher Services